The FEARLESS
BAKER

ALSO BY EMILY LUCHETTI

Stars Desserts
Four-Star Desserts
A Passion for Desserts
A Passion for Ice Cream
Classic Stars Desserts

The FEARLESS BAKER

EMILY LUCHETTI & LISA WEISS

Scrumptious Cakes, Pies, Cobblers, Cookies, and Quick Breads
That You Can Make to Impress Your Friends and Yourself

LITTLE, BROWN AND COMPANY
New York Boston London

Little, Brown and Company
Hachette Book Group
237 Park Avenue, New York, NY 10017
www.hachettebookgroup.com

First Edition: May 2011

Little, Brown and Company is a division of Hachette Book Group, Inc. The Little, Brown name and logo are trademarks of Hachette Book Group, Inc.

Library of Congress Cataloging-in-Publication Data
Luchetti, Emily.
   The fearless baker : scrumptious cakes, pies, cobblers, cookies, and quick breads that you can make to impress your friends and yourself / Emily Luchetti and Lisa Weiss.—1st ed.
       p. cm.
   ISBN 978-0-316-07428-5
   1. Baking. 2. Desserts. I. Weiss, Lisa. II. Title.
   TX763.L82 2011
   641.8'65—dc22   2010025987

10 9 8 7 6 5 4 3 2 1

Q-MA

Design: AdamsMorioka, Inc.

Printed in the United States of America

To Peter, Dan, Pilgrim, and Chita,
who always love whatever we feed them

Contents

Introduction

When I meet people at a party and tell them I'm a pastry chef, without fail someone will say, "That's so amazing. I love to cook but I never bake. It terrifies me." After hearing this more times than I can count, I began to wonder, what is it about baking — or really desserts in general — that is so intimidating to so many people?

Certainly it's not that there aren't plenty of ways to learn. There's the Food Network, Web sites, videos, and hundreds of baking and dessert cookbooks out there filled with some delicious and some not-so-delicious recipes and comprehensive instruction. I've written several books myself over the years, books people tell me have become dog-eared. But why is it some people—even good cooks—say that they don't bake because it scares them? It occurred to me that maybe those of us who bake for a living take a lot of cooking knowledge for granted, and don't really understand some of the basic questions a beginning baker might ask. Maybe we give too much information, so that it makes the recipes seem intimidating. I didn't know the answer, but I thought if I could put people in a real-life kitchen situation and work alongside them to find out what questions they have, what things scare them about baking, I could somehow translate that into a book that would turn them into Fearless Bakers.

When I ran my as-yet-unfocused idea of a beginners' book past a few of my nonprofessional friends, one sent back an email and said, "I'd love it. Even though I entertain and cook a great deal, I always end up buying dessert because I'm terrified by the thought of baking." Hyperbole maybe, but thus was born *The Fearless Baker*. Or as I thought of it, "How to turn a terrified baker into a fearless one."

People tend to assume that because I'm a professional pastry chef I must have inherited a baking legacy passed down through the generations: a grandmother who was the county-fair pie queen or a mother who won bake-offs for her ethereal cakes. Surely there must be some kind of baking gene in my DNA. It's true that I came from a family of eaters and passionate food lovers, but I was in my teens before I realized that all the cakes my mom made for our birthdays—spice cake was my favorite— came from box mixes. But that didn't make any difference. The fact that she took the time to create something special for us was all that mattered. My grandmother's best recipe was for a martini, but that's another story.

The truth is that anyone can learn to bake. When someone says to me that the thought of baking— using precise measurements and following specific techniques—scares them, I like to point out that if you

have a driver's license, can ride a bike, graduated from school, got a job, or raised a family, then, without question, you can bake a cake. Or a pie. Or a batch of cookies. It just requires a bit of patience and concentration.

Ah, patience and concentration: two commodities people seem very short on these days, with our hectic schedules and constant distraction. I can't tell you the number of reasons—besides fear—I've heard from people for why they don't make dessert. The most common are "It's easier to buy it," and "I don't have the time." I can identify with those: my life is just as hectic as everyone else's. And just because I make desserts for a living doesn't mean that I want to come home after an exhausting day and bake for my family. So that's why I'll often pick up some ice cream and dress it up with some of the homemade chocolate or caramel sauce I keep in the fridge. I'm also a big believer in store-bought shortcuts like puff pastry and ready-made pie dough. Cut up fresh fruit and you can have a tart on the table in no time.

Another reason people give for not baking is "I don't want to have tempting sweets in the house." I understand this as well; diet issues are a concern for all of us. The way I deal with it, for the most part, is to bake for occasions when I have people over so I don't end up with leftovers. If I do have leftovers (which is seldom), then I give them to my neighbors or bring them into work the next day. Temptation avoided!

There's one reason I will always keep baking. Nothing can compare to the satisfaction I get from seeing how chocolate chip cookies can turn a friend's bad day into a good one, how freshly baked muffins can brighten someone's morning, or how a frosted layer cake can make my husband smile.

To create this book I teamed up with a long-time friend, Lisa Weiss, a terrific home cook and coauthor of many chefs' cookbooks. Together we gathered a list of friends and family who had expressed to us their fear of baking. From the beginning we decided to call them our Fearful Bakers, or FBs. It was my job to turn them from Fearful Bakers into Fearless Bakers.

Each FB was invited to one of our home kitchens so that I could be their Baking Fairy Godmother (which

is what one of them called me) to stand alongside them as they followed my recipes. As they worked I would answer their questions and guide them in gentle instruction. A private baking lesson if you will, coaching them through simple things like whipping egg whites to a soft peak, folding whipped cream into a mousse, or something more challenging like caramelizing the crust on crème brûlée with a torch. I think I learned as much, or more, than they did. They went home with their apple pie or cherry cheesecake and I got a better understanding of the questions novice bakers might ask when they read a recipe. (For a complete list of our FBs and to show their diverse backgrounds, see page 283.)

Questions like "What is parchment paper and where do I get it?" (Nonstick paper: best bought in sheets, which can be found at a restaurant supply store, rather than in rolls.) "Can I use walnuts instead of pecans" or "I don't like bittersweet chocolate, can I use semisweet chocolate?" For many of the FBs, I had to help them

develop a strategy for tackling the recipe because they were so eager to just dive in. My first words to them always ran something along the lines of, "Before you do anything else, read the recipe through. You don't want to get to the end and find out that the custard has to be chilled for four hours when company is coming in thirty minutes."

During our baking sessions, Lisa took notes and recorded our conversations. What you'll read in these pages is the result. About a third of the recipes in the book have snippets of dialog that relate to a lesson that was learned by one of our FBs. Lisa and I rewrote and refined each recipe, incorporating their suggestions to make the recipes clearer and trying to give just the right amount of information—not so much as to overwhelm and yet enough that you won't be left asking questions. Read all the dialogs and you'll have had your own comprehensive baking lesson, or read them as you need them. No matter what, I hope you will be inspired to go in the kitchen and bake.

1. Before you begin, read the recipe through to the end. Make sure you have all your ingredients and can allot the time required.

2. Measure out all your ingredients accurately and have them ready to go. (Professional pastry chefs weigh their ingredients but I discovered that beginning bakers prefer to use measuring cups and tablespoons. Chocolate should always be weighed.)

3. Don't improvise on the instructions—at least the first time you make a recipe. You can make substitutions in ingredients if the recipe says you can, but don't otherwise.

4. Preheat the oven. Invest in an oven thermometer to check the accuracy of the temperature; ovens can be off many degrees, which can affect the results of your baking.

5. Use a kitchen timer and always check for doneness before the specified time in the recipe. Rely on the description of when something is done—skewer clean, golden brown, etc.

6. Relax and have fun!

Techniques You Need to Know:
How to Beat, Cream, Whip, and Fold

So what does a recipe mean when it says to "beat," or "cream," or "whip," or "fold"? Maybe you're so new to baking that you think cream comes from cows and sheets are folded. Maybe you're experienced enough to know the terms but wonder what is fully expected in the end. The terms actually refer to how something should be mixed and what it should be mixed with, but the techniques vary depending on what you're baking.

The terms **beat** and **cream** are used somewhat interchangeably. In both cases you want to make the mixture (usually including butter) smooth and homogeneous. Generally, when people say to "cream" a mixture, it takes longer than it would to "beat" it. In this book I instruct you to beat and not cream, and I tell you what the mixture should look like when you are finished. If you're mixing by hand, use a wooden spoon or a rubber spatula. If you're mixing with a handheld mixer, use the beaters; with a stand mixer, use the paddle (also called the beater blade) attachment. When making cookies, you want to mix the batter until it is evenly combined (using a standing mixer's paddle attachment). For cakes, you want to mix longer so air is incorporated, which makes a cake rise higher and taste lighter. (If you mix cookie batter as long as you do cake batter your cookies will come out higher and more cakey in texture.) Cookies can easily be done by hand. Cakes can be done by hand but I don't want physical exertion to stop you from baking. That's why in the cake recipes I recommend using a mixer. Stand mixers have more power than handheld mixers, so keep in mind you will have to mix longer with a hand mixer to get the same results. (To make things even more confusing, some

books, not this one, will tell you to "beat" egg whites rather than, say, "whip" egg whites; in either case, you will want to use a hand whisk or the whisk attachment to an electric mixer.)

The term **whip** is used when you need to create volume or a soft batter of eggs combined with sugar. If you're mixing by hand, use a whisk. If you're using a handheld mixer, the standard two whisks work; with a stand mixer, use the whisk attachment. For general whipping, but particularly when you need a lot of volume (say, when whipping egg whites for meringue), electric mixers save you a ton of work. (If I need to whip only a couple of whites or a cup of cream, for quick work and easy cleanup I use an old-fashioned handheld rotary beater, also called an egg beater.) When I use a handheld mixer I move the mixer around the bowl and with my free hand use a spatula to push the ingredients into the whisks of the mixer. This way everything gets evenly mixed and helps make the mixing go faster. While many desserts can be made without whipped egg whites, knowing how to do this simple fundamental technique opens up a whole other world of meringue-topped pies, macaroons, pavlovas, and angel food cakes.

It's true that you'll get more volume when you whip room-temperature eggs, but don't lose sleep if they're cold out of the fridge. Begin whipping the whites on medium-low speed. When they start to get foamy increase the speed to high. Egg whites behave differently when whipped with and without sugar. It is easier to over-whip egg whites if they don't have any sugar. There is nothing for the eggs to hold onto as they

During our baking sessions, Lisa took notes and recorded our conversations. What you'll read in these pages is the result.

increase in volume. Whipped egg whites without sugar should be billowy and soft, not clumpy, kind of like bubbles in a bubble bath. They should still look airy. If they separate in clumps, they have been over-mixed.

About a third of the recipes in the book have snippets of dialog that relate to a lesson that was learned by one of our FBs (and all are referenced on page 283). Lisa and I rewrote and refined each recipe, incorporating their suggestions to make the recipes clearer and trying to give just the right amount of information—not so much as to overwhelm and yet enough that you won't be left asking questions.

If the recipe calls for sugar, once the egg whites have turned opaque and start to hold their shape, continue to mix while adding the sugar in a slow but steady stream. Whipped egg whites with sugar will look satiny and very thick. When you lift the whisk the whites should hold their shape and not flop over. It will take longer to whip whites with sugar than without.

The term **fold** is used when two mixtures need to be gently combined. You don't want to lose any volume in either of the mixtures, especially the lighter one. Folding is usually done when one of the mixtures is whipped cream, whipped egg whites, or sometimes egg yolks and sugar. To fold correctly, put half of the lighter mixture on top of the other mixture, then with the flat side of a rubber spatula cut down through the two mixtures and at the bottom of the bowl turn the spatula flat-side up and bring the heavier batter over the lighter one. Continue this pattern until the two are almost combined. It helps to turn the bowl a quarter turn after each fold to help mix more efficiently. Add the second half of the lighter mixture and fold only until combined and you can no longer see streaks of either mixture.

Read all the dialogs and you'll have had your own comprehensive baking lesson, or read them as you need them. No matter what, I hope you will be inspired to go into the kitchen and bake.

Baking Equipment

In an effort to simplify the dessert-making process and make it seem less intimidating, the recipes have been written so that you're not asked for any fancy, esoteric, or expensive baking tools. In fact, many of our Fearful Bakers—who happen to be good cooks but just don't bake—have pretty well-equipped kitchens with stand mixers, food processors, convection ovens, and name-brand pots and pans. That's great if you have them, but to make the most of the recipes in this book all you really need are a few basic kitchen tools plus the necessary baking pans. The following equipment is what I consider to be basic:

An assortment of various sized bowls,
  preferably a few metal ones

Measuring cups and spoons

Good, sharp chef's knife, paring knife, and serrated knife

Vegetable peeler

Large wooden spoon

Flat spatula (wood, metal, or nonstick)

Whisks, a couple of sizes

Rubber spatula

Rimmed baking pans or cookie sheets

Small, medium, and large saucepans and medium
  and large skillets

Ruler (but there's a ruler printed on the back cover
  of the book if you need a quick reference)

Parchment paper

Here are some other tools you'll find used in the recipes and listed at the beginning under What You'll Need. Many of the tools are optional, but they will allow you to become more efficient, creative, and adventurous. If you're making a cake or pie, be careful about substituting one pan size for another. Volumes vary and can affect results.

Stand mixer or handheld mixer

Stand mixer attachments: whisk and flat paddle,
  or BeaterBlade by NewMetro Design
  or POURfect Scrape-A-Bowl

Food processor

Oven thermometer

Offset and narrow metal spatulas

Heat resistant rubber spatula

Medium mesh sieve

Small spring-loaded ice-cream scoop

Microplane grater

Straight-sided cake pans: 9- by 2-inch round,
  8- by 8- by 2-inch square, 9- by 9- by 2-inch square,
  9- by 13- by 2-inch

Tube pans: angel food, Bundt (12-cup), and 9-inch fluted
  tube pan (10-cup; sometimes called a *kugelhopf* pan)

Springform pan, 9-inch

Pie pans (not deep dish): 9-inch glass, ceramic, or metal

Tart pan, preferably with a removable bottom, 9-inch

Loaf pans: 9- by 5-inch, 8 1/2- by 4 1/2-inch

Standard muffin pan, 12-cup

Ingredients

Certain ingredients are staples in all pastry kitchens— flour, butter, sugar, eggs—and if you keep them on hand, you'll be much more likely to make a dessert on short notice. Many seasoned pastry chefs will work with only certain brands—particularly when it comes to chocolate—but I want you to feel comfortable using whatever is available to you in your local supermarket. Fancy names and labels don't make the dessert.

Standardization does make a difference when it comes to successfully re-creating a dessert recipe. That's why all the recipes in this book (and most other baking books as well) call for large eggs instead of extra-large, and unsalted butter rather than salted.

Here is a list of what you'll need to stock your Fearless Baker pantry and fridge, ingredients used throughout the book:

Unbleached all-purpose flour: Using bleached rather than unbleached flour will not affect the recipe noticeably, but you can never tell if it's been bleached naturally or chemically, and unless you're looking for white, white biscuits, why not choose the more natural?

Unsalted butter: If you use salted butter, you will have to cut down on the salt called for in the recipe. When a recipe calls for softened butter, leave it at room temperature for about an hour. If your kitchen is hot it will soften more quickly. You'll know if it's soft enough when you can press a dent in it with your finger. If it's greasy and shiny, it's too soft. Because unsalted

butter goes bad more quickly than salted, I keep it in the freezer so I don't have to run to the store when I need it. It keeps in the fridge for no longer than a week.

Sugars: White sugar is either granulated or powdered (also called confectioners' sugar). Make sure it says "cane sugar" on the package. If it doesn't, it might have been made with beet sugar, an inferior product. Confectioners' sugar often needs to be sifted before use because it gets clumps that don't dissolve when you stir them with other ingredients. I use light (also called golden) brown sugar rather than dark brown sugar, but if you already have dark brown sugar in your cupboard, use it. The molasses flavor will be more pronounced than if you used golden or light brown, but your dessert will come out fine. Brown sugar is measured in a cup and is firmly packed.

Eggs: All eggs should be Grade AA large. If you have leftover egg whites you can refrigerate them for 3 days or freeze them for up to 2 months. If you're not using the yolks right away, cover them with plastic wrap to prevent a skin from forming. They'll keep for 2 days in the fridge.

Kosher salt: I use it in all my baking and cooking because it has a cleaner taste and no additives. If you use table salt, decrease the amount called for in the recipe by one-half. If you've not tried kosher salt, get some and do your own side-by-side comparison with table salt. You'll discover that it gives all your dishes—both sweet and savory—more flavor without that salty taste.

Vanilla extract: The label should read "pure vanilla extract" to differentiate it from artificial vanilla or a product called vanillin flavoring.

Vanilla beans: The whole beans (or pods) are usually slit lengthwise in half and the teeny seeds scraped out with the back (dull) edge of a knife. The scraped bean can be saved and used to steep in cream or put into a container of granulated sugar to make vanilla sugar. Try to avoid jars with single beans. My experience is that they're too often dry. For the price of a bean, you want them plump and fresh.

Nonstick cooking spray and baking spray: Both are used to prepare pans for baking. The difference between the two is that baking spray has flour added (it is found in most supermarkets either with the baking products or in the section with oils and other sprays). If you use baking spray you won't have to dust a pan with flour after greasing. It won't hurt to use baking spray when nonstick spray is called for, but the reverse is not true. You can't use nonstick in place of baking spray unless you flour the pan. In general I find cooking spray is easier to use than butter but they both work fine.

Chocolate—this is where quality and personal preference come into play. Over the last few years the world of chocolate has exploded with terms like "cacao percentage," "single estate," "place of origin," "organic," and "fair trade," which has made it better for consumers but confusing at the same time. Here's a quick breakdown on kinds of chocolate for baking. The main rule to remember is that chocolate varies in how much cacao and cacao mass it contains. Cacao is anything from the bean—cocoa butter and chocolate liquor. Cacao mass is the chocolate paste (often called chocolate liquor) from the bean after the cocoa butter and other components have been removed. The higher the percentage of cacao a chocolate contains, the less sugar it contains.

Family and friends are always asking me to recommend chocolate brands. It's such a personal preference that I don't like to get too specific, and besides, there are so many good ones.

But I can generally say that the better supermarket brands—Ghirardelli, Guittard, Lindt, and Scharffen Berger—are consistently good and you can count on high-end brands to be good (though not necessarily better). One trick I use when I'm in an unfamiliar market is head for the candy aisle as well as the baking aisle because many stores put their higher-quality chocolates there. Just check the label to make sure they don't contain nuts or flavors. I like most high-end chocolates, but some I use often are TCHO, Valrhona, E. Guittard, and Scharffen Berger. (See page 282 for sources for specialty chocolates.)

Unsweetened chocolate is 100 percent chocolate liquor. It has no sugar added to it. People often think bittersweet does not have sugar in it but that's not true.

The next two levels—bittersweet and semisweet—get a bit broad. The amount of cacao in these chocolates varies from about 52 to 99 percent. The rest of the bar is sugar and a few stabilizers. Both are good to eat, but your preference will be influenced by how sweet you like it. Sometimes what you like for eating may be different from what you like in your cookies or chocolate pudding. I love to nibble on chocolate that's anywhere between 75 and 99 percent cacao, but wouldn't bake with it. The confusing part is that no two companies are consistent in their definition of bittersweet and semisweet. For example, Scharffen Berger has a 62 percent cacao that they label semisweet. Ghirardelli has a 60 percent cacao that they call bittersweet. So the best thing to do is not get caught up in the bittersweet versus semisweet nomenclature and pay attention to the percentage of cacao listed on the package. For the recipes in this book I use mostly 58 to 62 percent chocolate. The first time you make one of these recipes don't try substituting 70 percent or higher, or you may need to change other ingredients in the recipe for it to work. You can experiment once you know what the recipe is supposed to taste like. If you are adding chopped chocolate pieces to cookies, you can use 70 percent.

White chocolate is not really chocolate at all since it doesn't have any cacao solids. Good white chocolate brands list cocoa butter in the ingredient list. If not, pass it up. (Another way to tell is that if the chocolate is white-white, it doesn't contain cocoa butter which is creamy white. But unfortunately you usually can't see the color until you get it home and open the package. So make sure to read the ingredients label.) Those brands without cocoa butter are thick when they melt and have an artificial taste.

Milk chocolate, of course, has milk in it. It has less chocolate liquor and cocoa butter. I prefer milk chocolate brands that are less sweet and have a creamy flavor, such as E. Guittard, Valrhona, and Scharffen Berger.

Cocoa powder is basically what's left over after the cocoa butter is removed from the ground cocoa beans. There are two kinds of cocoa powder—natural and Dutch processed. You can use either in these recipes.

Cookies, Bars, and Bites

There's no better place for you to become a Fearless Baker than with cookies. Always welcomed, loved by young and old alike, enjoyed as a snack out of the cookie jar or as a casual dessert after dinner, cookies don't require any complicated techniques.

Frankly, it's kind of hard to screw up a cookie. A cake may not rise, custard can curdle, and pie dough might turn tough, but cookies are forgiving. As long as you add your ingredients and follow the basic instructions, they'll taste good—delicious even. Here are my top tips for successful cookie baking:

It's true that most cookies can be made entirely by hand, but if you have a mixer, use it. You'll be glad. It will save you time and elbow grease.

Ingredients need only be mixed until they just come together—don't overdo it.

Cookies don't require sifted flour. If the baking powder or baking soda has clumps, put it in a small bowl and stir it with your finger or a spoon to break it up.

The size of the cookies doesn't matter as long as all the cookies on one baking sheet are the same size so they bake in the same amount of time. You can go bigger or smaller than the recipe calls for—consistency is what's important. If you make them larger or smaller than is specified in the recipe, be sure to adjust the baking time accordingly. And if making cookies is something you love and you find yourself baking them often, consider getting a small spring-loaded ice cream scoop. The portions will be consistent and it's faster and easier.

If you're making several batches of cookies at a time and only have one or two baking sheets, you can form all the cookies and put them onto parchment. Just make sure to cool the sheet slightly before putting the parchment with the cookies onto the pans.

In a regular oven I prefer to cook one sheet of cookies at a time, but you can cook two pans of cookies at a time, one in the upper third and one in the lower third, if you switch the pans and rotate them halfway through baking. If you use a convection oven, you can bake two pans at once (you may still need to rotate the pans from front to back so they cook evenly) and reduce the temperature by 25°F.

Despite what other cookbook authors advise, I never bother cooling cookies on racks. In professional kitchens we don't have enough space and after many years I've learned it's an unnecessary step. When you remove the baking sheet from the oven simply slide the parchment with the cookies onto your counter.

Make-Ahead and Storage Tips

Most of the cookies here can be formed—rolled, dropped, or sliced—and refrigerated or frozen before baking. Once they're baked they will keep in an airtight container for a week, but you will notice their flavor diminish within a couple days' time. Of course they'll probably disappear before then!

3:00 PM Chocolate Pick-Me-Up Cookies

Makes about 42 cookies

Many people who don't know me well are surprised when they see me turn down dessert after dinner, but my friends know I'm usually burned out on sweets by the end of my workday so they understand. I do, however, indulge a daily weakness for chocolate, particularly in the afternoon around 3:00 PM when my energy flags. Just one of these cookies makes a perfect pick-me-up.

You'll need to toast nuts for this recipe as well as most recipes in this book. Toasting brings out the flavor of the nuts. I prefer to toast them in the oven, rather than in a pan on the stovetop, because the oven gives you much more even results. Just make sure to set a timer!

WHAT YOU'LL NEED

2 or 3 baking or cookie sheets

Parchment paper

Saucepan and metal bowl, or double boiler (if you have one)

Rubber spatula

Small spring-loaded ice cream scoop (if you have one)

1 1/2 cups pecan pieces

8 ounces dark chocolate (58 to 62 percent cacao), chopped or broken into 1-inch pieces

4 tablespoons unsalted butter

3 tablespoons all-purpose unbleached flour

1/4 teaspoon baking powder

2 large eggs

1 cup granulated sugar

1 1/2 teaspoons pure vanilla extract

5 ounces (1 cup) milk chocolate chips

FB: Whoops, we don't have any pecans. Looks like just walnuts.

EL: No big deal. Do you like walnuts?

FB: Yeah, it doesn't matter to me, I like all kinds of nuts (even the human kind).

EL: (Laughing) But let's toast them first to bring out the flavor. Put them in one layer on that baking sheet and put them in the preheated oven.

After a few minutes…

FB: Do you smell something burning?

EL: Oops. I think it's the nuts.

FB: Oh my God, they look a little brown.

EL: We were chatting so much we forgot to set the timer. Even professionals make mistakes in the kitchen. I've burned more nuts than I care to admit. That's why timers were invented.

FB: Do you think we should toss these?

EL: Taste one and tell me what you think.

FB: Yuck. Pretty bitter.

EL: I agree. Let's toss them.

FB: Should we make more?

EL: Sure, but this time let's use a timer.

1. Preheat the oven to 350°F. Line the baking sheets with parchment.

2. Spread the pecan pieces in one layer in a small baking pan and put in the (preheated) oven. Set a timer for 10 minutes and check the nuts to see if they're a light golden brown. If not, toast 2 minutes longer. Set aside to cool.

3. Melt the chocolate and the butter by putting them in a heat-proof bowl set over a saucepan of simmering water, making sure the bowl does not touch the water. (You can use a double boiler if you have one.) Stir and scrape the sides of the bowl occasionally with the rubber spatula until the chocolate is smooth and evenly melted. Remove the bowl from the heat. Let cool to room temperature.

4. In a small bowl, stir the flour and baking powder together and set aside.

5. With an electric mixer or by hand, beat the eggs with the sugar and vanilla until smooth. Mix in the melted chocolate. Add the flour mixture and continue to mix until everything is evenly combined. Scrape down the sides of the bowl once or twice with the rubber spatula. Stir in the pecans and chocolate chips, just until combined.

6. Put 2 racks in the upper and lower thirds of the (preheated) oven. Place 1-tablespoon (slightly rounded, not flat, not heaping) mounds of dough 2 inches apart on the parchment-lined baking sheets. If you have one you can also use a small ice cream scoop to form the cookies and plop them out onto the sheets (it's much faster and easier).

7. Bake the cookies for about 9 to 11 minutes, or until they've lost their sheen. Although they may seem underdone and kind of gooey, don't be tempted to let them bake longer—they'll firm up as they cool. So that the cookies bake evenly, you may need to rotate the pans in the oven or switch racks halfway through.

Almond–Chocolate Chip Cookies

Makes about 22 cookies

One of our Fearful Bakers called these "Grandma Cookies." I love that, but I would add that they're more like "Modern Grandma Cookies" because I swapped almond butter for peanut butter and butter for shortening. As it turned out it was not an easy recipe revision and it took me several tries to get them just right—buttery, nutty, and crumbly.

If your almond butter has separated, stir it before adding it to the mixer.

WHAT YOU'LL NEED

2 or 3 baking or cookie sheets

Parchment paper

Rubber spatula

Small spring-loaded ice cream scoop (if you have one)

1/2 cup sliced almonds

8 tablespoons (1 stick) unsalted butter, softened

1 cup granulated sugar

1 large egg

1 cup almond butter

1 1/2 cups unbleached all-purpose flour

1 teaspoon baking soda

1/2 teaspoon kosher salt

3 ounces dark chocolate (58 to 62 percent cacao), chopped or broken into 1-inch pieces

1. Preheat the oven to 350°F. Line the baking sheets with parchment paper.

2. Spread the almonds in one layer in a small baking pan and put it in the preheated oven. Set a timer for 10 minutes and check the almonds to see if they're a light golden brown. If not, toast 2 minutes more. Let cool, then chop into roughly 1/2-inch pieces. Set aside.

3. With an electric mixer or by hand, beat the butter and sugar together until smooth. Scrape down the sides of the bowl with the rubber spatula and mix in the egg until combined. Mix in the almond butter. Add the flour, baking soda, and salt. Mix until everything is smooth, scraping down the sides of the bowl once or twice. Stir in the chocolate and almonds.

4. Put 2 racks in the upper and lower thirds of the (preheated) oven. Arrange 2-tablespoon (slightly rounded, not flat, not heaping) mounds of dough 2 inches apart on the parchment-lined baking sheets. If you have one, you can also use a small ice cream scoop to form the cookies and plop them out onto the sheets (it's much faster and easier).

5. Flatten the mounds slightly with your hands or the bottom of a glass. Bake for 10 to 12 minutes, or until the cookies have browned lightly on the edges but still seem soft in the middle if you press them lightly with your finger. Although they may seem underdone, don't be tempted to let them bake longer—they'll firm up as they cool. So that the cookies bake evenly, you may need to rotate the pans in the oven or switch racks halfway through.

6. Let the cookies cool to room temperature (if you can wait that long).

Chocolate Chip Cookies

Makes about 42 cookies

I'm always skeptical when I see "Best-Ever" in a recipe title. What I think is delicious you may not, so I don't claim anything of the kind. What I will say is that I've been tinkering with this recipe for so many years that it's exactly the way I like it. The cookies are flat and crispy but still a little chewy. Try them and see what you think.

The chocolate "chips" I use here are pieces of chopped chocolate. Those perfect little chocolate chip kisses that you buy in the package have additives so that they keep their shape and don't melt.

WHAT YOU'LL NEED

2 or 3 baking or cookie sheets

Parchment paper

Rubber spatula

Small spring-loaded ice cream scoop (if you have one)

5 ounces dark chocolate (58 to 62 percent cacao)

8 tablespoons (1 stick) unsalted butter, softened

3/4 cup firmly packed light brown sugar

1/4 cup granulated sugar

1 large egg

1/2 teaspoon pure vanilla extract

1 cup plus 2 tablespoons unbleached all-purpose flour

1/2 teaspoon baking soda

1/2 teaspoon kosher salt

1. Preheat the oven to 350°F. Line the baking sheets with parchment paper.

2. Chop the chocolate into 1/4-to 1/2-inch pieces. You should have about 1 1/4 cups. Set aside.

3. With an electric mixer or by hand, beat the butter, brown sugar, and granulated sugar together until smooth. Scrape down the side of the bowl with the rubber spatula and mix in the egg and vanilla until combined. Add the flour, baking soda, and salt. Mix until everything is smooth, scraping down the side of the bowl once or twice. Stir in the chocolate pieces.

4. Put 2 racks in the upper and lower thirds of the (preheated) oven. Arrange 1-tablespoon slightly rounded, (not flat, not heaping) mounds of dough 2 inches apart on the parchment-lined baking sheets. If you have one, you can also use a small ice cream scoop to form the cookies and plop them out onto the sheets (it's much faster and easier).

5. Flatten the mounds slightly with your hands or the bottom of a glass. Bake for 10 to 12 minutes, or until the cookies have browned lightly on the edges but still seem soft in the middle if you press them lightly with your finger. Although they may seem underdone, don't be tempted to let them bake longer— they'll firm up as they cool. So that the cookies bake evenly, you may need to rotate the pans in the oven or switch racks halfway through.

6. Let the cookies cool to room temperature.

Apple Crisp Bars

Makes 15 (3- by 2 1/2-inch) bars

With these bars you have all the flavor and texture of an apple crisp contained in a package that you can pick up with your fingers—no fork required. They would be perfect for a box picnic or as sweet bites at a cocktail party.

WHAT YOU'LL NEED
Food processor

9- by 13-inch baking pan

8 tablespoons (1 stick) cold unsalted butter

1 1/2 cups plus 2 tablespoons unbleached all-purpose flour

1/2 cup confectioners' sugar

3 pounds Gala or Fuji apples (7 to 8 medium)

1/2 cup granulated sugar

1/4 teaspoon cinnamon

Pinch kosher salt

Streusel Topping (recipe follows)

1/2 cup water

1 teaspoon lemon juice

Streusel Topping
1/3 cup pecan pieces

1 cup unbleached all-purpose flour

1/3 cup firmly packed light brown sugar

7 tablespoons unsalted butter, melted and cooled

1. Preheat the oven to 375°F.

2. Cut the butter into 1/2-inch pieces. Put 1 1/2 cups of the flour and the confectioners' sugar in the bowl of a food processor and scatter over the butter pieces. Pulse just until the butter is the size of rolled oats.

3. Turn the mixture out into the baking pan and pat with your fingers to spread into an even layer. Bake the crust in the (preheated) oven until golden brown, about 25 minutes.

4. While the crust is baking, make the filling. Peel the apples and core each by cutting from the top down the sides and discarding the rectangular piece of core. Slice crosswise into 1/4-inch pieces. Combine the apples, granulated sugar, cinnamon, salt, water, and lemon juice in a large skillet (the water is to help the apples cook). Cook over medium heat until the apples are soft, 15 to 20 minutes. If the apples are dry, add a little more water. If there is still water in the pan and the apples have already softened, turn up the heat to evaporate the liquid. Let cool.

5. Coarsely chop the apples and stir in the remaining 2 tablespoons flour. Spread the apple filling over crust. Drop the streusel topping in small clumps on top of the apples, patting it down and spreading it out to cover the top.

6. Bake in the (preheated) oven until the streusel is golden brown, about 35 minutes.

7. Let cool to room temperature in the pan before cutting into bars.

Streusel Topping
8. In a medium bowl, stir together the pecans, flour, and brown sugar. Stir in the melted butter until well combined but still with some clumps. The streusel can be made ahead and kept in a covered container in the refrigerator for up to 2 weeks.

Blondies

Makes 9 (3-inch) or 16 (2-inch) bar cookies

I know most people think of these bars as blonde brownies, but to me they're more like the soft middle of a big, chewy chocolate chip cookie.

If you're not quite sure if these are done baking, leave the pan in the oven a couple of minutes. The extra time won't hurt them. Use any kind of chocolate chips you like, milk or dark, and any size, mini or chunk.

WHAT YOU'LL NEED

9-inch square baking pan

Rubber spatula

10 tablespoons (1 1/4 sticks) unsalted butter, softened

1 cup firmly packed light brown sugar

1 large egg

2 teaspoons pure vanilla extract

1 1/4 cups unbleached all-purpose flour

3/4 teaspoon baking powder

1/4 teaspoon kosher salt

1 cup chocolate chips

1. Preheat the oven to 350°F.

2. Grease the baking pan with nonstick cooking spray or butter and evenly coat with flour, tapping out the excess.

3. With an electric mixer or by hand, beat the butter and brown sugar together until smooth. Scrape down the side of the bowl with the rubber spatula, then mix in the egg. And the vanilla extract. Add the flour, baking powder, and salt and stir until everything is evenly blended. Stir in the chocolate chips.

4. Turn the batter out into the prepared pan and spread evenly with the spatula. Bake until a bamboo skewer or toothpick inserted into the center of the batter (and not a chocolate chip) comes out clean and it's a light golden brown, about 30 minutes.

5. Let cool to room temperature. Cut in the pan into 9 (3-inch) or 16 (2-inch) squares.

Chewy Brown Sugar Cookies

Makes about 32 cookies

These are perfect cookie jar cookies. For a special treat try using them to form ice cream sandwiches, filled with good-quality purchased vanilla ice cream. A word of caution: don't use blackstrap molasses. It's way too strong and would overwhelm the subtler flavor of the brown sugar.

WHAT YOU'LL NEED

2 or 3 baking or cookie sheets

Parchment paper

Rubber spatula

Small spring-loaded ice cream scoop (if you have one)

8 tablespoons (1 stick) unsalted butter, softened

1/2 cup plus 2 tablespoons firmly packed light brown sugar

2 tablespoons mild molasses

1 cup plus 2 tablespoons unbleached all-purpose flour

1/2 teaspoon kosher salt

1. Preheat the oven to 350°F. Line the baking sheets with parchment paper.

2. With an electric mixer or by hand beat the butter and brown sugar together until smooth. Scrape down the side of the bowl with the rubber spatula and mix in the molasses. Add the flour and salt and mix until everything is evenly blended.

3. Put 2 racks in the upper and lower thirds of the (preheated) oven. Arrange 2-tablespoon (slightly rounded, not flat, not heaping) mounds of dough, 2 inches apart on the parchment-lined baking sheets. If you have one you can also use a small ice cream scoop to form the cookies and plop them out onto the sheets (it's much faster and easier).

4. Flatten the mounds slightly with your hands or the bottom of a glass. Bake for 10 to 12 minutes, until the cookies have browned lightly on the edges but still are soft in the middle if you press them lightly with your finger. Although they may seem underdone, don't be tempted to let them bake longer—they'll firm up as they cool. So that the cookies bake evenly you may need to rotate the pans in the oven or switch racks halfway through.

5. Let the cookies cool to room temperature.

Mocha–Cream Cheese Brownies

Makes 16 (2-inch) or 9 (3-inch) brownies

Who could resist the tasty pleasure of two crowd-pleasers, brownies and cheesecake, along with the fun of blending two batters into marbleized swirls? With their hint of coffee they make a perfect midafternoon grown-up treat.

Eater beware: Even though you can cut these brownies into 3-inch squares, I like them better cut into smaller squares or rectangles. They're richer than they look.

WHAT YOU'LL NEED
9-inch square baking pan

Saucepan and metal bowl, or double boiler if you have one

Rubber spatula

Chocolate Layer
9 ounces dark chocolate (58 to 62 percent cacao), chopped or broken into 1-inch pieces

10 tablespoons (1 1/4 sticks) unsalted butter, softened

1 cup granulated sugar

3 large eggs

3/4 cup unbleached all-purpose flour

Large pinch of kosher salt

Coffee–Cream Cheese Layer
2 (8-ounce) packages cream cheese, softened

1/2 cup granulated sugar

2 large eggs

2 teaspoons instant coffee granules

1 teaspoon pure vanilla extract

1. Preheat the oven to 350°F. Grease the bottom and sides of the baking pan with nonstick cooking spray or butter.

Chocolate Layer
2. Melt the chocolate and butter by putting them in a heat-proof bowl set over a saucepan of simmering water, making sure the bowl does not touch the water. (You can use a double boiler if you have one.) Stir and scrape the side of the bowl occasionally with the rubber spatula until the chocolate is smooth and evenly melted. Set aside and let cool to room temperature.

3. In a medium bowl, whisk the sugar and eggs until smooth. Stir in the melted chocolate, then the flour and salt and mix until well blended. Turn the batter into the prepared pan and spread evenly with the spatula.

Coffee–Cream Cheese Layer
4. In another bowl, mix the cream cheese with the sugar until smooth. Add the eggs and stir until combined. Scrape down the side of the bowl with the rubber spatula. Stir in the instant coffee and vanilla until everything is well blended.

5. Using the rubber spatula, spread the cream cheese mixture on top of the chocolate layer, then run a table knife through the cream cheese to swirl it into large white ribbons throughout the brown batter (don't go crazy—you want the swirls to stay distinct).

6. Bake, until a bamboo skewer or toothpick inserted into the center of the batter comes out clean, 30 to 35 minutes.

7. Let cool to room temperature, then cut into 16 (2-inch) or 9 (3-inch) squares.

Caramelized Pinwheel Cookies

Makes about 32 cookies

You may have bought or seen *palmiers* at a French bakery: those shatteringly crisp cookies, crunchy with caramelized sugar inside and out. Sometimes called "palm leaves" or "elephant ears," which they resemble, the cookies are made with puff pastry dough and sugar. Though they're not difficult, I've simplified the recipe even further by using store-bought puff pastry dough and I've eliminated any complicated rolling. This is one recipe in the book where I think parchment is a must. Because the sugar in the pinwheels can burn quickly, once you remove the sheet from the oven the paper makes quick work of sliding all the cookies at once off the hot pan to keep them from browning further. That's also why I only bake one sheet of cookies at a time—when it comes to turning them you can do it more quickly.

1. Preheat the oven to 400°F. Line the baking sheets with parchment paper.

2. Unfold the thawed sheet of puff pastry by carefully opening it to see if it's cold but pliable. If it starts to crack, let it defrost on the counter 5 minutes and test it again. Once it's fully flexible, unfold it and check for any cracks along the seam. If there are any, simply push the edges back together and smooth them out.

3. Sprinkle a work surface with a little sugar and place the puff pastry on top of the sugar. Sprinkle the pastry with sugar and with the rolling pin, roll out to a 13-inch square. Lift it up occasionally to make sure the dough isn't sticking to the work surface; if it is, put more sugar underneath (or on top if it's sticking to the rolling pin). Don't be afraid to be generous with the sugar to prevent sticking.

WHAT YOU'LL NEED
1 or 2 baking or cookie sheets

Parchment paper

Rolling pin

Metal spatula

1 (9- by 9-inch) sheet store-bought puff pastry, defrosted according to the package directions

About 1/2 cup granulated sugar

The timer has just gone off after baking a batch of pinwheel cookies on the first side for 7 minutes.

FB: Umm, they smell so good and they're starting to color.

EL: Take the pan out and flip the cookies over with that spatula. And since they're popping up a little you can lightly press to flatten them after you turn them.

FB: Wow, that was quick.

EL: Look at the tops. They seem good, but you also need to check the bottoms.

FB: (Uses the spatula to look at the underside of a cookie.) Yikes, they're darker than the other side.

EL: These cookies can go from golden brown to burnt really fast. Take the pan out of the oven and slide the parchment onto the counter. Good. Now you see what I meant about looking underneath. You have to make sure to check the bottoms and not just look at the tops.

4. Sprinkle the dough with 2 tablespoons sugar.

5. Cut the dough in half lengthwise (in a vertical line perpendicular to your body) and starting at one of the ends closest to you, roll each piece of dough up like it's a carpet. Cut each log into 1/4-inch slices. Lay the slices flat-side up on your work surface and sprinkle them with sugar.

6. Transfer them to the parchment-lined baking sheets sugared-side down, leaving 1 inch between the pinwheels and being careful to not let them unroll (you can lightly press the open end into the cookie so it is less likely to spring open). Sprinkle each one once more with sugar.

7. Bake 1 sheet of cookies in the (preheated) oven until they just begin to turn golden brown, about 7 minutes. Remove the pan from the oven and, with a metal spatula, turn each cookie over. Return them to the oven and bake 2 to 5 minutes longer (depending on your oven), until they're nicely browned and caramelized—but watch them like a hawk, they can burn quickly. So that the pinwheels don't continue to cook, immediately slide the parchment paper off the baking sheet and onto the counter.

8. Bake the other pan of pinwheels.

Cardamom Shortbread

Makes 20 (about 2- by 1 1/2-inch) shortbread

Cardamom is not used much in American kitchens. The Nordic countries have had a long-standing love affair with this Asian Indian spice, and you'll often find it flavoring their baked goods. I like the way its sweet and spicy pungency gives an unexpected lift to what can be rather mundane desserts like shortbread and custard. What I don't like is how much work it can be to extract the tiny seeds from cardamom pods, so I use ground cardamom instead.

WHAT YOU'LL NEED
8-inch square baking pan

Aluminum foil

Electric stand mixer or a handheld mixer and medium bowl

16 tablespoons (2 sticks) cold unsalted butter

1/2 cup granulated sugar

1 3/4 cups unbleached all-purpose flour

1/4 cup cornstarch

1/2 teaspoon cardamom

1/4 teaspoon kosher salt

1. Preheat the oven to 300°F.

2. Grease the baking pan with nonstick cooking spray or butter. Line the sides and bottom with one piece of foil, pressing it into the corners.

3. Cut the butter into 1/2-inch cubes. In the bowl of an electric stand mixer or in a medium bowl if you're using a handheld mixer, stir the sugar with the flour, cornstarch, cardamom, and salt. Add the butter cubes and mix on low speed until the butter and flour come together into small clumps of "wet sand," but haven't formed a ball.

4. Turn the mixture out into the lined pan. Cover the dough with a piece of plastic wrap and with your fingers press it evenly over the bottom of the pan. Remove the plastic wrap.

5. Bake the shortbread in the (preheated) oven for 25 minutes. Remove from the oven and with a paring knife gently score three 1/2-inch-deep lines in one direction and then four perpendicular lines, to make twenty 2- by 1 1/2-inch rectangles. With a fork, prick holes all over the top. Continue to bake until the shortbread is evenly firm from the edges to the center, about 30 minutes longer. As the shortbread continues to bake some of the scored marks will disappear but you'll still see traces so you'll know where to cut when it has cooled.

6. Let cool completely in the pan. Lift up the foil removing the shortbread in one piece. Peel the foil back from the sides and cut the shortbread along the scored lines.

Cashew Currant Cookies

Makes about 30 cookies

I'm always trying to find ways to give new twists to familiar cookies, and here I think I have hit on a winner. For a basic drop cookie it's quite refined. In place of the usual chocolate chips I use white chocolate, and instead of raisins I use smaller and subtler currants. And also add salted cashews, which create a perfect balance.

WHAT YOU'LL NEED

2 or 3 baking or cookie sheets

Parchment paper

Rubber spatula

Small spring-loaded ice cream scoop (if you have one)

6 tablespoons unsalted butter, softened

1/2 cup firmly packed light brown sugar

1/3 cup maple syrup

2 tablespoons mild molasses

1 large egg

1 1/2 cups unbleached all-purpose flour

3/4 teaspoon kosher salt

1/2 teaspoon baking soda

1/2 teaspoon cinnamon

3/4 cup chopped cashews

3/4 cup white chocolate chips

1/2 cup currants

1. Preheat the oven to 350°F. Line the baking sheets with parchment paper.

2. With an electric mixer or by hand, beat the butter and brown sugar together until smooth. Scrape down the side of the bowl with the rubber spatula and mix in the maple syrup and molasses. Mix in the egg until combined. Add the flour, salt, baking soda, and cinnamon. Mix until everything is smooth, scraping down the side of the bowl once or twice. Stir in the cashews, chocolate chips, and currants.

3. Put 2 racks in the upper and lower thirds of the (preheated) oven. Arrange 1-tablespoon (slightly rounded, not flat, not heaping) mounds of dough 2 inches apart on the parchment-lined baking sheets. If you have one you can also use a small ice cream scoop to form the cookies and plop them out onto the sheets (it's much faster and easier).

4. Bake for about 12 minutes, or until the cookies have browned lightly on the edges but still are soft in the middle if you press them lightly with your finger. Although they may seem underdone, don't be tempted to let them bake longer—they'll firm up as they cool. So that the cookies bake evenly you may need to rotate the pans in the oven or switch racks halfway through.

5. Let the cookies cool to room temperature (if you can wait that long). They'll keep for up to 1 week in a covered container.

Cherry Pistachio Biscotti

Makes about 40 biscotti

It may be true that you can make most any dessert recipe by hand with only a spoon, whisk, and/or a sharp knife—that's all our grandmothers had—but who would want to when mixers and food processors make many baking chores so much easier? What I've found odd is that so many people have mixers sitting on their kitchen counters that they never use. I've concluded that part of the fear of baking has a lot to do with the fear of the mixer.

The other biscotti recipe in this book (Chocolate Biscotti, page 34) is mixed entirely by hand. The difference between the two recipes is that there is no butter in the Chocolate Biscotti and here you need to cream butter and sugar together, a process that is more easily accomplished with a mixer.

WHAT YOU'LL NEED
Baking or cookie sheet

Parchment paper

Electric stand mixer or a handheld mixer and medium bowl

Rubber spatula

4 tablespoons unsalted butter, softened

3/4 cup granulated sugar

1 large egg

1 1/3 cups unbleached all-purpose flour

1/2 teaspoon baking powder

1/4 teaspoon kosher salt

1/2 cup dried cherries

1/4 cup shelled dry-roasted pistachios

EL: Do you have a mixer at home?

FB: Um, I have a stand mixer, like that one, but I have to admit that since I rarely bake I keep it in the garage.

EL: That's okay; I'm going to show you how to work with it. Once you do it, you'll wonder why you haven't used it more often.

1. Preheat the oven to 350°F. Line the baking sheet with parchment paper.

2. Using the stand mixer, or a medium bowl and a handheld mixer, first on low speed and then increasing the speed gradually to medium, beat the butter and sugar together until smooth. Scrape down the side of the bowl with the rubber spatula and mix in the egg until combined.

3. Add the flour, baking powder, salt, cherries, and pistachios and mix on low speed until the mixture just comes together into a shaggy but cohesive dough.

4. Turn the dough out on a lightly floured work surface. Gather the dough into one piece and divide in half. Gently roll each half into a log about 12 inches long and 1 1/2 inches in diameter (the actual size doesn't matter too much; you just want them to be the same size so they bake evenly). Sprinkle the logs and work surface with more flour if they're sticking. Place the logs on the parchment-lined baking sheet with a few inches separating them. Bake until they're firm to the touch and a light golden brown, about 30 minutes.

5. Remove the pan from the oven and reduce the oven temperature to 300°F.

6. Let the biscotti cool for 10 minutes. Slice the logs on the diagonal into 3/4-inch pieces. Return to the baking sheet, cut-side down, and bake until the biscotti are golden, 15 minutes. Let cool to room temperature.

Chocolate Biscotti

Makes about 36 biscotti

You may be aware that biscotti are twice-baked cookies (it's the second baking that gives them their crisp, dry texture), but few novice bakers realize how easy they are to make. Everything can be done by hand. And I mean literally by hand. Once you've stirred the ingredients in a bowl to roughly combine them, don't be afraid to dump the shaggy dough out on a counter and finish gathering it together by hand. To make things even easier, the biscotti can be cut and baked the second time the next day.

I can't stress enough how important it is to read a recipe through before getting started. Even our best and brightest Fearful Bakers forget this rule.

WHAT YOU'LL NEED

Baking or cookie sheet

Parchment paper

Rubber spatula

1/3 cup pecan pieces

1 cup unbleached all-purpose flour

3/4 cup granulated sugar

1/3 cup cocoa powder

1 teaspoon baking soda

Large pinch kosher salt

2 large eggs

1/2 teaspoon pure vanilla extract

5 ounces dark chocolate (58 to 62 percent cacao), chopped or broken into 1-inch pieces

1 to 1 1/4 cups sweetened shredded coconut

When we join our Fearful Baker she is assembling and getting ready to combine the ingredients for the biscotti.

FB: Do we have the coconut? Can I add it now?

EL. It's in that little bag. But did you read the recipe?

FB: I really didn't read it through—I just looked at the list of ingredients.

EL: What you're going to do after the biscotti are baked is to dip them in chocolate and then top them with coconut. One of my top tips for bakers is to read the recipe through before you start, because, if you put the coconut in the dough it would make it too dry, and you wouldn't have any coconut to dip the cookies into.

FB: (Laughing) Oops, guess I won't be passing the final exam.

1. Preheat the oven to 350°F and line the baking sheet with parchment paper.

2. Put the pecan pieces in one layer in a small baking pan and put it in the (preheated) oven. Set a timer for 10 minutes and check the pecans to see if they're a light golden brown. If not, toast 2 minutes longer. Set aside to cool.

3. By hand in a medium bowl, stir the pecans with the flour, sugar, cocoa powder, baking soda, and salt. In another medium bowl whisk the eggs with the vanilla.

4. Switch to a spoon or rubber spatula and stir the eggs into the flour/cocoa mixture until the mixture comes together into a shaggy but cohesive dough. Since the dough can be difficult to stir, don't be afraid to finish gathering and mixing it together by hand. You don't want to see any big dry clumps.

5. Turn the dough out on a lightly floured work surface and divide in half. Gently roll each half into a log about 12 inches long and 1 1/2 inches in diameter. Sprinkle the logs and work surface with more flour if they're sticking. Place the logs on the baking sheet with a few inches separating them. Bake for about 15 minutes, or until they're firm to the touch and they no longer appear shiny or wet where the logs have cracked.

6. Remove the pan from the oven and reduce the oven temperature to 300°F.

7. Let the biscotti cool for 10 minutes. Slice the logs into 1/2- to 3/4-inch slices. Place on the baking sheet cut-side down and bake for 15 minutes. Let cool to room temperature.

8. While the biscotti are baking, melt the chocolate by putting it in a heat-proof bowl set over a saucepan of simmering water, making sure the bowl does not touch the water. (You can use a double boiler if you have one.) Put the coconut on a plate or in a wide bowl.

9. Dip a cut side of each cooled biscotto into the melted chocolate and then in the coconut. Place it chocolate side up on a rack or back on the baking sheet. Continue to dip all the biscotti.

10. The chocolate needs to harden before you serve them, so if you can resist, let them sit for at least an hour.

Chewy Oatmeal Cookies

Makes about 36 cookies

How do you make an old-fashioned oatmeal cookie more irresistible? Add chocolate chips to reel in those chocoholics, use dried cherries in place of raisins, and include lots of brown sugar to make the cookies chewy. I've never seen anyone turn down a second cookie once they've tasted one of these—even those who claim only to like their oatmeal cookies crisp.

WHAT YOU'LL NEED

2 or 3 baking or cookie sheets

Parchment paper

Rubber spatula

Small spring-loaded ice cream scoop (if you have one)

12 tablespoons (1 1/2 sticks) unsalted butter, softened

1 cup firmly packed light brown sugar

1/2 cup granulated sugar

1 large egg

1 teaspoon pure vanilla extract

3 cups old-fashioned oats

1 cup all-purpose unbleached flour

1 teaspoon baking soda

1/2 teaspoon kosher salt

2 tablespoons whole milk

1/2 cup dried cherries

1/2 cup chocolate chips

1. Preheat the oven to 350°F. Line the baking sheets with parchment paper.

2. With an electric mixer or by hand, beat the butter, brown sugar, and granulated sugar until smooth. Add the egg and vanilla, mixing until well combined. Stir in the oats, flour, baking soda, and salt until well blended, then stir in the milk, dried cherries, and chocolate chips.

3. Put 2 racks in the upper and lower thirds of the (preheated) oven. Place 1-tablespoon (slightly rounded, not flat, not heaping) mounds of dough 2 inches apart on the parchment-lined baking sheets. If you have one you can also use a small ice cream scoop to form the cookies and plop them out onto the sheets (it's much faster and easier).

4. Flatten the mounds slightly with your hands or the bottom of a glass. Bake for about 10 minutes, or until the cookies have browned lightly on the edges but still are soft in the middle if you press them lightly with your finger. Although they may seem underdone, don't be tempted to let them bake longer—they'll firm up as they cool. So that the cookies bake evenly you may need to rotate the pans in the oven or switch racks halfway through.

5. Let the cookies cool to room temperature (if you can wait that long).

Coconut-Chocolate-Almond Macaroons

Makes about 30 cookies

For the last couple of years French macaroons—or *macarons* as they spell it—have become quite the rage on bakery and restaurant dessert menus all over America. While I admit to adoring the authentic, airy, pastel-colored French confections, I like this style just as much. Not only are they intensely flavored clouds that melt on your tongue, they're much, much easier to make.

This and the Coffee-Chocolate Meringues (page 42) are two recipes for which an electric mixer is a must. Whipping the egg whites to achieve maximum volume is crucial to the success of the meringue (see page 12 for more information on whipping egg whites).

WHAT YOU'LL NEED

2 or 3 baking or cookie sheets

Parchment paper

Saucepan and metal bowl, or double boiler if you have one

Electric stand mixer or handheld mixer and medium bowl

Rubber spatula

1 cup whole almonds

4 ounces dark chocolate (58 to 62 percent cacao), chopped or broken into 1-inch pieces

2 large egg whites

1/2 cup sugar

2 cups sweetened shredded coconut

1 teaspoon pure vanilla extract

1. Preheat the oven to 350°F. Line the baking sheets with parchment paper.

2. Chop the almonds into pieces no larger than 1/4 inch. Reduce the oven temperature to 325°F. Spread the almond pieces in one layer in a small baking pan and put in the (preheated) oven. Set a timer for 10 minutes and check the nuts to see if they're a light golden brown. If not, toast 2 minutes longer. Set aside to cool.

3. Melt the chocolate by putting it in a heat-proof bowl set over a saucepan of simmering water, making sure the bowl does not touch the water. (You can use a double boiler if you have one.) Stir and scrape the side of the bowl occasionally with the rubber spatula until the chocolate is smooth and evenly melted. Let cool to room temperature.

4. In a stand mixer with the wire whisk attachment, or using a handheld mixer and a medium bowl, whisk the egg whites on medium speed until frothy. With the machine running, add the sugar in a slow, steady stream. Increase the speed to high and whip until the whites hold stiff glossy peaks on the whisk (stop the mixer and lift the whisk to check).

5. Using the rubber spatula, gently mix in the chopped almonds, chocolate, coconut, and vanilla until the mixture is evenly combined.

6. Put 2 racks in the upper and lower thirds of the (preheated) oven. With a spoon, scoop up generous tablespoons of the mixture and, with another spoon or your finger, scrape them off into mounds onto the parchment-lined baking sheets. You can space them fairly close together since they won't spread or puff up.

7. Bake until the surfaces of the macaroons look dry and seem somewhat firm if you give them a little squeeze, about 15 minutes. So that the cookies bake evenly, you may need to rotate the pans in the oven or switch racks halfway through. Let cool 10 minutes. Peel the macaroons off the parchment.

Chocolate-Orange Crinkle Cookies

Makes about 26 cookies

At the beginning of the baking sessions we held in preparing this book, invariably I would ask, "What kind of oven do you have? Regular or convection?" And most of the time I could predict the answer: "I don't know" or "convection, but I don't know how to use it." It was amazing to me how many of our bakers had well-equipped kitchens with new high-tech appliances, stand mixers, and food processors that were often not used at all or were simply underutilized.

1. Preheat the oven to 350°F.

2. Spread the hazelnuts in one layer in a small baking pan and put in the (preheated) oven. Set a timer for 10 minutes and check the nuts to see if they're a light golden brown. If not, toast 2 minutes longer. Put the warm nuts in a colander and rub them with a clean kitchen towel to remove some of the skins. (If you don't have a colander, just rub them in the towel.) Don't worry about getting all the skins—you just want to remove the loose pieces.

3. In the food processor, process the hazelnuts with the flour and baking powder until the nuts are finely ground and look like coarse sand. Transfer to a medium bowl and set it aside.

4. Melt the chocolate, butter, and liqueur by putting them in a heat-proof bowl set over a saucepan of simmering water, making sure the bowl does not touch the water. (You can use a double boiler if you have one.) Stir and scrape the side of the bowl occasionally with the rubber spatula until the chocolate is smooth and evenly melted. Remove the bowl from the heat and set aside.

5. Using the stand mixer, or a handheld mixer and medium bowl, beginning on low speed and then increasing to medium speed, beat the eggs with the 1/3 cup sugar and orange zest until they're well combined and the sugar has begun to dissolve. Reduce the speed to low and mix in the melted chocolate and then the ground hazelnut mixture until everything is

WHAT YOU'LL NEED

2 or 3 baking or cookie sheets

Parchment paper

Food processor

Saucepan and metal bowl, or double boiler if you have one

Electric stand mixer or a handheld mixer and medium bowl

Rubber spatula

2/3 cup hazelnuts

1/2 cup all-purpose unbleached flour

1/2 teaspoon baking powder

8 ounces dark chocolate (58 to 62 percent cacao), chopped or broken into 1-inch pieces

3 tablespoons unsalted butter

2 tablespoons orange flavor liqueur (such as Grand Marnier or Cointreau)

2 large eggs

1/3 cup plus 1/4 cup granulated sugar

Grated zest of 1 orange

About 1/4 cup confectioners' sugar

EL: So now that your kitchen remodel is done, what kind of oven did you finally decide on?

FB: That German one. It's really beautiful and is convection.

EL: Let's use the convection oven today for these cookies so I can give you a little lesson.

FB: I'd love that. I know it's supposed to be a great feature, but how is it different?

EL: Basically there is a fan in the oven that circulates the air so that the heat fills the entire oven evenly. In a regular oven the heat comes from the top and the bottom, often creating hot spots. In professional kitchens, where oven space can be at a premium because of the volume of things to bake, we almost exclusively use convection.

FB: What do you mean?

EL: You can fill a convection oven with racks of food and they'll all cook pretty evenly. In a regular oven you cook one rack at a time, usually in the middle of the oven, or if you use two racks, you have to switch halfway through baking. You'll see with these cookies. Let's put two baking sheets in the oven and you'll see the difference. You might need to turn the pans around front to back, because no oven is perfect, but the advantage is that you can bake more cookies at a time.

FB: Do you need to adjust the recipe for convection?

EL: Convection cooks a little faster and browns things more quickly, so I tend to lower the heat by twenty-five degrees with most recipes.

evenly combined. Scrape down the side of the bowl with the rubber spatula.

6. Transfer the dough to a bowl or wrap it in plastic and refrigerate until it's chilled and somewhat firm, about 1 hour (or you can leave it overnight).

7. Preheat the oven to 350°F. Line 2 baking sheets with parchment paper.

8. To form the cookies, gently roll (don't squash) pieces of the dough (about 1 generous tablespoon) into 1-inch balls. If the dough gets too soft to roll, put it back in the fridge for a few minutes to firm up. Put the 1/4 cup granulated sugar and the confectioners' sugar into 2 separate small bowls. Roll the balls first in the granulated and then in the confectioners' sugar, making sure they're heavily coated. Arrange the sugared balls about 2 inches apart on the parchment-lined baking sheets.

9. Put 2 racks in the upper and lower thirds of the (preheated) oven. Bake the cookies for 10 to 12 minutes, until they are firm on the edges but still soft in the middle if you press them lightly with your finger. Although they may seem underdone, don't be tempted to let them bake longer—you want them to be fudgy. So that the cookies bake evenly you may need to rotate the pans in the oven or switch racks halfway through.

10. Remove the pans from the oven and let the cookies cool to room temperature.

Cinnamon Sugar Cookies

Makes about 24 cookies

If you ever invite me over for dinner and are worried about what to make for dessert, just know that I will eat practically anything with cinnamon sugar on it.

There are three reasons for rolling the dough into logs rather than dropping mounds onto a cookie sheet: it's a quick way to coat them with the sugar and portion them out and they make a much neater cookie—perfect for presentation on a platter.

WHAT YOU'LL NEED

2 or 3 baking or cookie sheets

Parchment paper

Rubber spatula

8 tablespoons (1 stick) unsalted butter, softened

1/3 cup plus 1 tablespoon granulated sugar

1 large egg yolk

1/2 teaspoon pure vanilla extract

1 cup plus 2 tablespoons unbleached all-purpose flour

1/4 teaspoon kosher salt

3/4 teaspoon ground cinnamon

1. With an electric mixer or by hand, mix the butter with the 1/3 cup sugar until smooth. Scrape down the side of the bowl with the rubber spatula. Mix in the egg yolk and vanilla, then add the flour, salt, and 1/4 teaspoon cinnamon. Mix until everything is evenly combined.

2. Turn the dough out onto a floured surface and divide into 2 equal pieces. Sprinkle each piece with flour and roll into a 6-inch log. Wrap the logs in plastic and refrigerate until firm, about 45 minutes.

3. Preheat the oven to 350°F. Line the baking sheets with parchment paper.

4. Stir the remaining 1/2 teaspoon cinnamon and 1 tablespoon sugar in a small bowl and sprinkle onto a piece of parchment paper or your work surface. Roll the logs in the cinnamon sugar to coat evenly. Cut the logs into 1/2-inch slices.

5. Put 2 racks in the upper and lower thirds of the (preheated) oven. Arrange the slices on the parchment-lined baking sheets, leaving 2 to 3 inches between them.

6. Bake until the cookies are golden brown, about 12 minutes. So that the cookies bake evenly, you may need to rotate the pans in the oven or switch racks halfway through. Cool to room temperature.

Coconut Macadamia Bars

Makes 9 or 16 bars

Basically this is an amped-up version of blondies, made more delicious and complex with the addition of coconut and macadamias.

WHAT YOU'LL NEED

9-inch square baking pan

Rubber spatula

1 cup coarsely chopped macadamia nuts

1 1/3 cups firmly packed light brown sugar

2 large eggs

12 tablespoons (1 1/2 sticks) unsalted butter, melted

2 teaspoons pure vanilla extract

1 1/2 cups all-purpose unbleached flour

1/2 teaspoon kosher salt

1/2 cup bittersweet chocolate chips

1/3 cup sweetened shredded coconut

1. Preheat the oven to 350°F. Grease the baking pan with nonstick cooking spray or butter.

2. Spread the nuts in one layer in a small baking pan and put in the (preheated) oven. Set a timer for 10 minutes and check the nuts to see if they're a light golden brown. If not, toast 2 minutes longer. Set aside to cool.

3. In a medium bowl, whisk the brown sugar with the eggs until blended. Whisk in the melted butter and vanilla. With the rubber spatula or a spoon, stir in the flour and salt until smooth. Stir in the chocolate chips, coconut, and chopped macadamias until everything is evenly distributed.

4. Turn the batter into the prepared pan and spread it out evenly with the spatula.

5. Bake until a bamboo skewer or toothpick inserted into the center of the batter comes out clean, about 40 minutes.

6. Let cool to room temperature, then cut in the pan into 9 (3-inch) or 16 (2-inch) square bars.

Coffee-Chocolate Meringues

Makes about 48 meringue cookies

Shatteringly crisp and airy, these cookies are mostly about texture, but that's not to say that they're lacking in flavor. In fact it's amazing to me just how much chocolaty and nutty punch can be packed into such ephemeral little packages.

WHAT YOU'LL NEED

2 baking or cookie sheets

Parchment paper

Food processor

Electric stand or handheld mixer and medium bowl

Rubber spatula

1/2 cup sliced almonds

1/2 cup confectioners' sugar

1 tablespoon instant coffee granules

4 large egg whites, at room temperature

1/2 cup granulated sugar

1 1/2 ounces dark chocolate (58 to 62 percent cacao), chopped into small pieces, or 1/3 cup chocolate chips

The FB is reading the recipe through and Emily is gathering the ingredients.

FB: It says to process a half cup sliced almonds with a half cup powdered sugar. Why is that?

EL: Sometimes, as in this recipe, you'll see you're supposed to process nuts with flour or sugar. It's to keep the nuts dry when they start releasing their oils as they're chopped. If you left them by themselves and processed long enough they would turn to butter, which is not a bad thing if you like almond butter but not what you want here.

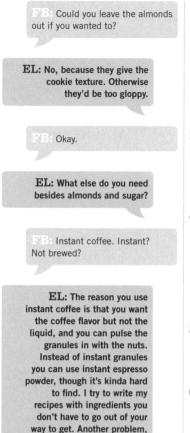

FB: Could you leave the almonds out if you wanted to?

EL: No, because they give the cookie texture. Otherwise they'd be too gloppy.

FB: Okay.

EL: What else do you need besides almonds and sugar?

FB: Instant coffee. Instant? Not brewed?

EL: The reason you use instant coffee is that you want the coffee flavor but not the liquid, and you can pulse the granules in with the nuts. Instead of instant granules you can use instant espresso powder, though it's kinda hard to find. I try to write my recipes with ingredients you don't have to go out of your way to get. Another problem, if you don't use it often, is that the espresso powder can go bad—either get really hard in the jar or go moldy—so once you open it I recommend you keep it in the freezer.

1. Preheat the oven to 300°F. Line the baking sheets with parchment.

2. Spread the almonds in one layer in a small baking pan and put in the (preheated) oven. Set a timer for 10 minutes and check the almonds to see if they're a light golden brown. If not, toast 2 minutes more. Set aside to cool.

3. In the food processor, process the almonds with the confectioners' sugar and instant coffee until the nuts are finely ground and look like coarse sand. Transfer to a bowl and set aside.

4. In a stand mixer with the wire whisk attachment or using a handheld mixer and a medium bowl, whisk the egg whites on medium speed until frothy. With the machine running, add the granulated sugar in a slow, steady stream. Increase the speed to high and whip until the whites hold stiff glossy peaks on the whisk (stop the mixer and lift the whisk to check).

5. Sprinkle half of the ground nuts over the egg whites and very gently stir them in with the rubber spatula. Stir in the remaining nuts and then the chopped chocolate.

6. Put 2 racks in the upper and lower thirds of the (preheated) oven. With a spoon, scoop up generous tablespoons of the meringue and with another spoon or your finger scrape them off into mounds onto the parchment-lined baking sheets. Don't fret if they're messy—that's their beauty. You can space them fairly close together since they won't spread or puff up.

7. Bake until the surfaces of the meringues look dry, about 30 minutes. So that the cookies bake evenly, you may need to rotate the pans in the oven or switch racks halfway through. Let cool 10 minutes. Peel the meringues off the parchment and store in an airtight container for up to 1 week.

Cornmeal Thumbprints

Makes about 56 (1 1/4-inch) cookies

This might be the sleeper cookie recipe in this book. The name "Cornmeal Thumbprints" isn't particularly sexy, but my co-author's husband, Dan, who is an admitted cookie monster and has tasted every cookie in this book, declared these his favorite. The cornmeal adds an unexpected crunch that is a nice contrast to the jam.

You can use your thumb to make the thumbprint; or the end of a large wooden spoon makes a nice, perfectly round mini-crater. Fill it with any kind of jam— I like raspberry—and if you have homemade jam so much the better.

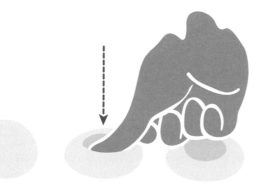

WHAT YOU'LL NEED

3 baking or cookie sheets

Parchment paper

Rubber spatula

1 1/2 cups all-purpose unbleached flour

1 1/2 cups cornmeal

1/2 teaspoon kosher salt

1/2 teaspoon baking powder

16 tablespoons (2 sticks) unsalted butter, softened

1/2 cup granulated sugar

1 large egg

1/4 cup honey

1 teaspoon pure vanilla extract

2/3 cup your favorite jam

FB: That's the timer for the cookies.

EL: Okay, let's take them out and make the thumbprint.

FB: With my thumb? Really?

EL: (Laughing) Yep. That's how they got their name. But I'll give you my very secret professional tip. Just use the end of this wooden spoon.

1. Preheat the oven to 350°F. Line the baking sheets with parchment paper.

2. In a medium bowl, whisk the flour, cornmeal, salt, and baking powder together.

3. With an electric mixer or by hand, beat the butter and sugar until smooth. Add the egg and mix until well combined and use the rubber spatula to scrape down the side of the bowl. Add the honey and vanilla and mix thoroughly, again scraping down the side of the bowl once or twice.

4. Add the flour mixture and mix until the dough comes together.

5. Pinch off dough into approximately 1 1/4-inch pieces and roll into balls. Arrange the balls on the parchment-lined baking sheets, leaving about 2 inches between them.

6. Bake 1 sheet at a time in the center of the oven until the cookies are no longer wet looking, about 10 minutes. Remove from the oven and, using your thumb or the end of a large wooden spoon, gently make a "thumb-sized" indentation in the center of each cookie. If a cookie breaks or starts to fall apart, simply push it back together. Return the pans to the oven and bake 5 to 7 minutes longer, until the undersides of the cookies are turning brown. Let cool completely.

7. Using a small spoon, drop jam into the center of each cookie's thumbprint.

Double Chocolate Thumbprints

Makes about 32 (1 1/4-inch) cookies

Chocolate ganache fills the little dimples of these chocolate butter cookies, giving them a two-for-one punch of chocolate in every bite. While "ganache" might sound very French (it is), and rich (it is), it may also sound difficult (it's not); it is simply chocolate melted with cream so that it can be poured for a glaze or used as a filling. It's also the basis for chocolate truffles.

WHAT YOU'LL NEED

2 baking or cookie sheets

Parchment paper

Rubber spatula

1 cup unbleached all-purpose flour

1/4 cup cocoa powder

1/4 teaspoon baking soda

1/4 teaspoon kosher salt

8 tablespoons (1 stick) unsalted butter, softened

1/3 cup granulated sugar

1/3 cup firmly packed light brown sugar

1 large egg yolk

2 1/2 ounces dark chocolate (58 to 62 percent cacao), chopped or broken into 1-inch pieces

1/4 cup heavy cream

1. Preheat the oven to 350°F. Line the baking sheets with parchment paper.

2. Over a bowl or piece of parchment, sift the flour, cocoa powder, and baking soda together with a sifter, or in a fine strainer by gently tapping your hand against the edge. Add the salt (you can just leave it on top of the flour pile because it gets mixed in later).

3. With an electric mixer or by hand, beat the butter, granulated sugar, and brown sugar on medium speed until smooth. Add the egg yolk and mix until well combined and use the rubber spatula to scrape down the side of the bowl. Add the sifted flour mixture and mix until the dough comes together, again scraping down the side of the bowl once or twice.

4. Pinch off dough into approximately 1 1/4-inch pieces and roll into balls. Arrange the balls on the parchment-lined baking sheets, leaving about 2 inches between them.

5. Bake 1 sheet at a time in the center of the oven until the cookies are no longer wet looking, about 10 minutes. Remove from the oven and, using your thumb or the end of a large wooden spoon, gently make a "thumb-sized" indentation in the center of each cookie. If a cookie breaks or starts to fall apart, simply push it back together. Return the pans to the oven and bake 3 minutes longer, or until the undersides are turning brown. Let cool completely.

6. While the cookies are cooling, make the chocolate ganache. Put the chopped chocolate in a bowl. Warm the cream in a saucepan over medium heat. As soon as it starts to bubble around the edge, pour the hot cream over the chocolate. Shake the bowl a little to submerge all the chocolate pieces, then cover the bowl for several minutes. Whisk until smooth. Let cool slightly.

7. Using a small spoon, drop ganache into the center of each cookie's thumbprint. Allow the ganache to set, about 1 hour, before you devour them.

Honey-Roasted Peanut Butter Cookies

Makes about 36 cookies

I've never been a big fan of peanut butter cookies and find most recipes pretty boring. Until now. These are positively addicting, which I attribute to the seemingly insignificant but big-on-flavor addition of chopped honey-roasted peanuts. One tip: err on the side of caution. If you can't decide if they need a minute or two more, take them out of the oven anyway. They're better undercooked than overcooked and dry.

WHAT YOU'LL NEED

2 or 3 baking or cookie sheets

Parchment paper

Rubber spatula

Small spring-loaded ice cream scoop (if you have one)

16 tablespoons (2 sticks) unsalted butter

1 cup granulated sugar

3/4 cup firmly packed light brown sugar

1 cup smooth peanut butter

2 large eggs

2 teaspoons pure vanilla extract

2 1/2 cups unbleached all-purpose flour

1 tablespoon plus 1 teaspoon baking powder

1/2 teaspoon kosher salt

2 cups honey-roasted peanuts, coarsely chopped

1. Preheat the oven to 350°F. Line the baking sheets with parchment paper.

2. With an electric mixer or by hand, beat the butter, granulated sugar, and brown sugar together until smooth. Scrape down the side of the bowl with the rubber spatula and mix in the peanut butter. Mix in the eggs and vanilla until combined. Add the flour, baking powder, and salt. Mix until everything is smooth, scraping down the side of the bowl once or twice. Stir in half of the peanuts.

3. Put 2 racks in the upper and lower thirds of the (preheated) oven. Arrange 1-tablespoon (not flat, not heaping) mounds of dough 2 inches apart on the parchment-lined baking sheets. If you have one you can also use a small ice cream scoop to form the cookies and plop them out onto the sheets (it's much faster and easier). Press the remaining nuts on the cookies (it's okay to flatten the cookies slightly as you press the nuts on).

4. Bake for 14 minutes, or until the cookies have browned lightly on the edges but still are soft in the middle if you press them lightly with your finger. Although they may seem underdone, don't be tempted to let them bake longer—they'll firm up as they cool and if baked too long they'll be dry. So that the cookies bake evenly you may need to rotate the pans in the oven or switch racks halfway through.

5. Let the cookies cool to room temperature.

Milk Chocolate–Walnut Drop Cookies

Makes about 24 cookies

Chocolate has become big business today and it seems as though everyone in the world has gone to the dark side. Overlooked in all this fervor is good old milk chocolate, now associated with vending-machine candy bars. That's too bad, because there are a number of chocolate producers turning out exceptional milk chocolate. In this cookie, milk chocolate is preferable because dark chocolate would overpower the flavor of the walnuts. But for you dark chocolate fans—don't worry. You will be amazed at how chocolaty these cookies are.

I don't measure chocolate in a measuring cup, because depending on how big the chopped pieces are, the quantity can vary greatly. Read the label of your chocolate bar in order to see how much it weighs. Most chocolate bars for baking come scored into ½-ounce or 1-ounce pieces. Read the label to see how it's marked. Do some grade-school math and divide the bar into the appropriate number of ounces needed for the recipe.

WHAT YOU'LL NEED

2 or 3 baking or cookie sheets

Parchment paper

Saucepan and metal bowl, or double boiler if you have one

Rubber spatula

Small spring-loaded ice cream scoop (if you have one)

1 cup walnuts

10 ounces milk chocolate

3 tablespoons unsalted butter

2 large eggs

3/4 cup granulated sugar

1 teaspoon pure vanilla extract

1/2 cup plus 2 tablespoons unbleached all-purpose flour

1/2 teaspoon baking powder

1. Preheat the oven to 350°F. Line the baking sheets with parchment paper.

2. Spread the walnuts in one layer in a small baking pan and put it in the (preheated) oven. Set a timer for 10 minutes and check the nuts to see if they're a light golden brown. If not, toast 2 minutes longer. Set aside to cool.

3. Break 6 ounces of the chocolate into 1-inch pieces. Chop the remaining 4 ounces chocolate into 1/4-inch pieces—about the size of chocolate chips—and set them aside.

4. Melt the 1-inch pieces of chocolate and the butter in a heat-proof bowl set over (but not touching) a saucepan of simmering water (or use a double boiler if you have one). Stir and scrape the side of the bowl occasionally with the rubber spatula until the chocolate is smooth and evenly melted. Remove from the heat. Let cool to room temperature.

5. With an electric mixer or by hand, beat the eggs with the sugar and vanilla until the mixture has thickened and lightened in color. Scrape down the side of the bowl with the rubber spatula and stir in the melted chocolate mixture. Add the flour and baking powder and mix until everything is smooth, scraping down the side of the bowl once or twice. Stir in the walnuts and reserved chocolate pieces.

6. Put 2 racks in the upper and lower thirds of the (preheated) oven. Arrange 1-tablespoon (not flat, not heaping) mounds of dough 2 inches apart on the parchment-lined baking sheets. If you have one you can also use a small ice cream scoop to form the cookies and plop them out onto the sheets (it's much faster and easier).

7. Bake until the cookies are set and no longer shiny, about 12 minutes. Although they may seem underdone, don't be tempted to let them bake longer—they'll firm up as they cool and if baked too long they'll be dry. So that the cookies bake evenly you may need to rotate the pans in the oven or switch racks halfway through.

8. Let the cookies cool to room temperature.

Oatmeal-Almond Cookies

Makes about 36 cookies

Many of our Fearful Bakers asked about the differences among sheet pans, baking sheets, rimmed baking sheets, and cookie sheets. Sheet pans and baking sheets are the same thing: flat pans of choice in professional kitchens. They come in full size (18- by 24-inch), half size (12- by 18-inch), and quarter size (9- by 12-inch) and always have a 1-inch rim, which is why they're often called in recipes "rimmed baking sheets." Home cooks are more familiar with cookie sheets, flat pans that are rimless except for a small lip on one or two sides. For the cookie recipes in this book, any flat pan will do.

WHAT YOU'LL NEED

2 or 3 baking or cookie sheets

Parchment paper

Small spring-loaded ice cream scoop (if you have one)

1 cup sliced almonds

16 tablespoons (2 sticks) unsalted butter, softened

1 cup granulated sugar

1/2 cup firmly packed light brown sugar

2 large eggs

2 1/4 cups old-fashioned oats

1 1/4 cups unbleached all-purpose flour

1 teaspoon baking soda

1/2 teaspoon kosher salt

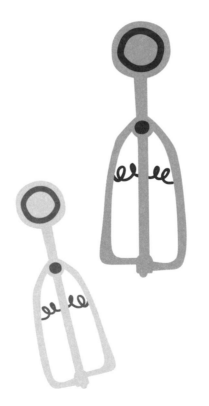

FB: Okay, so making this cookie dough is pretty easy. In fact I think I've transitioned from Fearful Baker to Tentative Baker based on how unintimidating your recipes are.

EL: Well, that's one of the best things about cookie baking. It's not hard and makes a new baker feel accomplished. So let's go on to forming the cookies. Do you have an ice cream scoop at home?

FB: No. I think we just scoop ice cream with a spoon when we're eating it out of the carton.

EL: You and me both! But one of the best uses for a small ice cream scoop is making cookies. But let's just use a tablespoon measure like you would at home.

FB: The recipe says "slightly rounded, not flat, not heaping" tablespoons. Do you really need to be that precise?

EL: It is important to make them all the same size so they cook evenly. Be careful not to put them too close together because the cookies will spread.

1. Preheat the oven to 350°F. Line the baking sheets with parchment paper.

2. Spread the almonds in one layer in a small baking pan and put in the (preheated) oven. Set a timer for 10 minutes and check the almonds to see if they're a light golden brown. If not, toast 2 minutes longer. Set aside to cool.

3. With an electric mixer or by hand, beat the butter, granulated sugar, and brown sugar until smooth. Add 1 egg, mix until well combined, and then add the second egg. Stir in the toasted almonds, oats, flour, baking soda, and salt until well combined.

4. Put 2 racks in the upper and lower thirds of the (preheated) oven. Place 1-tablespoon (slightly rounded, not flat, not heaping) mounds of dough 2 inches apart on the parchment-lined baking sheets. If you have one you can also use a small ice cream scoop to form the cookies and plop them out onto the sheets (it's much faster and easier).

5. Flatten the mounds slightly with your hands or the bottom of a glass. Bake for 10 to 12 minutes, until the cookies have browned lightly on the edges but still are soft in the middle if you press them lightly with your finger. Although they may seem underdone, don't be tempted to let them bake longer—they'll firm up as they cool. So that the cookies bake evenly you may need to rotate the pans in the oven or switch racks halfway through.

6. Let the cookies cool to room temperature before removing them from the parchment (if you can wait that long).

Orange Butter Cookies

Makes about 24 cookies

Rather than rolling out this butter cookie dough and cutting it into shapes, I've developed this recipe so that they're "slice and bakes." The logs can be refrigerated or frozen, so on a moment's notice you can slice them off and bake. You could use lemon instead of orange.

WHAT YOU'LL NEED

2 or 3 baking or cookie sheets

Parchment paper

Electric stand mixer or a handheld mixer and medium bowl

1 medium navel orange

8 tablespoons (1 stick) unsalted butter, softened

1/3 cup granulated sugar

1 large egg yolk

1/2 teaspoon pure vanilla extract

1/4 teaspoon kosher salt

1 cup plus 2 tablespoons all-purpose unbleached flour

1. Zest the rind of the orange, then cut the orange in half and squeeze the juice into a bowl (you'll only need 1 1/2 teaspoons of juice and can drink the rest).

2. In a stand mixer or using a handheld mixer and a medium bowl, beat the butter and sugar on medium speed until smooth. Add the orange zest, 1 1/2 teaspoons of the juice, the yolk, vanilla, and salt and stir until combined.

3. Reduce the speed to low, add the flour, and mix until everything is combined and comes together into a dough.

4. Turn the dough out onto a well-floured work surface, gather together with your hands, and divide into 2 pieces. Sprinkle one of the pieces with flour and roll it with your hands into a 6-inch, evenly thick log. Repeat with the second piece of dough. Wrap the logs in plastic wrap and refrigerate for at least 1 hour or until firm. (The dough can be kept in the fridge for 2 days or frozen for 2 months.)

5. Preheat the oven to 350°F. Line the baking sheets with parchment paper.

6. Slice the logs into 1/2-inch-thick large coins and arrange on the parchment-lined baking sheets about 2 inches apart.

7. Put 2 racks in the upper and lower thirds of the (preheated) oven. Bake until the cookies are golden brown, about 13 minutes. So that the cookies bake evenly, you may need to rotate the pans in the oven or switch racks halfway through. Let cool completely.

Pecan Sandies

Makes about 24 cookies

Although these sandies—aka nut butter cookies—have the same ingredients as shortbread, they're much lighter and crumblier. They're wonderful on their own but also make great accompaniments to ice cream.

WHAT YOU'LL NEED

2 or 3 baking or cookie sheets

Parchment paper

Food processor

Small spring-loaded ice cream scoop (if you have one)

1 cup (about 4 ounces) pecans

1/4 cup cornstarch

16 tablespoons (2 sticks) unsalted butter, softened

1/2 cup granulated sugar

1 cup all-purpose unbleached flour

1 teaspoon pure vanilla extract

1/2 teaspoon kosher salt

1. Preheat the oven to 350°F. Line the baking sheets with parchment paper.

2. Spread the pecans in one layer in a small baking pan and put in the (preheated) oven. Set a timer for 10 minutes and check the nuts to see if they're a light golden brown. If not, toast 2 minutes longer. Let cool.

3. In the food processor, process the pecans with the cornstarch until they're finely ground and look like coarse sand.

4. With an electric mixer or by hand, beat the butter and sugar until smooth. Stir in the ground pecans, flour, vanilla, and salt until well combined.

5. Put 2 racks in the upper and lower thirds of the (preheated) oven. Place 1-tablespoon (slightly rounded, not flat, not heaping) mounds of dough 2 inches apart on the parchment-lined baking sheets. If you have one you can also use a small ice cream scoop to form the cookies and plop them out onto the sheets (it's much faster and easier).

6. Flatten the mounds slightly with your hands or the bottom of a glass. Bake until the cookies are a light golden brown but still soft in the middle if you press them lightly with your finger, 12 to 15 minutes. Although they may seem underdone, don't be tempted to let them bake longer—they'll firm up as they cool. So that the cookies bake evenly you may need to rotate the pans in the oven or switch racks halfway through.

7. Let the cookies cool to room temperature.

Pecan Shortbread

Makes about 24 cookies

What makes shortbread so delicious? In a word: butter. And since butter is one of only five ingredients in this recipe, it's important that it—as well as the pecans—be fresh and of the highest quality. Sometimes I'll even buy artisan butter with a higher fat content for making shortbread.

For the lightest, crumbliest texture, note that the butter needs to be cold from the fridge before it's mixed in with the dry ingredients. Most other cookie recipes in this book call for softened, room-temperature butter.

WHAT YOU'LL NEED
Food processor

2 or 3 baking or cookie sheets

Parchment paper

Electric stand or handheld mixer and medium bowl

1/4 cup (about 1 ounce) pecans

1/2 cup granulated sugar

16 tablespoons (2 sticks) unsalted butter, cold

2 cups all-purpose unbleached flour

Large pinch kosher salt

1. Preheat the oven to 350°F.

2. Spread the pecans in one layer in a small baking pan and put in the (preheated) oven. Set a timer for 10 minutes and check the nuts to see if they're a light golden brown. If not, toast 2 minutes longer. Let cool. Turn off the oven.

3. In the food processor, process the pecans with 1 tablespoon of the sugar until they're finely ground and look like coarse sand.

4. Cut the butter into small—about 1/2-inch square—pieces. In the bowl of an electric stand mixer, or in a medium bowl if you're using a handheld mixer, mix the ground pecans, remaining sugar, flour, and salt on low speed. Add the butter pieces and mix until everything comes together into a dough.

5. Turn the dough out onto a well-floured work surface, gather together with your hands, and divide into 2 pieces. Sprinkle one of the pieces with flour and roll it with your hands into a 6-inch-long, evenly thick log. Repeat with the second piece of dough. Wrap each log in plastic wrap and refrigerate for at least 1 hour or until firm. (The dough can be kept in the fridge for 2 days or frozen for 2 months.)

6. Preheat the oven to 350°F. Line the baking sheets with parchment paper.

7. Slice the logs into 1/4-inch-thick large coins and arrange on the parchment-lined baking sheets about 2 inches apart.

8. Put 2 racks in the upper and lower thirds of the (preheated) oven. Bake until the cookies are golden brown on the edges, about 15 minutes. So that the cookies bake evenly, you may need to rotate the pans in the oven or switch racks halfway through. Let cool completely on the pans.

Pine Nut–Fig Cookies

Makes about 30 cookies

Pine nuts are often associated with savory dishes—think pesto—but their buttery and rich flavor makes them ideal for baked goods as well.

Because pine nuts are so oily, they can go bad quickly. Smell or taste them to make sure they're fresh.

A little helpful tip: I find it easier to cut dried fruit with scissors because it's so sticky.

WHAT YOU'LL NEED

2 or 3 baking or cookie sheets

Parchment paper

Small spring-loaded ice cream scoop (if you have one)

1/2 cup pine nuts

12 tablespoons (1 1/2 sticks) unsalted butter, melted

1 1/4 cups firmly packed light brown sugar

1/4 cup granulated sugar

1 teaspoon pure vanilla extract

1 large egg

1 large egg yolk

2 1/4 cups all-purpose unbleached flour

1/4 cup white cornmeal

1/2 teaspoon baking soda

1/2 teaspoon kosher salt

1/2 cup dried figs, cut into 1/4-inch pieces

1. Preheat the oven to 350°F. Line the baking sheets with parchment.

2. Spread the pine nuts in one layer in a small baking pan and put in the (preheated) oven. Set a timer for 10 minutes and check the nuts to see if they're a light golden brown. If not, toast 2 minutes longer. Let cool and then coarsely chop.

3. Put the melted butter in a medium bowl and, with a rubber spatula or wooden spoon, stir in the brown sugar, granulated sugar, and vanilla until everything is well combined. Stir in the egg and egg yolk, then the flour, cornmeal, baking soda, and salt. Last, stir in the pine nuts and figs.

4. Put 2 racks in the upper and lower thirds of the (preheated) oven. Place 2-tablespoon (not flat, not heaping) mounds of dough 2 inches apart on the parchment-lined baking sheets. If you have one you can also use a small ice cream scoop to form the cookies and plop them out onto the sheets (it's much faster and easier).

5. Bake until the cookies are golden brown, about 12 minutes. So that they bake evenly you may need to rotate the pans in the oven or switch racks halfway through.

6. Let the cookies cool to room temperature.

Ranger Cookies

Makes about 36 cookies

No one knows for certain how these cookies got their name. I've heard that they were originally called Texas Ranger Cookies or Lone Ranger Cookies and are similar to a 1930s recipe for Cowboy Cookies. Whatever. Personally I think they should be rechristened Kitchen Sink Cookies, because they have a little bit of everything but that proverbial sink. Instead of the sugary corn flakes that most recipes use, I've substituted healthier bran-flake cereal. Some cooks throw in chocolate chips. You can too.

WHAT YOU'LL NEED

2 or 3 baking or cookie sheets

Parchment paper

Small spring-loaded ice cream scoop (if you have one)

8 tablespoons (1 stick) unsalted butter, softened

1/2 cup granulated sugar

1/2 cup firmly packed light brown sugar

1 large egg

1/4 teaspoon pure vanilla extract

1 cup all-purpose unbleached flour

1/2 teaspoon baking soda

1/8 teaspoon baking powder

1/2 teaspoon kosher salt

1 cup old-fashioned oats

1 cup bran-flake cereal

1/2 cup sweetened shredded coconut

1. Preheat the oven to 350°F. Line the baking sheets with parchment paper.

2. With an electric mixer or by hand, beat the butter, granulated sugar, and brown sugar until smooth. Add the egg and vanilla, mixing until well combined. Stir in the flour, baking soda, baking powder, and salt until well blended, then stir in the oats, bran, and coconut.

3. Put 2 racks in the upper and lower thirds of the (preheated) oven. Place 1-tablespoon (not flat, not heaping) mounds of dough 2 inches apart on the parchment-lined baking sheets. If you have one you can also use a small ice cream scoop to form the cookies and plop them out onto the sheets (it's much faster and easier).

4. Flatten the mounds slightly with your hands or the bottom of a glass. Bake for 16 minutes, or until the cookies have browned lightly on the edges but still seem soft in the middle if you press them lightly with your finger. Although they may seem underdone, don't be tempted to let them bake longer—they'll firm up as they cool. So that the cookies bake evenly you may need to rotate the pans in the oven or switch racks halfway through.

5. Let the cookies cool to room temperature (if you can wait that long).

Roll-Out Sugar Cookies

Makes about 24 (3-inch) cookies

If you need a basic sugar cookie recipe that you can roll out and cut into shapes for any holiday, look no further. Your finished cookies will be tender, sweet, and ready to decorate.

WHAT YOU'LL NEED
Rubber spatula

2 or 3 baking or cookie sheets

Parchment paper

Rolling pin

Cookie cutter(s)

16 tablespoons (2 sticks) unsalted butter, softened

2/3 cup granulated sugar

1/4 cup firmly packed light brown sugar

2 large eggs

2 teaspoons pure vanilla extract

2 1/2 cups all-purpose unbleached flour

1/2 teaspoon kosher salt

1. With an electric mixer or by hand, mix the butter, granulated sugar, and brown sugar until smooth. Scrape down the side of the bowl with the rubber spatula and mix in the eggs and vanilla, then add the flour and salt and mix until it comes together into a dough.

2. Turn the dough out onto a well-floured work surface, gather together with your hands, and divide into 2 equal pieces. Shape the pieces into 2 rough squares about 1 inch thick and wrap them individually (and tightly) in plastic. Refrigerate the squares for at least 2 hours or until firm. (The dough can be kept in the fridge for 2 days or frozen for 2 months.)

3. Preheat the oven to 350°F. Line the baking sheets with parchment paper.

4. Sprinkle a work surface with flour. With the rolling pin, roll one of the squares 1/4 inch thick. Using a cookie cutter, cut out shapes and place them on the parchment-lined baking sheets about 1 inch apart (these cookies do not spread very much). The scraps can be gathered up and rolled out one more time. Repeat with the other dough square.

5. Put 2 racks in the upper and lower thirds of the (preheated) oven. Bake until the cookies are golden brown on the edges, about 10 minutes. So that the cookies bake evenly, you may need to rotate the pans in the oven or switch racks halfway through. Let cool completely on the pans.

6. When the cookies are cool you can decorate them to your heart's delight.

Thin Crispy Ginger Cookies

Makes about 48 cookies

Besides the triple hit of fresh, ground, and crystallized ginger, the texture of these cookies is what makes them so appealing. Take care not to overbeat the dough as you're mixing the ingredients or the cookies will turn out "cakey" and not thin and crisp.

WHAT YOU'LL NEED

2 or 3 baking or cookie sheets

Parchment paper

Microplane or cheese grater

Rubber spatula

Small spring-loaded ice cream scoop (if you have one)

1 (2-inch) piece fresh ginger

14 tablespoons (1 3/4 sticks) unsalted butter, softened

1 1/4 cups granulated sugar

1 large egg

1/4 cup molasses

2 1/4 cups unbleached all-purpose flour

1/4 cup finely chopped candied ginger

4 teaspoons ground ginger

1 teaspoon baking soda

1/4 teaspoon kosher salt

FB: Four dozen cookies! Now we're talkin'.

EL: Uh-huh, this recipe will really fill up your cookie jar. And the cookies spread a lot, so you can put only a few on each cookie sheet. They need to be spaced three inches apart.

FB: Is there a way to form all the cookies in advance and then bake them as the others come out of the oven?

EL: That's one of the great things about parchment paper, besides the fact that you don't have to grease your pan. You can put the dough mounds on the parchment paper, leave them on the counter, and then as the cookie sheets come out of the oven slide the baked cookies off and slide the unbaked ones on.

FB: Do you need to cool the cookies on a rack? I notice a lot of recipes say to do that.

EL: Actually, I never do. I just slide the parchment off the pan and let the cookies cool on the counter. Once they're cool I peel them off the paper by hand or with a spatula.

1. Preheat the oven to 350°F. Line the baking sheets with parchment paper.

2. With the back of a spoon or small sharp knife, remove the peel from the fresh ginger. Finely grate it with a Microplane or on the small holes of a cheese grater onto a piece of parchment or into a small bowl. Set aside.

3. With an electric mixer or by hand, beat the butter and sugar together on medium-low speed until smooth. Scrape down the side of the bowl with the rubber spatula and mix in the egg until combined. Mix in the molasses. Add the grated fresh ginger, the flour, candied ginger, ground ginger, baking soda, and salt and mix until everything is combined. Be careful to not overbeat the dough.

4. Put 2 racks in the upper and lower thirds of the (preheated) oven. Place level tablespoons of dough 3 inches apart on the parchment-lined baking sheets. If you have one, you can also use a small ice cream scoop to form the cookies and plop them out onto the sheets (it's much faster and easier). They spread quite a bit as they bake so leave plenty of room. So that the cookies bake evenly you may need to rotate the pans in the oven or switch racks halfway through.

5. Bake for 16 to 18 minutes, until the cookies are evenly golden brown (they will puff up and sink when they're cooled). Though it's not necessary, so they cool faster, you can transfer the cookies to a wire rack, or do as I do: just leave them on their baking sheets or parchment to cool. They will crisp up as they cool.

Truffle Brownies

Makes about 16 (2 1/4-inch) brownies

The trick to making these brownies is to not bake them until a skewer or toothpick inserted comes out clean, as in the usual test for doneness. What you want is to see some fudgy stuff still clinging to the skewer or toothpick. They should take about 30 minutes, but I start testing them after 20 just to be on the safe side. The brownies will continue to firm up as they cool and end up deliciously moist and super chocolaty.

For spreading frosting and batters, baker's spatulas are the tool of choice. These are spatulas that are like knives, but with thinner blades and rounded blunt ends. They come in varying lengths and two types: straight and offset. Offset spatulas are handier because their blades are lower than the handle and slightly bent, enabling you to maneuver more easily inside a pan (as in this recipe where you need to spread the brownie batter).

WHAT YOU'LL NEED
9-inch square cake pan

Saucepan and metal bowl, or double boiler if you have one

Rubber spatula

Baking spatula, preferably one that's offset

8 ounces unsweetened chocolate, roughly chopped or broken into 1-inch pieces

8 tablespoons (1 stick) unsalted butter

4 large eggs

1 cup granulated sugar

3/4 cup firmly packed light brown sugar

3/4 cup all-purpose unbleached flour

1 teaspoon pure vanilla extract

Large pinch kosher salt

FB: I'm reading this recipe over, and it's making me nervous. All this stuff about a double boiler. The few times I've needed to melt chocolate I do it in the microwave, but boy does it smell when it's burned!

EL: I know a lot of cooks who have mastered the microwave thing, but I prefer the double boiler. I think that once you try the double-boiler method you will find it more reassuring than melting chocolate in the microwave, because you have more control.

1. Preheat the oven to 350°F. Grease the bottom and sides of the baking pan with nonstick cooking spray or butter.

2. Melt the chocolate and butter by putting them in a heat-proof bowl set over a saucepan of simmering water, making sure the bowl does not touch the water. (You can use a double boiler if you have one.) Stir and scrape the side of the bowl occasionally with the rubber spatula until the chocolate is smooth and evenly melted. Let cool to room temperature.

3. In a medium bowl, whisk the eggs, granulated sugar, and brown sugar until combined, then whisk in the melted chocolate. Add the flour, vanilla, and salt and continue to whisk until the mixture is smooth and evenly combined. Pour into the prepared pan and smooth the surface with the baking spatula. An offset spatula (see headnote), if you have one, works the best.

4. Bake the brownies for 20 minutes and check for doneness by inserting a bamboo skewer or toothpick in the middle. When it comes out a little fudgy, not quite clean, the brownies are done. If they're a little too wet, bake 5 minutes longer and check again.

5. Let the brownies cool in the pan, then cut into 16 squares, each about 2 1/4 inches. Or cut 12 brownies if you like them really big.

Walnut Sandwich Cookies
with Milk Chocolate Filling

Makes about 24 (2-inch) sandwich cookies

I really believe there is something about a sandwich cookie that brings out the kid in us. Maybe it's because we all seem to have memories of pulling them apart and licking the filling before eating the cookie. Or still do. All I know is that making sandwich cookies also appeals to the baker in me. There's something fun about rolling out the shortbread dough, cutting it into shapes, and then sandwiching a creamy sweet filling between the finished cookies. And if you want to eat the filling separately from the cookie, go ahead.

1. Preheat the oven to 350°F. Line the baking sheets with parchment paper.

Cookies
2. Spread the walnuts in one layer in a small baking pan and put in the (preheated) oven. Set a timer for 10 minutes and check the nuts to see if they're a light golden brown. If not, toast 2 minutes longer. Let cool. Turn off the oven.

3. In the food processor, process the walnuts with 1/4 cup of the flour until they're finely ground and look like coarse sand. Transfer to a medium bowl with the remaining 1 3/4 cups flour, add the salt, and whisk it all together.

4. Cut the cold butter into 1/2-inch cubes (it's the cold butter that makes the dough crumblier, or "shorter"). Using the stand mixer, or a handheld mixer and a medium bowl, beat the cold butter and sugar on medium speed until smooth. Reduce the speed to low, add the walnut mixture, and mix until everything is combined and begins to just come together into a dough. Don't mix it so much that it forms a ball.

WHAT YOU'LL NEED
3 baking or cookie sheets

Parchment paper

Food processor

Electric stand mixer or handheld mixer and medium bowl

Rolling pin

2-inch round cookie cutter

Cookies
2/3 cup walnuts

2 cups all-purpose unbleached flour

1/2 teaspoon kosher salt

16 tablespoons (2 sticks) unsalted butter, cold

1/2 cup granulated sugar

Chocolate Filling
6 ounces milk chocolate, chopped or broken into 1-inch pieces

1/2 cup heavy cream

EL: Which rolling pin do you use at home? This plain one or the kind with handles?

FB: I don't know, I don't have experience with either one.

EL: Well, do you have a rolling pin?

FB: Yes, and I think it's that kind (pointing to the one with handles). Although the one I have is a lot smaller.

The Fearful Baker rolls out the shortbread dough.

5. Using your hands, gather the dough into a ball. Put the ball on a lightly floured work surface. With the rolling pin, roll the dough out so that it is evenly 1/4 inch thick. With the cookie cutter, cut out rounds and place them on the parchment-lined sheets, spacing them 1 1/2 inches apart. (If the dough sticks to the work surface, use a small spatula to slide under and lift them.) The remaining dough scraps may be gathered into a ball and rolled once more. If you've used a 2-inch cutter you should have about 48 cookies.

6. Put the sheets with the dough in the refrigerator and chill for 1 hour or until firm.

7. Preheat the oven to 350°F.

8. Put 2 racks in the upper and lower thirds of the (preheated) oven. Bake the cookies until the edges are lightly golden, 12 to 14 minutes. So that the cookies bake evenly, you may have to rotate the pans in the oven or switch racks halfway through baking. Let the cookies cool completely on the pans.

Chocolate Filling

9. Put the chopped milk chocolate in a bowl. Warm the cream in a saucepan over medium heat. As soon as it starts to bubble around the edges, pour the hot cream over the chocolate. Shake the bowl a little to submerge all the chocolate pieces. Cover the bowl for several minutes. Whisk the cream with the chocolate until smooth. Allow the filling to cool to room temperature, about 45 minutes or until it's thick enough to spread.

10. Separate the cookies into two equal batches. For one batch, place 1 1/2 to 2 teaspoons of the filling on the bottom side of each cookie. Use the remaining cookies to create a sandwich, putting the cookies bottom-side down on the filling and gently pressing the 2 together gently until the filling spreads out almost to the edge.

Cakes

I think there are few endeavors in the kitchen as rewarding as baking a cake, though it does require a little more effort in terms of time and technique than whipping up a batch of cookies. However, cakes shouldn't be reserved just for special occasions. "I made this cake from scratch" is a proud moment for any cook, and not just beginners.

I still remember how accomplished I felt the first time I made a delicious and moist white layer cake that wasn't from a mix. Really all a cake mix provides is the pre-mixture of the dry ingredients—you still have to add the liquids. And bakery cakes may save time, but they're expensive and all too often the frostings are excessively sweet, the cake itself dry and flavorless.

Many of you who have followed my career or bought my other cookbooks know that my personal taste in desserts falls decidedly on the homey side, so you'll find no fancy restaurant cakes here, just good old-fashioned, time-tested cake recipes that you'll probably recognize as your own or your family's favorites.

For organizational purposes I've loosely grouped the recipes according to the kinds of cake pans that are used. There are white and chocolate layer cakes, pound cakes, angel food cakes, cheesecakes, and Bundt cakes. Some have frostings—and others can be simply dusted with confectioners' sugar.

Make-Ahead and Storage Tips
Unless specified in the recipe, cakes can be wrapped tightly in plastic and kept at room temperature for 3 days or frozen for a month (the exceptions are any cakes with custard, cream cheese, or whipped cream). Layer cakes can be made a day ahead and frosted the day you want to serve them. They are easier to store overnight if they are unfrosted.

1. For many of the cake recipes you'll need to butter the pan. Use softened butter or nonstick spray and coat the inside of the pan. (When you spray a cake pan, spray into the dishwasher or over the sink so you don't have to wipe up the spray that gets on the counter.) Some recipes ask you to butter and flour the pan in which case you should coat the pan with flour after it's been greased, turning the pan to make sure all surfaces are coated with the flour and then tapping out the excess. When you need to butter and flour the pan, a nifty trick I've learned is to coat the pan with the kind of nonstick spray that has flour added—it's widely available and is called baking spray.

2. Dry ingredients (flour, baking soda, and/or baking powder) for cakes are usually sifted, but if the recipe doesn't call for sifting, put the baking powder or baking soda in a small bowl and stir it with your finger or a spoon to break up any clumps.

3. While having room-temperature eggs will help make a better cake, don't let the fact that they have been in the fridge stop you from making a cake. Either use them as is or put them (still in the shell) in a bowl of hot water for 10 minutes before you need to add them to the batter.

4. When whipping egg whites for cakes, add the sugar slowly and steadily until the whites form glossy, billowy peaks.

5. It's easy to tell when a cake is done because an inserted bamboo skewer or toothpick will come out clean, except in a couple of recipes where I say it should come out "a little fudgy" or "still gooey." (And, by the way, I use a skewer because toothpicks aren't long enough to reach into the center of a tall tube or Bundt cake.)

6. Always let cakes cool completely in the pan before unmolding or releasing them.

Basic White Cake

Makes 2 (9 by 2-inch) round cakes

There are so many ways to dress up a Basic White Cake that every baker should have this recipe in his or her arsenal. Make it a few times and you'll be a pro, able to whip up a layer cake on a moment's notice. The wrapped cake layers keep at room temperature for a few days, or frozen for a couple of months.

WHAT YOU'LL NEED
2 (9- by 2-inch) round cake pans

Electric stand mixer or a handheld mixer and medium bowl

Rubber spatula

2 1/2 cups unbleached all-purpose flour

1 teaspoon baking soda

1 teaspoon baking powder

1/2 teaspoon kosher salt

16 tablespoons (2 sticks) unsalted butter, softened

2 cups granulated sugar

4 large eggs

1 cup buttermilk, or 1 cup whole milk mixed with 1 teaspoon lemon juice

2 teaspoons pure vanilla extract

1. Preheat the oven to 350°F. Grease the bottoms and sides of the cake pans with nonstick cooking spray or butter and coat evenly with flour, tapping out the excess.

2. Over a bowl or piece of parchment, sift the flour, baking soda, and baking powder together with a sifter or with a fine strainer by gently tapping your hand against the edge. Add the salt (you can just leave it on top of the flour pile because it gets mixed in later).

3. Using the stand mixer, or a handheld mixer and medium bowl, first on low speed and then gradually increasing the speed to medium, beat the butter and sugar together until smooth. Scrape down the side of the bowl with the rubber spatula and mix in the eggs, one at a time, until combined.

4. Stir the buttermilk or milk and lemon juice mixture with the vanilla in a measuring cup. On medium-low speed, add half of the milk mixture to the butter mixture. Mix until incorporated and then scrape down the side of the bowl. Add half of the sifted ingredients. Mix until combined and scrape down the side of the bowl. Add the remaining milk mixture and the sifted ingredients in the same manner.

5. Divide the batter between the pans and, using the spatula, evenly spread it in the pan. Bake the cakes on the middle rack of the (preheated) oven until a bamboo skewer inserted in the middle comes out clean or the cake has slightly pulled away from the side of the pan, about 20 minutes. If you had to put the cake pans on two different racks in the oven, switch the pans halfway through baking so they'll bake evenly.

6. Cool the cakes in their pans. Unmold them by running a small knife around the edge of the pans. Place a plate on top of each cake and invert the cake and plate. Remove the pans and let the cakes cool completely.

White Layer Cake with Chocolate Frosting

Makes 1 layer cake, serving about 12

I think people tend to overlook this classic combination of white cake with chocolate frosting, particularly if given a chocolate-chocolate option. It's perfect for people who straddle the fence between chocolate and vanilla.

WHAT YOU'LL NEED
Cake plate or platter large enough to hold a 9-inch cake

Large wide spatula

Table knife or narrow metal spatula (if you have one)

2 Basic White Cake layers (page 66)

Easy Chocolate Frosting
10 ounces bittersweet chocolate, chopped (no bigger than 1/2-inch pieces)

1 cup heavy cream

2/3 cup granulated sugar

12 tablespoons (1 1/2 sticks) unsalted butter, softened and cut into 1-inch pieces

EL: So, we're going to go ahead and make the frosting and let that sit while the cakes cool.

FB: Okay. We have eight ounces of chocolate here and the recipe calls for ten ounces.

EL: Ooh. (Emily goes to the pantry). Here's two more ounces.

FB: If you didn't have ten ounces could you adjust the recipe?

EL: No, you need the ten ounces for the frosting to be thick enough. The important thing with frosting is that it's thick but soft enough to be spreadable and not so thin it's runny.

FB: Now, am I chopping the chocolate correctly?

EL: You want kind of small pieces, because if they're too big they won't melt in the cream. Yes, that's about right, nothing bigger than half-inch. Make sure you keep your free hand on top of the knife blade so you don't cut your finger.

FB: Got it. Now what?

EL: Heat the cream on the stove until it's really hot. You'll see other recipes that ask you to scald the cream. What I like to say is get it to the point where the cream is just starting to think about boiling. Once that happens you pour it over the chopped chocolate in the bowl. After the chocolate is melted and cools a bit, you're going to whisk in the butter, one tablespoon at a time.

FB: That's all there is to it?

EL: Almost. You need to let the frosting sit at room temperature to firm up to the point that it's spreadable.

FB: How long does that take?

EL: An hour at least. Once it's the right consistency you can leave it for six hours or so.

To assemble the cake, put one of the cake layers bottom-side up on the cake plate or platter. Using the narrow metal spatula, spread with about 1 cup of the frosting (see below). With the wide spatula, place the other layer (also bottom-side up) on top of the frosting. Spread the frosting over the side and then the top of the cake.

Easy Chocolate Frosting

1. Put the chopped chocolate in a medium bowl. Heat the cream with the sugar in a small saucepan over medium-high heat until small bubbles form at the edge, stirring to dissolve the sugar. Pour the warm cream over the chopped chocolate. Shake the bowl a little to submerge all the chocolate pieces. Then cover the bowl for several minutes. (You can cover the bowl with anything that's handy, like a pan lid.) Whisk until smooth. Let sit for 5 minutes to cool slightly.

2. Whisk the butter into the chocolate, adding only 1 or 2 pieces at a time and whisking until they're blended before adding the next. Once all the butter is added, give the mixture a final whisk to smooth it out. Let sit at room temperature until it seems spreadable. This step may take up to an hour, but you can prepare the frosting up to 6 hours ahead of time. If you try to rush it by putting it in the refrigerator, stir every 10 minutes and keep a close eye on it so it doesn't get hard.

Strawberry Cream Cake

Makes 1 layer cake, serving 12 to 16

This is a celebration cake, one to make for an anniversary or birthday or even to celebrate the arrival of spring strawberries in the market. Once you've made the components, the cake layers, the whipped cream, and the strawberries, it's not difficult to assemble the cake. The cake layers can be made way ahead and even frozen, the cream can be whipped and the strawberries chopped a few hours ahead.

When the cake is assembled, make sure to put the berries on the bottom layer before the whipped cream so the berry juice soaks into the cake. Just the opposite on the top layer: spread on the whipped cream and then the chopped berries so they show.

WHAT YOU'LL NEED
Electric stand mixer or a handheld mixer and medium bowl

Cake plate or platter large enough to hold a 9-inch cake

Large wide spatula

Table knife or narrow metal spatula (if you have one)

3 pints (about 1 1/2 pounds) strawberries

About 7 tablespoons granulated sugar

1 1/2 cups heavy cream

1/2 teaspoon pure vanilla extract

2 Basic White Cake layers (page 66)

EL: Do you want a smaller knife to chop those strawberries?

FB: No, I like living on the wild side.

EL: Good for you. A bigger knife moves quicker. A large chef's knife works well when you are roughly chopping things. You want to rough-chop them no bigger than a half-inch.

1. Just before you're ready to use them, rinse the strawberries. Remove the stems and coarsely chop. Put them in a bowl and stir in 3 tablespoons of the sugar. Taste for sweetness and add another tablespoon of sugar if needed. Set aside for up to 2 hours.

2. In the stand mixer fitted with the wire whisk, or using a handheld mixer and medium bowl, whip the cream with 3 tablespoons sugar and the vanilla until it forms softly mounded peaks—not pourable but not grainy either.

3. To assemble the cake, place one of the layers on the cake plate or platter bottom-side up. Distribute half of the chopped strawberries evenly on top. Then, with the narrow metal spatula, spread half of the whipped cream over the berries. With the large spatula, top with the second cake layer, bottom-side up, and spread the remaining cream over the top of the cake. Distribute the rest of the berries.

4. Although you can assemble this cake a few hours before serving and keep it in the fridge, it tastes best when it's put together just before serving. (You can, however, chop the strawberries and whip the cream a few hours ahead.) If it has been refrigerated, let it sit at room temperature for 20 minutes or so before cutting it into wedges.

Boston Cream Pie

Makes 1 layer cake, serving about 12

I'll bet you know that this classic American dessert is really not a pie at all, that it's a layer cake filled with pastry cream and topped with a shiny glaze of chocolate. What you may not know is that it was invented at a historic hotel in Boston and was proclaimed the official Massachusetts State Dessert in 1996, beating out other desserts such as the Toll House cookie and Indian pudding. I took my nieces to the hotel many years ago. I wanted to sample the original "pie," and while I won't say I wasn't disappointed, what I realized is that with so few components the key to the cake's successful interpretation is in the quality of the chocolate used in the glaze, the tender crumb of the cake, and the smooth richness of the pastry cream.

WHAT YOU'LL NEED

Cake plate or platter large enough to hold a 9-inch cake

Wide or large spatula

Table knife or narrow metal spatula (if you have one)

2 Basic White Cake layers (page 66)

Pastry Cream
6 large egg yolks

1/2 cup granulated sugar

1 teaspoon pure vanilla extract

3 1/2 tablespoons plus 1 1/2 teaspoons cornstarch

2 1/4 cups whole milk

Chocolate Glaze
1/2 cup plus about 3 tablespoons heavy cream

4 ounces dark chocolate (58 to 62 percent cacao), chopped or broken into 1-inch pieces

FB: What is pastry cream, really?

EL: It's simply custard, like crème anglaise, but thickened. Usually people think of it as the filling for cream puffs and éclairs.

FB: Oh, of course. Lots of times fruit tarts have pastry cream, huh?

EL: Yes. The French, who invented it, call it crème pâtissière. It's used for all kinds of desserts and is fundamental in professional pastry kitchens.

FB: Why do you say to heat the milk, whisk it into the eggs, and then put it all back in the pan on the stove? Why can't I just put the yolks into the hot milk in the saucepan? It would save a step.

EL: It's called tempering and you want to warm the yolks by slowly pouring in the milk. If you dump them into the large amount of hot milk they will curdle.

FB: Oh, okay. But here's another question. How can you cook the custard without it curdling?

EL: Because you stir it all the time and it has cornstarch, which stabilizes it. Some recipes use flour as a thickener. You just need to be careful to stir and scrape all over the bottom and into the corners of the pan so the custard cooks and thickens without scorching. It's really an easy procedure, and pastry cream is great to have on hand. I love it lightened with whipped cream folded in.

FB: Will you teach me how to make éclairs?

EL: Of course. But another day. Let's make the pastry cream first.

1. To assemble the dessert, place one of the cake layers bottom-side up on the cake plate or platter. Spread the chilled pastry cream on top. Using the wide spatula, place the other cake bottom-side up, on top of the pastry cream.

2. Pour the glaze (see below) onto the middle of the upper cake and, with a knife or a narrow metal spatula, spread it out so it runs a little over and down the side of the cake layers. Refrigerate until serving time but let sit at room temperature for 30 minutes before cutting it into wedges.

Pastry Cream

1. In a medium bowl, whisk the yolks with the sugar and vanilla and then whisk in the cornstarch.

2. In a medium saucepan, heat the milk until it just begins to bubble around the edge of the pan. Then whisk it into the egg mixture. Pour the milk back into the saucepan.

3. Over medium-low heat, stirring constantly with a rubber spatula or wooden spoon, cook the egg/milk mixture until it thickens, about 10 minutes. Make sure you scrape the bottom of the pan so that the mixture doesn't scorch. When it's done it will have a mayonnaise-like consistency.

4. Pour the mixture through a mesh strainer into a clean bowl to remove any lumps. Press plastic wrap onto the surface of the pastry cream to prevent a skin from forming. Refrigerate until the pastry cream is cold, at least 1 hour and as long as 2 days.

Chocolate Glaze

1. In a small saucepan, heat 1/2 cup of the cream until it's very hot but not bubbling. Remove the pan from the heat, add the chopped chocolate, and cover the pan with a lid. Let sit 5 minutes.

2. Stir with a spoon until the chocolate and cream are combined. Let sit a little longer to cool, then add as much of the remaining 3 tablespoons cream as necessary to make the chocolate pourable but not so thin it will run off the top of the cake (you may not need any additional cream at all). Transfer the glaze to a glass measuring cup with a spout.

Basic Chocolate Cake

Makes 2 (9- by 2-inch) round cakes

Just as you can with the Basic White Cake, get this recipe down and you can dress it up endlessly with various frostings, turning it each time into what seems like a new dessert. It gets its deep, dark flavor from both chopped unsweetened chocolate and cocoa powder.

WHAT YOU'LL NEED

2 (9- by 2-inch) round cake pans

Saucepan and metal bowl, or double boiler if you have one

Rubber spatula

Electric stand mixer or a handheld mixer and medium bowl

3/4 cup cocoa powder

3/4 cup water

4 ounces unsweetened chocolate, chopped or broken into 1-inch pieces

2 cups all-purpose unbleached flour

1 1/2 teaspoons baking soda

1/4 teaspoon kosher salt

12 tablespoons (1 1/2 sticks) unsalted butter, softened

2 cups granulated sugar

5 large eggs

1 cup whole milk

1. Preheat the oven to 350°F. Grease the bottoms and sides of the cake pans with cooking spray or butter and coat evenly with cocoa powder, tapping out the excess.

2. In a small bowl, stir the 3/4 cup cocoa powder with the water to make a paste and set aside.

3. Melt the chocolate by putting it in a heat-proof bowl set over a saucepan of simmering water, making sure the bowl does not touch the water. (You can use a double boiler if you have one.) Stir and scrape the side of the bowl occasionally with the rubber spatula until the chocolate is smooth and evenly melted. Cool to room temperature.

4. Over a bowl or piece of parchment, sift the flour and baking soda together in a sifter or in a fine strainer by gently tapping your hand against the edge. Add the salt. Set aside.

5. Using the stand mixer, or a handheld mixer and medium bowl, on medium speed, beat the butter and sugar together until smooth. Scrape down the side of the bowl with the spatula and mix in the eggs, 1 at a time, until combined. On low speed, add the cocoa paste. Add the melted chocolate and mix until thoroughly combined.

6. On low speed, add half of the sifted flour, mixing thoroughly, then half the milk. Repeat with the remaining flour and then the milk, mixing well.

7. Divide the batter between the pans and, using the spatula, spread it out. Bake the cakes on the middle rack of the oven until a bamboo skewer inserted in the middle comes out clean, about 20 minutes. If you put the cake pans on 2 different racks in the oven, switch the pans halfway through baking so they'll bake evenly.

8. Cool the cakes in their pans. Run a small knife around the inside edges. Place a plate on top of each cake and invert the cake and plate. Remove the pans. Cool the cakes completely.

Chocolate Layer Cake with Choice of Frostings

Makes 1 layer cake, serving 10 to 12

I'm always suspicious when I see white frosting on a cake. I can usually count on it to be too sweet or too fluffy. The secret to this recipe is in the white chocolate, which gives the frosting a depth of flavor and spreadable consistency that makes it perfect in my book. I've also included a White Chocolate–Coconut Frosting variation that has a double hit of both shredded coconut and coconut extract.

A word of caution: Don't use white chocolate chips—they have additives that prevent them from melting properly. Read the label and steer away from brands that don't contain cocoa butter. Here are some other tips to bear in mind when making this frosting:

- Touch the meringue to make sure it's at room temperature before adding the softened butter. Although you add the butter in pats, they don't have to be completely incorporated before you add the next pat. A visible 1/2-inch or so piece is fine.

- Make sure the white chocolate is completely melted, lump-free, and at room temperature before adding it to the meringue.

- If you want to frost the cake right after you've made the frosting and it's too soft to spread, put it in the fridge for 10 to 15 minutes, stirring it often until it has firmed up to the right consistency. Next time make sure the butter isn't too soft or the chocolate too warm.

WHAT YOU'LL NEED

Cake plate or platter large enough to hold a 9-inch cake

Table knife or narrow metal spatula (if you have one)

Large wide spatula

2 Basic Chocolate Cake layers (page 74)

Easy Chocolate Frosting (page 68), or

White Chocolate Frosting
Saucepan and metal bowl, or double boiler if you have one

Rubber spatula

Electric stand mixer or handheld mixer and medium bowl

12 ounces white chocolate, chopped or broken into 1-inch pieces

4 large egg whites

1 cup granulated sugar

20 tablespoons (2 1/2 sticks) unsalted butter

Variation:
White Chocolate–Coconut Frosting
2 1/4 cups loosely packed sweetened shredded coconut

1/2 teaspoon coconut extract

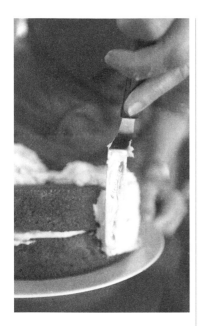

To assemble the cake, put one of the cake layers, bottom-side up, on the cake plate or platter. Using the narrow metal spatula, spread about 1 cup of the frosting (see below) on top. Using the wide spatula, place the other cake (also bottom-side up) on top of the frosting. Spread the remaining frosting over the side and then the top of the cake.

White Chocolate Frosting

1. Melt the chocolate by putting it in a heat-proof bowl set over a saucepan of simmering water, making sure the bowl does not touch the water. (You can use a double boiler if you have one.) Stir and scrape the side of the bowl occasionally with the rubber spatula until the chocolate is smooth and evenly melted. Remove the bowl and let the chocolate cool while you mix the egg whites.

2. In a medium metal (don't use Pyrex) bowl, whisk the egg whites with the sugar to combine. Put the bowl over the pot of simmering water you used to melt the chocolate, again making sure the bottom of the bowl doesn't touch the water. Whisk until the eggs are hot (bath-water temperature), then transfer to the bowl of the stand electric mixer (or leave them in the bowl if you're using a handheld mixer). Whip the whites on high speed until they've thickened and cooled.

3. Cut the butter into tablespoon pats. With the mixer on low speed, add the butter to the egg whites, one pat at a time.

4. Mix in the white chocolate. The frosting at this point should be spreadable. If it's too soft, put it in the fridge for 30 minutes, stirring occasionally, but be careful not to let it get too firm. Test it once or twice by moving a spatula through it.

Variation: White Chocolate–Coconut Frosting

1. Make the White Chocolate Frosting. After the melted white chocolate has been added with a rubber spatula, fold in 1 1/2 cups of the shredded coconut and the coconut extract. The frosting at this point should be spreadable. If it's too soft, put it in the fridge for 30 minutes, stirring occasionally, but be careful not to let it get too firm. Test it once or twice by moving your narrow metal spatula through it.

2. Use the remaining 3/4 cup coconut to decorate the sides of the frosted cake.

German Chocolate Cake

Makes 1 layer cake, serving 10 to 12

Cake plate or platter large enough to hold a 9-inch cake

Table knife or narrow metal spatula (if you have one)

Large wide spatula

2 Basic Chocolate Cake layers (page 74)

German Chocolate Frosting

This is a pretty sweet and rich, albeit yummy, frosting. Actually it's more of a filling, because you don't spread it on the side. Contradictory as it may sound, serving the cake with whipped cream is the best way to cut the richness.

It's much easier to spread the frosting right after it has been made, while it is still soft. If you do opt for making the frosting ahead of time, mix it up with a spoon to soften it. Once the cake is assembled and frosted, leave it at room temperature and serve it the same day.

1/2 cup pecan pieces

4 large egg yolks

1 (12-ounce) can evaporated milk

3/4 cup granulated sugar

1/2 cup firmly packed light brown sugar

6 tablespoons (3/4 stick) unsalted butter

2 cups sweetened shredded coconut

To assemble the cake, put one of the cake layers bottom-side up on a cake plate or platter. Using the narrow metal spatula, spread with half of the frosting (see below). Using the large spatula, place the other cake (also bottom-side up) on top of the frosting. Spread the remaining frosting over the top of the cake.

German Chocolate Frosting

1. Preheat the oven to 350°F.

2. Spread the pecan pieces in one layer in a small baking pan and put in the (preheated) oven. Set a timer for 10 minutes and check the nuts to see if they're a light golden brown. If not, toast 2 minutes longer. Set aside to cool.

3. In a medium saucepan, whisk the egg yolks, evaporated milk, granulated sugar, and brown sugar. Add the butter.

4. Cook over medium heat, stirring frequently with a rubber spatula or wooden spoon, until the sugar is dissolved and the butter is melted. Turn the heat up to medium-high and cook, stirring constantly, about 5 minutes, or until the mixture thickens. The frosting should thickly coat the spatula or spoon without running off.

5. Remove from the heat and stir in the coconut and pecan pieces. Transfer to a bowl and let cool completely before frosting the cake. The frosting will keep at room temperature for a few hours or overnight.

Chocolate Cake with Peanut Butter Frosting

Makes 1 layer cake, serving 10 to 12

WHAT YOU'LL NEED
Cake plate or platter large enough to hold a 9-inch cake

Table knife or narrow metal spatula (if you have one)

Large wide spatula

1 cup honey-roasted peanuts

2 Basic Chocolate Cake layers (page 74)

Peanut Butter Frosting

I prefer the flavor of sugar- and preservative-free natural peanut butter—the kind that has just peanuts and salt; but if you use Skippy or Jif, decrease the sugar in this recipe from 2 1/4 cups to 1 3/4 cups.

The sides of this cake are not frosted, so you can see the peanut butter filling.

Electric stand mixer or handheld mixer and medium bowl

Rubber spatula

1 (8-ounce) package cream cheese, at room temperature

2 1/4 cups confectioners' sugar (see headnote)

1 cup natural peanut butter (see headnote)

8 tablespoons (1 stick) unsalted butter, softened

1 teaspoon pure vanilla extract

To assemble the cake, put one of the cake layers bottom-side up on the cake plate or platter. Using the narrow spatula, spread the top with half of the frosting (see below). Using the large spatula, place the other cake (also bottom-side up) on top of the frosting. Spread the remaining frosting over the top of the cake. Sprinkle the honey-roasted peanuts over the top of the cake.

Peanut Butter Frosting

Using the stand mixer, or a handheld mixer and medium bowl, first on low speed and then gradually increasing the speed to medium, beat the cream cheese and sugar together until smooth. Scrape down the side of the bowl with the rubber spatula. Add the peanut butter, butter, and vanilla and, on medium speed, mix until creamy and spreadable.

Spice Layer Cake with Cream Cheese Frosting

Makes 1 layer cake, serving 8 to 10

I always looked forward to the spice cake my mother made every year for my birthday, but it wasn't until my early teens that I realized it came from a mix. When I first tried to duplicate the flavor of those box mixes in a cake made from scratch, I discovered it wasn't all that easy to get the right balance of spices. The cake method is easy—it's just a white cake after all—but it wasn't until many cakes later that I got the spice flavor balance I so dearly loved.

1. Preheat the oven to 350°F. Grease the cake pans with nonstick cooking spray or butter and evenly coat with flour, tapping out the excess.

2. Over a bowl or piece of parchment, sift the flour, baking soda, baking powder, cinnamon, cardamom, ginger, and nutmeg together in a sifter or in a fine strainer by gently tapping the edge. Add the salt (you can just leave it on top of the flour pile because it gets mixed in later). Set aside.

3. Using the stand mixer, or a handheld mixer and medium bowl, first on low speed and then gradually increasing the speed to medium, beat the butter and sugar together until smooth. Scrape down the side of the bowl with the rubber spatula. Mix in the eggs and then the molasses, again scraping down the side of the bowl.

4. In a small bowl, whisk the buttermilk and vanilla until well blended.

5. Add half of the sifted flour mixture to the butter mixture and, on low speed, mix until thoroughly combined. Add half of the buttermilk mixture and again mix until blended. Repeat with the remaining flour mixture and then the buttermilk.

WHAT YOU'LL NEED

2 (9-inch) round cake pans

Electric stand mixer or handheld mixer and medium bowl

Rubber spatula

Table knife or narrow metal spatula (if you have one)

Large wide spatula

Cake plate or platter large enough to hold a 9-inch cake

2 1/4 cups all-purpose unbleached flour

3/4 teaspoon baking soda

3/4 teaspoon baking powder

1 tablespoon ground cinnamon

3/4 teaspoon ground cardamom

2 teaspoons ground ginger

1/4 teaspoon nutmeg

1/2 teaspoon kosher salt

20 tablespoons (2 1/2 sticks) unsalted butter, softened

1 3/4 cups granulated sugar

4 large eggs

2 tablespoons molasses

1 cup buttermilk or 1 cup whole milk mixed with 1 teaspoon lemon juice

1 teaspoon pure vanilla extract

Cream Cheese Frosting
Electric stand mixer or handheld mixer and medium bowl

Rubber spatula

1 3/4 cups confectioners' sugar

12 ounces cream cheese, softened

12 tablespoons (1 1/2 sticks) unsalted butter, softened

1 teaspoon pure vanilla extract

Large pinch kosher salt

6. Evenly divide the batter between the prepared pans and spread evenly with the narrow spatula. Bake until a bamboo skewer inserted in the middle of the cakes comes out clean, about 40 minutes. Let cool completely in their pans.

7. To remove a cake from the pan, run a knife around the inside edge, then invert it and gently tap one side against the counter, letting the cake gently fall out of the pan onto a platter or piece of parchment paper. The cakes can be wrapped in plastic and kept at room temperature for 2 days or frozen for 2 months.

8. To assemble the cake, put one of the cake layers bottom-side up on the cake plate or platter. Using the narrow spatula, spread with about 1 cup of the frosting (see below). Using the large spatula, place the other cake (also bottom-side up) on top of the frosting. Spread the frosting over the side and then the top of the cake.

Cream Cheese Frosting

1. Sift the confectioners' sugar through a strainer to remove any lumps.

2. Using the stand mixer, or handheld mixer and medium bowl, on medium speed whip the cream cheese and butter until smooth. Add the sugar, vanilla extract, and salt and mix in thoroughly.

Carrot Cake with Cream Cheese Frosting

Makes 1 layer cake, serving 8 to 10

To quote Mary Poppins, "A spoonful of sugar helps the medicine go down." If you're not a big fan of carrots but want to get your quota of beta carotene, this is the recipe for you. It's loaded with carrots.

1. Preheat the oven to 350°F. Grease the cake pans with nonstick cooking spray and butter and evenly coat with flour, tapping out the excess.

2. Coarsely grate the carrots (you should have about 3 cups) and set aside.

3. Spread the walnuts in one layer in a small baking pan and put in the (preheated) oven. Set a timer for 10 minutes and check the nuts to see if they're a light golden brown. If not, toast 2 minutes longer. Let the nuts cool. Chop by hand into 1/4-inch pieces and set aside.

4. Over a bowl or piece of parchment, sift the flour, baking soda, cinnamon, and ginger together in a sifter or in a fine strainer by gently tapping your hand against the edge. Add the salt (you can just leave it on top of the flour pile because it gets mixed in later). Set aside.

5. Using the stand mixer, or a handheld mixer and medium bowl, first on low speed and then gradually increasing the speed to medium, beat the butter, granulated sugar, and brown sugar together until smooth. Scrape down the side of the bowl with the rubber spatula.

6. In a small bowl, whisk the eggs and vanilla together until well blended.

WHAT YOU'LL NEED

2 (9-inch) round cake pans

Electric stand mixer or handheld mixer and medium bowl

Rubber spatula

Cake plate or platter large enough to hold a 9-inch cake

Table knife or narrow metal spatula (if you have one)

Large wide spatula

1 pound carrots (6 to 7)

1 cup walnuts

2 cups all-purpose unbleached flour

2 teaspoons baking soda

1 1/2 teaspoons ground cinnamon

1/2 teaspoon ground ginger

1/2 teaspoon kosher salt

12 tablespoons (1 1/2 sticks) unsalted butter

1 1/2 cups granulated sugar

1/2 cup firmly packed light brown sugar

4 large eggs

1 teaspoon pure vanilla extract

Cream Cheese Frosting (page 80)

7. Alternating between the sifted dry ingredients and the eggs, add them to the butter/sugar mixture in thirds, making sure the batter is combined before the next addition.

8. With the rubber spatula, stir in the grated carrots and chopped walnuts.

9. Evenly divide the batter between the prepared pans and spread evenly with the spatula. Bake until a bamboo skewer inserted in the middle of the cakes comes out clean, about 40 minutes. Let cool completely.

10. To remove a cake from the pan, run a knife around the inside edge, then invert it and gently tap one side against the counter, letting the cake gently fall out of the pan onto a platter or piece of parchment paper. The cakes can be wrapped in plastic and kept at room temperature for 2 days or frozen for 2 months.

11. To assemble the cake, put one of the cake layers bottom-side up on the cake plate or platter. Using the narrow spatula, spread with about 1 cup of the frosting. Using the large spatula, place the other cake (also bottom-side up) on top of the frosting. Spread the frosting over the side and then the top of the cake.

Chocolate Hazelnut Torte

Makes 1 cake, serving 8 to 10

A torte is a fairly dense cake that uses ground nuts for structure in place of flour (or with very little flour). I like to grind the nuts finely so they're almost indiscernible in the finished cake, except for the flavor they impart. That said, if you'd like to taste a few crunchy nut pieces, grind them more coarsely. Serve with whipped cream or ice cream.

1. Preheat the oven to 350°F. Butter the bottom and side of the cake pan or spritz with nonstick cooking spray.

2. Spread the hazelnuts in one layer in a small baking pan and put in the (preheated) oven. Set a timer for 10 minutes and check the nuts to see if they're a light golden brown. If not, toast 2 minutes longer. Put the warm nuts in a colander and rub them with a clean kitchen towel to remove some of the skins. (If you don't have a colander, just rub them in the towel.) Don't worry about getting all the skins—you just want to remove the loose pieces.

3. In the food processor, process the hazelnuts with the flour until they're finely ground and look like coarse sand with a few larger visible pieces of hazelnut. Set aside.

4. Melt the chocolate and butter by putting them in a heat-proof bowl set over a saucepan of simmering water, making sure the bowl does not touch the water. (You can use a double boiler if you have one.) Stir and scrape the side of the bowl occasionally with the rubber spatula until the chocolate is smooth and evenly melted. Remove from the heat. Let cool to room temperature.

5. Using the stand mixer, or a handheld mixer and medium bowl, first on low speed and then gradually increasing the speed to medium, beat the egg yolks with 1/2 cup of the sugar and the salt until the mixture is very thick and pale yellow, 3 to 5 minutes. On low speed, stir in the melted chocolate and then the ground-nut mixture.

WHAT YOU'LL NEED

9-inch round cake pan

Food processor

Saucepan and metal bowl, or double boiler if you have one

Rubber spatula

Electric stand mixer or handheld mixer and medium bowl

3/4 cup hazelnuts

2 tablespoons unbleached all-purpose flour

6 ounces dark chocolate (58 to 62 percent cacao), chopped or broken into 1-inch pieces

12 tablespoons (1 1/2 sticks) unsalted butter

4 large eggs, separated

3/4 cup granulated sugar

1/8 teaspoon kosher salt

6. In a clean, dry bowl and with clean, dry beaters or the whisk attachment, whip the egg whites on medium-low speed until foamy. Increase the speed to high, add the remaining 1/4 cup sugar in a steady stream, and whip until the egg whites are thick and hold a firm peak.

7. Using the rubber spatula, gently fold the whites into the batter until well blended. Spread it evenly into the prepared pan. Bake on the middle rack of the (preheated) oven until a bamboo skewer or toothpick inserted in the middle of the cake still comes out a little gooey, about 25 minutes.

8. Let the cake cool in the pan to room temperature. Unmold it by running a small knife around the edge of the pan. Put a plate or platter on top of the cake and invert the cake and plate together in one move. Lift off the pan and let the cake cool completely.

9. Cut into wedges and serve with whipped cream or ice cream.

Walnut Torte with Caramel-Vanilla Oranges

Makes 8 servings

Tortes are elegant enough for a dinner party, but simple enough to be served plain with tea or coffee in the afternoon. When I have the time and want to dress this torte up a little, I serve orange segments in a caramel-vanilla sauce alongside. Once you learn how to quickly and easily segment citrus fruit you'll want to make this recipe often. Serve with vanilla ice cream.

1. Preheat the oven to 350°F. Grease the bottom and side of the cake pan with nonstick cooking spray or butter and coat evenly with flour, knocking out the excess.

2. Spread the walnuts in one layer in a small baking pan and put in the (preheated) oven. Set a timer for 10 minutes and check the nuts to see if they're a light golden brown. If not, toast 2 minutes longer.

3. In the food processor, process the walnuts with 1/4 cup of the flour until they're finely ground and look like coarse sand, with a few larger visible pieces of walnut. By hand, stir in the remaining 1/2 cup flour and the baking powder and set aside.

4. In the stand mixer with the paddle or handheld mixer and medium bowl, beat the butter and sugar on medium speed until smooth. Add the egg, rum, and orange zest and mix until well combined, using the rubber spatula to scrape down the side of the bowl. Add the flour-walnut mixture; reduce the speed to low and mix until the batter is smooth and well combined.

5. With the rubber spatula, scrape the batter into the prepared cake pan and spread evenly. Bake until a bamboo skewer or toothpick inserted in the center comes out clean and the cake springs back in the center if you press it with your finger, 20 to 25 minutes.

WHAT YOU'LL NEED
Food processor

9-inch round cake pan

Electric stand mixer or handheld mixer and medium bowl

Rubber spatula

1 1/2 cups (6 ounces) walnuts

3/4 cup unbleached all-purpose flour

1 1/2 teaspoons baking powder

6 tablespoons (3/4 stick) unsalted butter, softened

2/3 cup granulated sugar

1 large egg

2 tablespoons dark rum

Zest of 1 orange

Caramel-Vanilla Oranges
6 navel oranges

1/3 cup granulated sugar

2 tablespoons water

1/4 cup orange juice

1 teaspoon pure vanilla extract

FB: How do you cut orange segments?

EL: Cut a quarter-inch slice off both ends to flatten the orange and expose the flesh. Put the orange on the cutting board with one of the cut sides down. Cut along the curve of the orange between the rind and the flesh. After your first cut, you'll be able to see where you're cutting so you don't take off too much flesh.

6. Cool the cake to room temperature. Cut around the inside edge with a knife, then remove the cake by inverting it onto a platter or plate.

7. To serve, cut the torte into 8 wedges. Put a spoonful of the caramel oranges (see below) alongside each piece. Vanilla ice cream would make a good accompaniment.

Caramel-Vanilla Oranges

1. Peel and segment the oranges into a medium bowl (see dialog).

2. In a medium saucepan, cook the sugar and water over medium heat until the sugar dissolves and the liquid is clear, about 2 minutes. Increase the heat to medium-high and continue to cook until the sugar is a *pale* gold caramel color, about 2 minutes. Do not stir once the sugar begins to boil; it may cause the sugar to crystallize. But once it starts to color, you can gently swirl the pan so that it colors evenly.

3. When the caramel is a medium tan color, remove from the heat and slowly and carefully add 1 tablespoon of the orange juice. The hot liquid will bubble up and sputter. Once it has stopped sputtering, add a couple more tablespoons of orange juice and again wait until the caramel stops sputtering. With a wooden spoon, gently stir in the rest of the orange juice and the vanilla.

4. Pour the orange caramel over the orange sections. Let marinate for at least 10 minutes before serving, or cover the bowl with plastic wrap and leave at room temperature overnight.

Lemon Angel Food Cake

Makes 1 cake, serving 8 to 10

Since the main ingredient in angel food cake is egg whites, whipped to an airy stiffness with sugar and folded with flour, right from the get-go the beginning baker needs to know how to separate eggs. Though many novice bakers have learned the technique at some point and don't find it intimidating, I've learned it's something many others fear, particularly when you need as many as a dozen, which you do for angel food. Cake flour is used because it has less gluten than all-purpose flour and will produce a lighter cake. Serve with fresh or frozen berries.

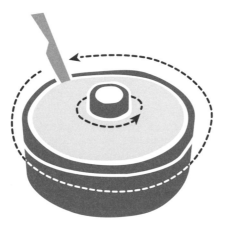

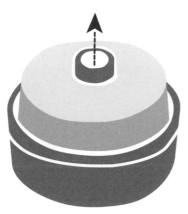

FB: My mom used to say you have to separate eggs when they're cold but that you whip them when they're room temperature.

EL: She was right, but the truth is I rarely have time in the restaurant kitchen to let the eggs warm up. The principle she's talking about is that when eggs are cold it's easier to separate the whites from the yolks, and then when the whites are warmer they whip to a higher volume. If you have the time, I say great. Your cake will come out higher. But if you don't you'll still end up with a nice cake. So, if you have the time, separate the eggs right out of the refrigerator and then let the whites sit for fifteen to twenty minutes to warm up a little before you beat them.

FB: What about an egg separator? I have one someone gave me.

EL: Frankly I think they're silly. They take too long. Here, let me show you how to do this. Start by cracking the egg on a flat surface.

FB: I thought you were supposed to use the side of a bowl.

EL: You can but the egg shell can shatter, and you're more likely to get little pieces of shell into the white. Crack the egg on the counter in one or two decisive taps—don't be timid but don't smash it either—and then transfer the yolk back and forth between the shells, letting the white run out into a bowl and reserving the yolk in another. Some chefs like to hold the egg in their hand and let the white run through their fingers.

FB: No, that would be too messy for me. But what if some of the yolk gets into the white? Do I have to throw them all out?

EL: Not at all. Just use one of the pointy shell edges to attract the yolk and scoop it out.

1. Preheat the oven to 350°F.

2. Over a bowl or piece of parchment, sift the flour in a sifter or in a fine strainer by gently tapping your hand against the edge. Add the salt (you can just leave it on top of the flour pile because it gets mixed in later).

3. Put the egg whites into a clean, dry, large bowl and, using the stand or hand mixer, begin beating on medium speed until frothy. Add the cream of tartar and increase the mixer speed to high. Slowly add the sugar in a steady stream and continue to whip. When the egg whites have reached a stiff, shiny peak that looks like thick marshmallow fluff, decrease the mixer speed to low and mix in the lemon zest, lemon juice, and vanilla.

4. Add all of the sifted flour, and with the mixer on the lowest speed, stir the flour into the whites until the mixture is almost but not quite completely combined—you still want to see some streaks of flour. Make sure you move the beaters around to reach all the edges of the bowl. Using the large rubber spatula, finish folding the flour into the whites by hand so that the mixture is thoroughly combined and no pockets of flour are visible.

5. Again using the spatula, drop big scoops of the batter evenly into the ungreased angel food cake pan. Gently smooth out the top of the batter and then lift the pan up a couple of inches from the counter and let it drop to get rid of any air pockets.

6. Bake until a bamboo skewer inserted into the center of the cake comes out clean, 35 minutes. Turn the pan upside down onto its "legs" if the pan has them, or invert it over a wine bottle and let the cake cool completely. To remove the cake from the pan, use a serrated knife and move it in a sawing up-and-down motion along the inside of the outer edge. Holding the pan by the tube, lift the cake out. Next, "saw" along the bottom surface to release the cake from the pan entirely (you won't need to cut around the tube). The cake can be made 3 days in advance and kept at room temperature wrapped in plastic.

7. To serve, cut the cake with a serrated knife using a sawing back and forth motion. Or, if your grandmother left you one, use an angel food cake cutter.

Coffee-Orange Angel Food Cake

Makes 1 cake, serving 8 to 10

As good as angel food cake can be plain, oftentimes it's just too plain and needs some adornment like fruit or sauce. Not this one. The coffee and orange turn this angel food into a stand-alone cake special enough for most any occasion. Well, you can never go wrong with a dollop of whipped cream.

Don't grease the angel food cake pan or use a nonstick pan because the cake needs the ungreased sides to stick to as it rises.

WHAT YOU'LL NEED

Two-piece or removable-bottom angel food or tube cake pan, *not nonstick*

Electric stand mixer or handheld mixer and a large bowl

Large rubber spatula

1 1/4 cups cake flour

1/4 teaspoon kosher salt

2 teaspoons instant coffee granules

12 large egg whites

1 teaspoon cream of tartar

1 1/2 cups granulated sugar

Grated zest of 2 oranges

2 1/2 tablespoons orange juice

1. Preheat the oven to 350°F.

2. Over a bowl or piece of parchment, sift the cake flour in a sifter or in a fine strainer by gently tapping your hand against the edge. Add the salt and coffee granules. Set aside.

3. Put the egg whites into a clean, dry, large bowl and, using the stand or hand mixer, begin beating on medium speed until frothy. Add the cream of tartar and increase the mixer speed to high. Slowly add the sugar in a steady stream. When the egg whites have reached a stiff, shiny peak that looks like thick marshmallow fluff, decrease the mixer speed to low and mix in the orange zest and juice.

4. Add half of the sifted flour and, with a rubber spatula fold the flour into the whites until they're almost but not quite completely combined—you still want to see some streaks of flour. Add the remaining flour and finish folding it into the whites so that the mixture is thoroughly combined and no pockets of flour are visible.

5. Using the spatula, drop big scoops of the batter evenly into the pan. Gently smooth out the top of the batter. Lift the pan up a couple of inches from the counter and let it drop to get rid of any air pockets.

6. Bake until a bamboo skewer inserted into the center of the cake comes out clean, about 35 minutes. Turn the pan upside down onto its "legs" or invert over a wine bottle and let the cake cool completely. To remove the cake from the pan, use a serrated knife and move it in a sawing up-and-down motion along the inside of the outer edge. Holding the pan by the tube, lift the cake out. Next, "saw" along the bottom surface to release the cake from the pan entirely. The cake can be made 3 days in advance and kept at room temperature wrapped in plastic.

7. To serve, cut the cake with a serrated knife using a sawing back-and-forth motion.

Lisa's Macaroon Cake

Makes 1 cake, serving 12 to 16

My coauthor, Lisa, found this recipe in a Jewish women's fund-raising cookbook. The original recipe used only shortening, but Lisa added butter for flavor. She serves it with a big bowl of berries and whipped cream.

The best pan for this cake is a nonstick tube pan with a removable bottom. If your pan is not nonstick, make sure it's generously coated with nonstick cooking spray.

WHAT YOU'LL NEED

10-inch tube cake pan with removable bottom, preferably nonstick

Electric stand mixer or handheld mixer and medium bowl

Rubber spatula

3 cups cake flour

6 large eggs, separated

1/4 cup vegetable shortening (preferably organic), at room temperature

8 tablespoons (1 stick) unsalted butter, softened

3 cups granulated sugar

1/2 teaspoon almond extract

1/2 teaspoon pure vanilla extract

1 cup whole milk

2 cups unsweetened shredded coconut

1. Preheat the oven to 300°F.

2. Generously grease the nonstick tube pan with nonstick cooking spray or butter and evenly coat with flour, tapping out excess.

3. Over a bowl or piece of parchment, sift the flour in a sifter or in a fine strainer by gently tapping your hand against the edge.

4. Using the stand mixer, or a handheld mixer and medium bowl, first on medium speed and then gradually increasing the speed to high, beat the egg yolks, shortening, and butter together until smooth. Gradually add the sugar, continuing to beat on high until the mixture is light and fluffy. Scrape down the side of the bowl with the rubber spatula and on low speed stir in the almond and vanilla extracts until blended.

5. On low speed, add the flour in thirds, alternating with half of the milk. Mix in the coconut and scrape down the side of the bowl with the rubber spatula. Transfer to a large bowl.

6. In a separate clean bowl with clean beaters, whip the egg whites until firm—which means they hold their shape and are not wet looking. With the rubber spatula gently fold the egg whites into the cake batter until the mixture is evenly blended.

7. Turn the batter into the cake pan and spread it out evenly with the spatula. Bake the cake until a bamboo skewer inserted in the middle comes out clean, 2 hours.

8. Let the cake cool in the pan for at least 30 minutes, then lift out the cake on the bottom tube section and let cool completely. Run a thin knife around the bottom to release the cake from the tube section. The cake will keep, wrapped in plastic, at room temperature for up to 3 days. It tastes even better if served the day after it is made.

Buttermilk Cheesecake

Makes 1 cheesecake, serving 10 to 12

Although cheesecake is usually served cold, when we were testing this recipe, we grew tired of waiting to cut into it and decided to taste it while it was still warm from the oven. What a happy surprise that was! And it was just as light after being reheated the next day.

Most cookbooks will tell you to bake cheesecake in a larger pan of water so it doesn't crack. So what if it does? Unless you're putting a whole cake on a buffet and want it picture perfect, slice it before serving.

WHAT YOU'LL NEED
Food processor

9-inch springform pan

Electric stand mixer or handheld mixer and medium bowl

Rubber spatula

5 ounces (one-third of a 15-ounce package), or 7 graham crackers

4 tablespoons (1/2 stick) unsalted butter, melted

1 1/2 pounds cream cheese, at room temperature

1 3/4 cups granulated sugar

1/4 teaspoon kosher salt

6 large eggs

1/4 cup unbleached all-purpose flour

3/4 cup sour cream

3/4 cup buttermilk or 3/4 cup milk mixed with 1 teaspoon lemon juice

1. Preheat the oven to 350°F.

2. Pulse the graham crackers in the food processor until finely ground. Transfer to a bowl and stir in the melted butter. Using your fingers or the bottom of a glass, evenly press the crumbs into the bottom of the springform pan. Bake the crust for 10 minutes. Let cool to room temperature.

3. Reduce the oven temperature to 300°F.

4. Using the stand mixer, or a handheld mixer and medium bowl, first on low speed and then gradually increasing the speed to medium, beat the cream cheese until smooth. Mix in the sugar and salt. Scrape down the side of the bowl with the rubber spatula and mix in the eggs one at a time, mixing well before adding the next one. With the mixer on low speed, stir in the flour and then the sour cream and buttermilk.

5. Spread the batter into the pan with the crust and bake for 1 hour to 1 hour and 15 minutes. When the cake is done it will have puffed up and browned and if you shake it carefully it still will be a little loose in the very center.

6. Run a knife around the inside edge of the pan as soon as you remove it from the oven and then let the cake cool for 30 to 45 minutes. Don't worry if it sinks as it cools. Open the latch to release the pan side from the cake and bottom pan. Cut and serve the cake while it's still warm—which is the way I like it (see headnote)—or refrigerate the cheesecake for several hours or up to 3 days and serve cold.

Gingerbread with Apples

Makes 1 cake, serving about 9

One of my favorite flavor combinations is apples and gingerbread, and what I usually do is serve sautéed apples alongside the cake. One time, I thought: why not put the apples right into the cake? Ta-da! I don't know why I hadn't thought of it before.

You don't even need to pull out the mixer for this recipe. Stir the dry ingredients in one bowl, the liquid ingredients in another bowl, then stir them all together.

Serve with whipped cream.

WHAT YOU'LL NEED

9-inch square cake pan

2 apples (any kind you like)

2 cups unbleached all-purpose flour

1 1/2 teaspoons baking soda

1 tablespoon ground ginger

1 teaspoon ground cinnamon

1/4 teaspoon nutmeg

1/2 teaspoon kosher salt

8 tablespoons (1 stick) unsalted butter

1/2 cup molasses

1/2 cup maple syrup

1/4 cup firmly packed brown sugar

2 large eggs

3/4 cup boiling water

1. Preheat the oven to 350°F. Grease the cake pan with nonstick cooking spray or butter.

2. Peel the apples and from the top core them by cutting off the sides and removing the rectangular piece of core. Cut into small (1/2-inch) pieces. Set aside.

3. Over a bowl or piece of parchment, sift the flour, baking soda, ginger, cinnamon, and nutmeg together in a sifter or in a fine strainer by gently tapping your hand against the edge. Add the salt (you can just leave it on top of the flour pile because it gets mixed in later). Transfer to a medium bowl.

4. In a medium saucepan over medium heat, melt the butter with the molasses, maple syrup, and brown sugar. With a whisk, stir into the flour mixture until well combined. Whisk in the eggs. Stir in the boiling water and then the apple pieces.

5. Pour the batter into the prepared cake pan. Bake on the middle rack of the (preheated) oven until a bamboo skewer or toothpick inserted in the middle comes out clean, about 45 minutes. Cool to room temperature.

6. Cut the cake in the pan into 3-inch squares.

Cherry-Topped Cheesecake

Makes 1 cake, serving about 12

Traditionally, cheesecake is baked in a water bath so it cooks evenly and gently and doesn't crack. (See Buttermilk Cheesecake recipe, page 92, for baking without a water bath.) A water bath, or *bain marie,* is essentially a large pan filled with water that can hold a smaller dish (or several small dishes). While it's a simple concept, the tricky part for a novice baker is filling the larger pan with hot water and getting it to the oven.

1. Preheat the oven to 350°F.

2. Pulse the cookies in the food processor until they're like coarse sand. (You should have about 1 1/4 cups.) In a bowl, stir the crumbs with the melted butter until well mixed.

3. With your fingers, evenly press the crumbs onto the bottom of the springform pan. Wrap the pan in aluminum foil so it covers the bottom and comes up the side (this prevents water from getting into the pan). Bake for 13 minutes, or until the crust is brown. Let cool to room temperature.

4. Reduce the oven temperature to 300°F.

5. Using the stand mixer, or a medium bowl and handheld mixer, on low speed beat the cream cheese until smooth, about 1 minute. Scrape down the side of the bowl with the rubber spatula, add the sugar, and start mixing on low speed. Increase the speed to medium and mix until incorporated. Break the whole eggs and egg yolks into a small bowl. Pour a couple at a time into the cream cheese, mixing them in before adding the next. Add the flour and cream and mix until well combined.

6. Pour the batter into the pan over the crust. Put the springform pan in the larger pan (see headnote) and find a space near your oven to fill the larger pan with water so you don't have to walk too far. Fill a large measuring cup with a spout with hot tap

WHAT YOU'LL NEED

9-inch springform pan

Large roasting pan that can hold the springform pan

Electric stand mixer or handheld mixer and medium bowl

Rubber spatula

7 ounces (27 two-inch) store-bought crispy ginger snaps (I use Nabisco)

4 tablespoons (1/2 stick) unsalted butter, melted

2 1/2 pounds cream cheese, at room temperature

1 1/4 cups granulated sugar

5 large whole eggs, at room temperature

2 large egg yolks, at room temperature

2 tablespoons unbleached all-purpose flour

1/3 cup heavy cream

Cherry Topping

1 1/2 pounds ripe cherries, stemmed and pitted (see page 172)

1/3 cup granulated sugar

1 1/2 tablespoons cornstarch

1/3 cup water

EL: Now that you have the springform wrapped with foil, and before you pour in your batter, you need to do one more thing.

FB: What's that?

EL: Before you dump everything in the pan, reread the recipe and ask yourself, "Did I put in the blah, blah, and blah?" As a double check I always read over the list of ingredients. You don't want to say later, "Oh shoot, I forgot the cream."

FB: Okay, I have the cream cheese, sugar, egg yolks, whole eggs, flour, and cream. Don't need the cherries for the topping yet.

EL: Use your spatula to scrape and pour the mixture into the pan.

FB: The recipe says to fill the larger pan half-full of hot water.

EL: Yes, you can fill the pan now, while it's on the counter, or put it in the oven and then fill it. Which would you want to do?

FB: I think I'd rather fill it first and carry the pan to the oven.

EL: Whatever makes you comfortable. First, fill a measuring cup with a spout with hot tap water. Good. Now, put the larger pan with the pan of cheesecake near the stove so you don't have to walk so far. Pour in the hot water. Open the oven and pull out the oven rack so you don't hit your hand on the roof or sides of the oven. Transfer the pan to the oven. Just be careful to not slosh it.

FB: Whew! I did it.

water and pour it into the larger pan to come halfway up the side of the springform. Carefully transfer the large pan to the (preheated) oven (you don't want any water splashing into the cheesecake). Bake the cheesecake until 2 1/2 inches in from the side is set and a 2-inch area in the center is still jiggly, about 1 hour and 20 minutes.

7. Carefully remove the water-filled pan from the oven and lift the cheesecake pan out of the water. Remove the foil. Gently run a paring knife around the inside edge of the pan, loosening the cheesecake from the side. Cool at room temperature for 1 hour, then refrigerate until cold and firm, at least 5 hours.

8. Open the latch and release the pan side from the cake and bottom pan. Place on a serving platter and top with the cherry topping (see below). Slice into wedges to serve.

Cherry Topping

Put the pitted cherries, sugar, cornstarch, and water in a medium saucepan. Cook over medium heat, stirring frequently but gently and scraping the bottom of the pan with a rubber spatula to prevent sticking as the liquid simmers. After about 8 minutes, the cherries should have given off juices and thickened and you should still see some whole cherries in the thickened juice. Remove from the heat and let cool. Transfer to a covered storage container and refrigerate for up to a week.

Chocolate–Peanut Butter Mousse Cake

Makes 1 cake, serving about 12

I really should have called this the Gilded Lily Cake because I've served the mousse cake on its own—without the nut crust—and called it Chocolate Silk. It's really so delicious it needs no adornment, but I think the nut crust adds a textural component that is a welcome contrast to the smooth richness of the mousse. This dessert is simple to prepare and utterly indulgent. Also, if you're looking for something to serve to guests who have wheat allergies, it's perfect. Serve with whipped cream.

WHAT YOU'LL NEED
9-inch springform pan

Saucepan and metal bowl, or double boiler if you have one

Electric stand mixer or handheld mixer and medium bowl

Rubber spatula

Crust
6 ounces nuts, any combination of whole natural almonds, pecans, and salted dry-roasted peanuts

1/2 cup firmly packed light brown sugar

6 tablespoons (3/4 stick) unsalted butter, melted

Filling
6 ounces bittersweet chocolate (58 to 62 percent cacao), broken into 1-inch pieces

2 ounces milk chocolate, broken into 1-inch pieces

1/2 cup smooth peanut butter

8 tablespoons (1 stick) unsalted butter

1/3 cup granulated sugar

Pinch kosher salt

4 large eggs

1/4 cup heavy cream

1/2 teaspoon pure vanilla extract

FB: Why do recipes always ask you to toast the nuts?

EL: Toasting dries them out so they don't get soggy and also brings out their nutty flavors.

FB: What are natural almonds?

EL: They are almonds with the skin still on. I prefer them for their color and taste.

FB: Can I put the different nuts on one pan or do I have to toast them separately?

EL: You can put walnuts and pecans together. But almonds, for instance, which are less oily than the other nuts, take longer and should be done separately. You don't need to toast the peanuts since we're using dry-roasted peanuts.

FB: What about hazelnuts?

EL: They take longer too and they also have skins that you want to rub off with a towel, so I like to keep them separate.

FB: Do I chop them before roasting or after?

EL: I chop them after. In this recipe I want them not too finely ground so I like to chop them by hand rather than throw them in a food processor.

Crust

1. Preheat the oven to 350°F. Spread the almonds and pecans separately in single layers on rimmed baking sheets. Bake for about 10 minutes, or until lightly browned. Cool to room temperature.

2. Combine with the peanuts and chop the nuts into small pieces, no bigger than 1/4 inch. Toss in a bowl with the brown sugar and melted butter, then transfer to the springform pan. Using the bottom of a glass or a measuring cup, press the nuts evenly into the bottom of the pan to form a crust. Set aside while you make the filling, or refrigerate for up to 8 hours.

Filling

3. Melt the bittersweet and milk chocolates with the peanut butter in a heat-proof bowl set over (but not touching) a saucepan of simmering water (or use a double boiler if you have one). Stir and scrape the side of the bowl occasionally with the rubber spatula until the chocolate is smooth and evenly melted.

4. Using the stand mixer, or a medium bowl and handheld mixer, on medium speed, beat the butter with the sugar and salt until the mixture is light and fluffy, about 2 minutes. Add the eggs one at a time and continue to beat on medium speed, stopping occasionally to scrape down the side of the bowl with the rubber spatula. It's okay if the mixture is separated.

5. Stir the chocolate mixture into the egg mixture until thoroughly combined. Stir in the cream and vanilla.

6. Pour the filling into the springform pan with the crust and refrigerate until firm, about 6 hours or overnight.

7. Cut the cake into wedges, wiping the knife with a damp towel after each slice. Every dessert tastes better with whipped cream and this cake is no exception.

Dark Chocolate Cake
with Mocha–Milk Chocolate Frosting

Makes 1 cake, serving about 12

When I tested this cake I was at home alone. I tasted it and I kept returning to take another taste. I came to my senses and put it in my car, to get it out of sight. I could have eaten the whole cake. Baked and frosted in the pan it's a great cake to take to friends.

WHAT YOU'LL NEED
9- by 13-inch cake pan

Rubber spatula

1 2/3 cups unbleached all-purpose flour

3/4 cup cocoa powder

2 teaspoons baking soda

1 teaspoon baking powder

1/4 teaspoon kosher salt

2 cups firmly packed light brown sugar

1/2 cup vegetable or canola oil

2 large eggs

1 cup strong coffee or espresso,
at room temperature

1 cup buttermilk

Mocha–Milk Chocolate Frosting
Saucepan and metal bowl, or double boiler
if you have one

Rubber spatula

6 ounces milk chocolate, chopped
or broken into 1-inch pieces

2 tablespoons instant coffee granules

6 tablespoons whole milk

2 2/3 cups confectioners' sugar

Pinch kosher salt

10 tablespoons (1 1/4 sticks) unsalted
butter, softened

1. Preheat the oven to 350°F. Grease the bottoms and sides of the cake pan with nonstick cooking spray or butter.

2. Over a bowl or piece of parchment, sift the flour, cocoa powder, baking soda, and baking powder together in a sifter or in a fine strainer by gently tapping your hand against the edge. Add the salt. Transfer to a large bowl. Whisk in the brown sugar, breaking up any lumps if necessary.

3. In another bowl, whisk together the oil, eggs, coffee, and buttermilk. Add to the bowl with the flour and cocoa, whisking until evenly blended. Pour the batter into the pan and spread it evenly with the rubber spatula in the pan.

4. Bake the cake on the middle rack of the oven until a bamboo skewer or toothpick inserted in the middle comes out clean, about 30 minutes.

5. Cool the cake to room temperature. Spread the frosting (see below) on top of the cake. Cut the cake into approximate 3-inch squares for serving.

Mocha–Milk Chocolate Frosting

1. Melt the milk chocolate in a heat-proof bowl set over (but not touching) a saucepan of simmering water (or use a double boiler if you have one). Stir and scrape the side of the bowl occasionally with the rubber spatula until the chocolate is smooth and evenly melted. Let cool to room temperature.

2. In a medium bowl, stir the coffee into the milk until dissolved. Sift the confectioners' sugar in a sifter or by gently tapping your hand against the edge of a fine strainer directly into the bowl. Add the salt. Cut the butter into tablespoons and add to the bowl a few pieces at a time, stirring them in until they're smooth. Add the cooled melted milk chocolate and stir in until combined.

3. Refrigerate the frosting until it's spreadable, about 30 minutes.

Brownie Pecan Cake

Makes 1 cake, serving about 12

This dessert is not quite as fudgy as a brownie or as light as a cake; it's somewhere in between. It does, however, make a delicious midmorning or afternoon snack, is perfect to take on a road trip or picnic. If you serve it for dessert, I recommend coffee ice cream or whipped cream and caramel sauce alongside.

WHAT YOU'LL NEED

9- by-13-inch baking pan

Saucepan and metal bowl, or double boiler if you have one

Electric stand mixer or handheld mixer and medium bowl

Rubber spatula

1 cup pecan pieces

3/4 cup unbleached all-purpose flour

3/4 cup cocoa powder

1 teaspoon baking powder

1/4 teaspoon kosher salt

2 ounces dark chocolate (58 to 62 percent cacao), chopped or broken into 1-inch pieces

12 tablespoons (1 1/2 sticks) unsalted butter, at room temperature

3/4 cup granulated sugar

3 large eggs

1/3 cup whole milk

1/2 cup chocolate chips

1. Preheat the oven to 350°F. Grease the bottom and sides of the baking pan with nonstick cooking spray or butter and evenly coat with flour, tapping out the excess.

2. Spread the pecans in one layer in a small baking pan and put in the (preheated) oven. Set a timer for 10 minutes and check the nuts to see if they're a light golden brown. If not, toast 2 minutes longer. Set aside to cool.

3. Over a bowl or piece of parchment, sift the flour, cocoa, and baking powder together in a sifter or in a fine strainer by gently tapping your hand against the edge. Add the salt (you can just leave it on top of the flour pile because it gets mixed in later). Set aside.

4. Melt the dark chocolate in a heat-proof bowl set over a saucepan of simmering water, making sure the bowl does not touch the water. (You can use a double boiler if you have one.) Stir and scrape the side of the bowl occasionally with the rubber spatula until the chocolate is smooth and evenly melted.

5. Using the stand mixer, or a handheld mixer and medium bowl, first on low speed and then gradually increasing the speed to medium, beat the butter and sugar together until smooth. Scrape down the side of the bowl with the rubber spatula. Add the eggs one at a time, mixing well each time before adding the next.

6. On low speed, mix in the melted chocolate and the milk. Add the sifted flour/cocoa mixture and mix until evenly blended. Stir in the pecans and chocolate chips.

7. Spread the batter with the spatula into the prepared pan. Bake the cake on the middle rack of the (preheated) oven until a bamboo skewer or toothpick inserted in the middle comes out a little fudgy, not completely clean, about 20 minutes.

8. Cool the cake in the pan to room temperature, then cut it into approximate 3-inch squares for serving.

Pineapple-Raspberry Upside-Down Cake

Makes 1 cake, serving about 12

I wanted to give this classic American dessert—one of my favorites—a more contemporary flavor, so I substituted fresh pineapple for canned and fresh raspberries for preservative-laden maraschino cherries. And I added a little cornmeal to the cake batter for texture. If you're stymied when confronted by a fresh pineapple, I think you'll find it not too difficult to cut once you try it.

You only need 1 1/2 cups of pineapple pieces for this recipe so you will have some left over for your morning fruit salad.

WHAT YOU'LL NEED
Rubber spatula

9-inch square cake pan

Electric stand mixer or handheld mixer and medium bowl

Cake platter or serving plate large enough for a 9-inch cake

Brown Sugar Topping
6 tablespoons (3/4 stick) unsalted butter

3/4 cup firmly packed light brown sugar

1 tablespoon light corn syrup

1 1/2 cups fresh pineapple pieces
(1/2 to 3/4 inch)

1/2 pint raspberries

Cake
1 1/2 cups unbleached all-purpose flour

1/2 cup white or yellow cornmeal

1 teaspoon baking powder

1/2 teaspoon kosher salt

16 tablespoons (2 sticks) unsalted butter, softened

1 3/4 cups granulated sugar

4 large eggs

1/4 cup buttermilk or 1/4 cup whole milk mixed with 1/4 teaspoon lemon juice

1/2 teaspoon pure vanilla extract

FB: So, we're going to do the pineapple now. Hmm. Never hacked at one before.

EL: With a sharp knife, first you cut off the green crown and then cut a half inch off the bottom.

FB: Like so?

EL: Turn the pineapple upright and, following the contour of the fruit, slice the skin off in strips. Now go back and dig out any black pieces (they're called eyes) with the tip of a peeler or with a paring knife.

FB: Another question. How do you know a ripe pineapple?

EL: First, look at the leaves to make sure they're fresh and green, with no brown spots or withering. I like to smell them. You shouldn't pick up any fermented odors. Buy the one that smells like pineapple. Sounds obvious, I know.

FB: Or you just get a can and open it (laughing).

EL: Fresh is so much better. To cut the trimmed pineapple into pieces, leave it standing on end and then cut down lengthwise through the center, cutting it into four wedges. Leave the wedges standing and cut down to remove the core. Cut the wedges into pieces and you're done.

1. Preheat the oven to 350°F.

Brown Sugar Topping

2. In a small saucepan, melt the butter over medium heat. Add the brown sugar and corn syrup. Whisking constantly, cook until the brown sugar is melted and the mixture is smooth. With the rubber spatula, spread onto the bottom of the cake pan. Evenly scatter the pieces of pineapple and then the raspberries over the mixture.

Cake

3. In a medium bowl, whisk the flour, cornmeal, baking powder, and salt. Set aside.

4. Using the electric stand mixer, or a handheld mixer and a medium bowl, beginning on low speed and increasing it to medium, beat the softened butter and granulated sugar until smooth. Add the eggs one at a time, mixing well after each addition. Stir in the buttermilk and vanilla. Finally, mix in the cornmeal mixture, scraping down the side of the bowl once or twice.

5. Using the rubber spatula, spread the cake batter over the pineapple and raspberries. Bake the cake until a skewer inserted in the middle comes out clean, about 45 minutes.

6. Let the cake cool for 10 minutes. Run a small knife around the inside edge of the cake pan. Place the large plate or platter on top and flip the cake and the pan to invert the cake onto the platter. Remove the pan and let cool to warm or room temperature before serving.

7. Store the cake at room temperature wrapped in plastic wrap for up to 3 days.

Warm and Gooey Chocolate Cake

Makes 8 servings

This is the dessert to make if you or someone you love is an avowed chocoholic. Even though I call it a cake, it's actually hard to describe. It's somewhere between a dense and sliceable flourless chocolate cake and a spoonable pudding. With only six ingredients whisked together by hand, it can be easily put together on short notice. You just have to make sure that one of your pantry ingredients is good-quality dark chocolate—a must in any true chocoholic's kitchen anyway. But choosing the chocolate can be a dilemma for bakers, with so many varieties available today.

WHAT YOU'LL NEED

9-inch square or round ceramic baking dish

Saucepan and metal bowl, or double boiler if you have one

Rubber spatula

Roasting pan or larger baking dish that will hold the baking dish

2 tablespoons plus 1 cup granulated sugar

8 ounces dark chocolate (58 to 62 percent cacao), chopped or broken into 1-inch pieces

10 tablespoons (1 1/4 sticks) unsalted butter

4 large eggs

Large pinch kosher salt

2 tablespoons unbleached all-purpose flour

FB: I am such a total chocoholic. I can't believe this is the recipe I'm going to make. So I see here that you say, "dark chocolate, fifty-eight to sixty-two percent cacao." Whenever I go to buy chocolate, not the candies, but the stuff in the baking aisle, I get so confused. I understand that the higher percentage of cacao, the less sweet and more chocolaty it tastes. But what about semisweet and bittersweet? The percentages seem to vary a lot.

EL: I'll tell you, it's confusing. A cocoa bean is made up of chocolate liquor and cocoa butter. This is called cacao. When you see percentages, they refer to the percentage of cacao to other ingredients. There isn't an industry standard in terms of labeling semisweet or bittersweet. Unsweetened chocolate is one hundred percent chocolate liquor.

FB: What do you like to use? What percentage, I mean?

EL: I like to nibble on dark chocolate, seventy-two to ninety percent, but it's not appropriate for many desserts. For the desserts in this book that call for dark chocolate, I use fifty-eight to sixty-two percent. More than that won't work as well. Since bittersweet or semisweet labels vary among companies, I don't say "bittersweet" or "semisweet."

FB: Any brands you recommend?

EL: Yes there are many good chocolates available. I encourage you to buy a few and conduct your own taste test. On pages 16 and 17 we list a few brands I use regularly.

1. Preheat the oven to 350°F. Grease the baking dish with nonstick cooking spray or butter. Use the 2 tablespoons of sugar to coat the bottom and sides of the dish by rotating and turning it and then tapping it over the sink to remove excess sugar.

2. Melt the chocolate and butter by putting them in a heat-proof bowl set over a saucepan of simmering water, making sure the bowl does not touch the water. (You can use a double boiler if you have one.) Stir and scrape the sides of the bowl occasionally with the rubber spatula until the chocolate is smooth and evenly melted.

3. In a large bowl, whisk the eggs by hand with the 1 cup remaining sugar and the salt until well blended. Whisk in the melted chocolate and then the flour. (Measure the flour into a small bowl and rather than sifting it, simply crush any lumps with your fingers.) With the rubber spatula, spread the batter evenly into the prepared baking dish.

4. Find a space near your oven to fill the roasting pan with water so you don't have to walk too far. Using very hot tap water (it's not necessary to bring a kettle of water to the boil), carefully— so that it doesn't splash into the cake—pour water into the roasting pan to come halfway up the sides of the baking dish. Moving carefully, transfer the roasting pan to a rack in the (preheated) oven.

5. Bake the pudding cake until a bamboo skewer or toothpick inserted in the middle comes out a little fudgy, 25 to 30 minutes (start checking at 20 minutes). Remove the roasting pan from the oven and set it aside to cool for 10 minutes before lifting the dish with the cake out of the water.

6. Serve scoops of the warm cake in dessert bowls with whipped cream. The cake can be made a day ahead and kept at room temperature. Reheat for 10 minutes in a 325°F oven, but be careful not to overheat it or it will lose its gooeyness.

Honey-Cinnamon Pound Cake

Makes 1 loaf cake, serving 8 to 12

With its fine texture and delicate aroma of honey and cinnamon, this pound cake makes a great any-time-of-day treat. Dress it up for dessert with whipped cream and fruit, or serve it simply with a cup of tea.

Loaf pan sizes can be inconsistent, so if your pan is smaller than the one specified, make sure you don't fill it more than one-half to two-thirds full.

WHAT YOU'LL NEED

8 1/2- by 4 1/2-inch loaf pan

Electric stand mixer or handheld mixer and medium bowl

Rubber spatula

2 cups unbleached all-purpose flour

1/2 teaspoon baking soda

1/2 teaspoon baking powder

1/2 teaspoon ground cinnamon

1/2 teaspoon kosher salt

10 tablespoons (1 1/4 sticks) unsalted butter, softened

3/4 cup granulated sugar

2 large eggs

1/4 cup honey

2/3 cup buttermilk or 2/3 cup whole milk mixed with 1 teaspoon lemon juice

1 teaspoon pure vanilla extract

EL: Let me measure that loaf pan before we get started.

FB: Where do you measure it?

EL: Well, like anything, by length and width.

FB: What if the top is wider than the bottom?

EL: For a loaf pan the difference between the two measures is not so great as to affect the recipe's outcome. A pie plate, though, you would measure by its top width. What is so frustrating is that if you go into a store to buy a loaf pan, whether it's a cookware shop or your local hardware store, they're all such different sizes. As a recipe writer you can't just say "loaf pan." With pie plates you can specify eight- or nine-inch for instance, or specify deep-dish and cooks will know what size to use.

FB: And it matters, because if you're a new baker like me, you worry if it doesn't come out right that it's something you've done wrong.

EL: The thing that really matters is how much you fill it. If you fill it too full, it will rise up and there'll be too much batter for the cake to cook properly. It would be overdone on the outside and too gooey in the middle. In a pinch, you can substitute a larger pan for a smaller one. The cake will take less time to bake and will come out flatter.

FB: So we're going to use this eight-and-a-half-inch pan?

EL: That's what the recipe calls for.

1. Preheat the oven to 350°F. Grease the loaf pan with nonstick cooking spray or butter and evenly coat with flour, tapping out the excess.

2. Over a bowl or piece of parchment, sift the flour, baking soda, baking powder, and cinnamon together in a sifter or in a fine strainer by gently tapping your hand against the edge. Add the salt (you can just leave it on top of the flour pile because it gets mixed in later).

3. Using the stand mixer, or a medium bowl and handheld mixer, on medium speed, beat the butter with the sugar until smooth and light in color. Add the eggs, scrape down the side of the bowl with the rubber spatula, and mix until combined. Mix in the honey.

4. In a small bowl, stir the buttermilk with the vanilla extract.

5. Add half of the sifted flour mixture to the butter mixture and mix on low speed until thoroughly combined. Add half of the buttermilk and again mix until blended. Repeat with the remaining flour mixture and then the rest of the buttermilk.

6. Evenly spread the batter into the prepared pan with the rubber spatula. Bake until a bamboo skewer or toothpick inserted in the middle of the cake comes out clean, about 1 hour. Begin checking after 50 minutes. Let cool for 15 minutes.

7. Run a small knife around the inside edge of the pan, then unmold by inverting the cake and pan onto a cutting board, cake platter, or plate. Cool completely before serving. The cake can be wrapped in plastic and kept at room temperature for up to 3 days.

8. Cut the cake into 3/4- to 1-inch slices.

Toasted Pecan Pound Cake

Makes 1 loaf cake, serving 8

Pound cakes are wonderfully versatile and great to have on hand. You can eat them on the run or turn them into a plated dessert for a dinner party with the addition of a sauce or ice cream. During the summer I like to slice pound cake, grill it lightly on the barbecue, and serve it with fresh fruit.

WHAT YOU'LL NEED

9- by 5-inch loaf pan

Electric stand mixer or handheld mixer and medium bowl

Rubber spatula

1 cup pecan pieces

1 1/2 cups unbleached all-purpose flour

1 teaspoon baking powder

1/4 teaspoon kosher salt

16 tablespoons (2 sticks) unsalted butter, softened

1 cup granulated sugar

1 teaspoon grated lemon zest

2 large eggs

3/4 cup buttermilk or 3/4 cup whole milk mixed with 1 teaspoon lemon juice

1 teaspoon pure vanilla extract

1. Preheat the oven to 350°F. Grease the bottom and sides of the loaf pan with nonstick cooking spray or butter.

2. Spread the pecan pieces in one layer in a small baking pan and put in the (preheated) oven. Set a timer for 10 minutes and check the nuts to see if they're a light golden brown. If not, toast 2 minutes longer. Set aside to cool.

3. In a medium bowl, whisk the flour with the baking powder and salt. Set aside.

4. Using the stand mixer, or a medium bowl and handheld mixer, on medium-low speed, beat the butter, sugar, and lemon zest until smooth. Add the eggs one at a time, mixing on medium speed until well combined before adding the second egg. Scrape down the side of the bowl with the rubber spatula.

5. In a small bowl, stir the buttermilk with the vanilla.

6. With the mixer on low speed, add half of the flour mixture to the butter mixture and mix until just combined. Add half of the buttermilk, again mixing until combined. Add the remaining flour, then the buttermilk, mixing well after each addition. Stir in the pecans.

7. Using the rubber spatula, scrape the batter into the prepared pan and spread evenly, nudging the batter into the corners of the pan. Bake until a bamboo skewer or toothpick inserted in the middle comes out clean, about 1 hour 15 minutes.

8. Let cool in the pan for 15 minutes. Run a small knife around the cake to loosen it from the pan and invert it onto a piece of parchment or plate. Let the cake cool to room temperature before slicing.

Olive Oil–Pecan Bundt Cake

Makes 1 cake, serving about 12

The key to this cake is the quality of olive oil you use. I've made it several times with various grades and flavors and found that it's best with the more pronounced olive flavor of fruity extra-virgin oil.

Though they're not absolutely necessary, the bread crumbs give the cake a nice crust. You can also dust the cake pan with flour. Serve the cake after dinner with whipped cream, or plain alongside your morning coffee.

WHAT YOU'LL NEED

12-cup, 10-inch Bundt cake pan

Food processor

Cake plate or platter large enough for a 10-inch cake

1/3 cup fine dry bread crumbs

1 cup pecans

2 cups unbleached all-purpose flour

1 cup good-quality fruity extra-virgin olive oil

1 1/2 cups granulated sugar

1 cup plain yogurt (I like 2 percent Greek yogurt for its richness but any kind except nonfat will work)

2 large eggs

2 teaspoons baking soda

1. Preheat the oven to 350°F. Grease the Bundt pan with nonstick cooking spray or brush with olive oil. Sprinkle the side, bottom, and tube with the bread crumbs, rotating and tilting the pan to coat well. Tap out any excess crumbs.

2. Spread the pecans in one layer in a small baking pan and put in the (preheated) oven. Set a timer for 10 minutes and check the nuts to see if they're a light golden brown. If not, toast 2 minutes longer. Let the nuts cool.

3. In the food processor, process the pecans with 1/2 cup of the flour until they're finely ground and look like coarse sand.

4. In a medium bowl, whisk the olive oil with the sugar until combined. Whisk in the yogurt with the eggs and then stir in the remaining 1 1/2 cups flour, the baking soda, and ground nuts until everything is well blended.

5. Evenly spread the batter into the prepared pan. Bake until a bamboo skewer inserted in the middle comes out clean, about 35 minutes.

6. Let the cake cool for 20 minutes. Unmold the cake by inverting the pan onto the cake plate or platter. If necessary, lift the plate and give it a tap on the counter to release the cake.

Vanilla Pound Cake

Makes 1 loaf cake, serving 8

It's not that I want to appear partisan—after all, as a professional I must maintain some air of neutrality—but if it came down to a choice between chocolate and vanilla, I would have to confess that I'm a vanilla girl. That's why I've embellished this perfectly wonderful vanilla pound cake with a syrup made from vanilla beans. Sometimes, too much of a good thing can be delicious.

To make sure the cake is really saturated with the vanilla syrup, poke holes on the top, spoon on the syrup, and then flip the cake over and repeat the poking and drizzling.

This pound cake and the Lemon Pound Cake variation that follows are similar. Both are finely textured cakes saturated with syrup, making them more flavorful and better keepers than unsyruped pound cakes. They'll stay fresh at room temperature for several days.

1. Preheat the oven to 350°F. Grease the bottom and sides of the loaf pan with nonstick cooking spray or butter.

2. In a medium bowl, whisk the flour with the baking soda and baking powder. Add the salt (you can just leave it on top of the pile because it gets mixed in later). Set aside.

3. Using the stand mixer, or a medium bowl and handheld mixer, on medium-low speed, beat the butter and sugar until smooth. Add the eggs one at a time, mixing on medium speed until well combined before adding the second egg. Scrape down the side of the bowl with the rubber spatula.

4. Stir the vanilla extract into the buttermilk. With the mixer on low speed, add half of the flour mixture to the butter mixture and mix until just combined. Add half of the buttermilk, again mixing until combined. Add the remaining flour, then the buttermilk, mixing well after each addition.

WHAT YOU'LL NEED
8 1/2- by 4-inch loaf pan

Electric stand mixer or handheld mixer and medium bowl

Rubber spatula

2 cups unbleached all-purpose flour

1/2 teaspoon baking soda

1 teaspoon baking powder

1/4 teaspoon kosher salt

10 tablespoons (1 1/4 sticks) unsalted butter, softened

1 cup granulated sugar

2 large eggs

1 1/2 teaspoons pure vanilla extract

2/3 cup buttermilk or 2/3 cup whole milk mixed with 1 teaspoon lemon juice

Vanilla Syrup
1/3 cup granulated sugar

3 tablespoons water

1/2 vanilla bean

The syrup had been set aside and the FB had just taken the cake out of the oven.

FB: This syrup has gotten a little thick.

EL: No problem. It's cooled down. Since it's still in the saucepan you can put it back on a low burner to warm it up. You could also put it in the microwave to warm it and thin it out. You don't want it so thick that it won't soak into the cake.

FB: So I just poke holes? All over, right?

EL: Yep. And then brush over the warm vanilla syrup. Flip the cake over and poke some more holes. Good. Now brush with some more of the syrup.

FB: Whoo, sticky. But sticky delicious.

EL: Wait till you taste it once it cools, when the vanilla syrup has had a chance to really work its magic.

5. Using the rubber spatula, scrape the batter into the prepared pan and spread evenly, nudging the batter into the corners of the pan. Bake until a bamboo skewer or toothpick inserted in the middle comes out clean, about 40 minutes.

6. Right after you remove the cake from the oven, run a small knife around the cake to loosen it from the pan and invert it onto a piece of parchment or aluminum foil on the counter. Poke a dozen or so holes in the bottom of the cake with a bamboo skewer. Then, with a pastry brush, brush half of the vanilla syrup (see below) onto the cake (if the syrup is too thick to spread, warm it up over low heat). Turn the cake over, poke some more holes in the top of the cake, and brush on the remaining syrup. Let the cake cool to room temperature before slicing.

Vanilla Syrup

Stir the sugar and water together in a small saucepan. Slit the bean in half lengthwise and, with the bean on the countertop, hold the bean on one end and scrape out the seeds with the back of a knife. Add the bean pod and seeds to the sugar and water. Cook over medium-high heat until the sugar is dissolved and turn off the heat. Don't let it boil. Set aside until the cake has finished baking. Remove the bean pod before brushing the syrup on the cake.

Variation: Lemon Pound Cake

Skip the vanilla extract and instead add the grated zest of 3 lemons to the mixing bowl with the eggs.

Instead of Vanilla Syrup make Lemon Syrup: In a small saucepan, combine 1/3 cup granulated sugar with 1/4 cup freshly squeezed lemon juice. Cook the mixture over medium-high heat until the sugar is dissolved, then turn off the heat. Don't let it boil. Set aside until the cake has finished baking.

Individual Lemon Cakes with Oranges and Vanilla Mascarpone Cream

Makes 6 servings

Your guests may not believe you made these elegant little cakes yourself until you show them the recipe, but I guarantee they'll be impressed. Not only are they pretty, they're pretty delicious. While the cakes can be made early in the day, it's best to assemble them right before serving. In the winter, I like to use blood oranges for a change of color and flavor.

1. Preheat the oven to 350°F. Grease the bottoms and sides of 6 muffin cups with nonstick cooking spray or butter and coat evenly with flour, tapping out the excess. With a 12-cup pan, you can use just 6; or use a 6-cup pan. It doesn't matter.

2. Over a bowl or piece of parchment, sift the flour and baking powder together in a sifter or in a fine strainer by gently tapping your hand against the edge. Add the salt (you can just leave it on top of the flour pile because it gets mixed in later).

3. Using the stand mixer, or a handheld mixer and medium bowl, first on low speed and then gradually increasing the speed to medium, beat the butter, sugar, and lemon zest together until smooth. Scrape down the side of the bowl with the rubber spatula and mix in the egg until combined.

4. In a small bowl, stir the buttermilk and vanilla together until well blended.

5. On low speed, alternating between the sifted dry ingredients and the buttermilk mixture, add them to the butter mixture in thirds, making sure the batter is combined before the next addition. Evenly divide the batter among the 6 prepared cups.

6. Bake on the middle rack of the (preheated) oven until a bamboo skewer inserted in the middles of the cakes comes out clean, about 20 minutes.

WHAT YOU'LL NEED

Standard 6- or 12-cup muffin pan

Electric stand mixer or handheld mixer and medium bowl

Rubber spatula

1 cup unbleached all-purpose flour

1 teaspoon baking powder

Large pinch kosher salt

6 tablespoons (3/4 stick) unsalted butter, softened

1/3 cup granulated sugar

Grated zest of 3 lemons

1 large egg

1/4 cup buttermilk or 1/4 cup whole milk mixed with 1/4 teaspoon lemon juice

1 teaspoon pure vanilla extract

4 large or 6 medium navel oranges, peeled and segmented (see page 86)

Vanilla Mascarpone Cream

1/2 vanilla bean

2/3 cup mascarpone, softened

1/2 cup heavy cream

1 tablespoon granulated sugar

Zest of 1 lemon

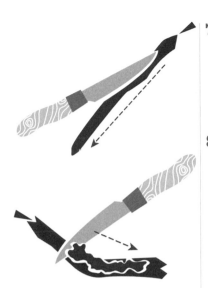

7. Let cool for 15 minutes. Run a small knife around the inside edge of each cup and, with the tip of the knife at the bottom of the cup, gently lift the little cakes out of their cups and turn them upside down, so the wider part of the cake is on the bottom. The cakes can be made ahead and kept in a covered container for several hours or overnight at room temperature.

8. To serve, cut the cakes in half horizontally. Place a wider half on each of 6 dessert plates. Spoon some orange segments on top and dollop with some of the Vanilla Mascarpone Cream. Repeat with the second cake layer, more oranges, and more cream. Serve immediately.

Vanilla Mascarpone Cream
Slit the bean half lengthwise and, while holding the bean on one end, scrape out the seeds with the back of a knife. Put the seeds in a medium bowl with the mascarpone, cream, sugar, and lemon zest. With an electric mixer, whip the cream until it forms softly mounded peaks. You can whisk it by hand with a wire whisk, but the mixer is faster and easier.

Walnut–Chocolate Chip Tube Cake

Makes 1 cake, serving about 10

There's a complexity of flavors in this cake that belies its homey appearance. Yes, it looks like an ordinary Bundt cake, maybe even made from a mix, but on first bite you'll taste brown butter, toasted nuts, and dark chocolate bits. It's so good that I wouldn't hesitate to serve it plain after dinner, with a scoop of ice cream.

See the recipe for Shelly's Pumpkin Cake (page 114) for information on tube pans.

WHAT YOU'LL NEED

9-inch, 10-cup fluted tube pan

Platter or plate large enough to hold a 9-inch cake

1 cup walnuts

16 tablespoons (2 sticks) unsalted butter

3 large eggs

1 1/2 cups granulated sugar

2 cups unbleached all-purpose flour

1 teaspoon baking powder

1/2 teaspoon kosher salt

1 cup buttermilk or 1 cup whole milk mixed with 1 teaspoon lemon juice

1 teaspoon pure vanilla extract

4 ounces dark chocolate (58 to 62 percent cacao), finely chopped, or 3/4 cup chocolate chips

FB: Here's the thing that always concerns me about baking: I know you need to be precise in measuring, but I admit that I can be a little careless. I'd really like to know how to measure.

EL: Not measuring accurately is one of the biggest problems beginning bakers have, and why recipes don't turn out. The best way to measure flour is first to put your measuring cup in the flour canister and, because the flour has been sitting a while and is kind of compacted, get in there and loosen it up. Now, with the cup, scoop up an overflowing measure. Then, with your finger just level it off. You can also use a knife or the canister lid if you're more comfortable with that. Often, though, fingers are the most convenient.

FB: What about sugar?

EL: Because sugar doesn't get compacted as it sits you don't need to "fluff it up" first, so just put your measuring cup in the bag or canister, scoop it up, and level it off. With baking soda and baking powder I just put the teaspoon in the box or can and use that edge as a leveler.

1. Preheat the oven to 350°F. Grease the pan with nonstick cooking spray or butter, making sure you coat the center tube and crevices of the pan well.

2. Spread the walnuts in one layer in a small baking pan and put in the (preheated) oven. Set a timer for 10 minutes and check the nuts to see if they're a light golden brown. If not, toast 2 minutes longer. Let cool, then chop them by hand into 1/4-inch (or so) pieces. Set aside.

3. Melt the butter in a small saucepan over medium heat. After the foam subsides and the liquid bubbles, let the butter continue to cook until it turns golden brown and you can see brown bits on the bottom of the pan and the butter is a nutty brown color, about 5 minutes. Remove from the heat. Pour the browned butter into a bowl or liquid measuring cup. (See pages 160–161 for brown butter tips.)

4. In a large bowl, whisk the eggs with the sugar until smooth. Whisk in the browned butter.

5. Over a bowl or piece of parchment, sift the flour and baking powder together in a sifter or in a fine strainer by gently tapping your hand against the edge. Add the salt (you can just leave it on top of the flour pile because it gets mixed in later).

6. In a small bowl, stir in the buttermilk with the vanilla.

7. Add half of the flour mixture to the egg/sugar mixture and whisk it until smooth. Whisk in half of the buttermilk mixture. Repeat with the remaining flour and buttermilk mixtures, whisking each in before adding the next. Stir in the chocolate.

8. Pour the batter into the prepared pan. Bake the cake until a bamboo skewer or toothpick inserted in the middle comes out clean, 55 to 60 minutes. Let the cake cool completely in the pan.

9. Turn the cake out of the pan onto a platter or plate and cut into wedges for serving. The cake will keep at room temperature wrapped in plastic for 3 to 4 days.

Shelly's Pumpkin Cake

Makes 1 cake, serving about 10

Shelly, one of the former servers at Farallon Restaurant, used to love to spend time watching us in the pastry kitchen. She is a fabulous baker and once during the holidays she brought in this pumpkin cake to share with the staff.

There are two kinds of *fluted* tube cake pans—as opposed to the straight sided, flat-bottomed angel food pans—that I use over and over again. One is the familiar and classic Bundt pan, and the other is a 9-inch fluted tube pan, sometimes called a *kugelhopf* pan (for the Austrian yeasted cake of that same name). The difference between the two pans is capacity. A Bundt holds 12 cups and a *kugelhopf* holds 10 cups. The trick with any fluted tube cake is to get it to unmold in one piece, so it's important to make sure the pan is well greased. I even grease nonstick pans for added assurance.

WHAT YOU'LL NEED
9-inch, 10-cup fluted tube pan

Table knife or narrow metal spatula
(if you have one)

4 large eggs

2 cups granulated sugar

1 cup vegetable oil

1 can (15 ounces) pumpkin puree

2 cups unbleached all-purpose flour

2 teaspoons baking soda

2 teaspoons ground cinnamon

1/2 teaspoon ground ginger

1/2 teaspoon kosher salt

1/3 cup pecan pieces

Cream Cheese Glaze
Electric stand mixer or handheld mixer
and medium bowl

8 ounces cream cheese, at room
temperature

3 cups confectioners' sugar

2 teaspoons pure vanilla extract

FB: Let's see, you say a nine-inch fluted tube pan. What is that? Oh, here it is. Well, that's another pan I've never seen before.

EL: They're sold in good cookware shops and even grocery stores. They usually offer a ten- or a twelve-cup pan but not both. Do you have a Bundt pan at home?

FB: Yes, I think so, collecting dust in the back of the cabinet.

1. Preheat the oven to 350°F. Grease the tube pan with nonstick cooking spray or butter.

2. In a large bowl, whisk the eggs by hand with the sugar until the mixture is well combined and the sugar has begun to dissolve. Whisk in the oil and then the pumpkin puree.

3. In another bowl, whisk together the flour, baking soda, cinnamon, ginger, and salt. Using the whisk, stir the flour mixture into the pumpkin mixture until everything is well combined.

4. Pour the batter into the prepared pan. Bake the cake until a bamboo skewer inserted in the middle comes out clean, 55 to 60 minutes. Let cool completely in the pan.

5. To remove the cake from the pan, invert it and gently tap one side against the counter, letting the cake gently fall out of the pan onto a platter or piece of parchment paper. Transfer the cake to a platter or plate.

6. Using a narrow metal spatula, or a table knife, spread the glaze (see below) over the top of the cake and down the sides a little, leaving a portion of the cake exposed at the bottom. Sprinkle the top of the cake with the pecan pieces. Cut into wedges for serving.

Cream Cheese Glaze
Using the stand mixer or a handheld mixer and medium bowl, on medium speed, beat the cream cheese until smooth. Add the sugar and vanilla extract and mix in thoroughly.

Pies and Tarts

In all the years I've been teaching people to bake, I've come to realize that at the heart of every non-baker lurks a fear of pastry dough. It's not cakes, cookies, puddings, or quick breads that (even experienced) cooks are afraid of. It's pie dough, or the thought of making it.

And perhaps not surprisingly, that's what people tell me they *want* to learn how to make. They want to make their own pies and tarts because there's nothing that tastes as good as one that's homemade.

To make a pie or tart, you don't even need to make a crust from scratch. Several recipes in this chapter have cookie crusts or use store-bought puff pastry. Basic Sugar Short Dough is made in a processor or mixer, but instead of being rolled out, it is simply pressed in a tart pan. Even if a recipe does call for a pie or tart shell, you can use store-bought dough. When I'm short on time I use store-bought dough and rarely bother making my own puff pastry. It's one of my favorite shortcuts, particularly now that I've found some good brands (see Purchased Pie and Tart Dough, page 117).

If you're a beginning baker, purchased dough is a great way for you to ease yourself into making pies and tarts. That way you can take baby steps by first concentrating on fitting the dough into a pan and making the filling. Once you've mastered those steps, the next is to make your own dough. I can't deny that your first attempt won't be as good as your tenth, but it's not as difficult

as one might imagine. And as convenient as store-bought dough is, once you have tackled making your own, you'll discover that homemade tastes the best. When the Fearful Baker who made apple pie for this book finished, he said, "I don't know what I was afraid of. It wasn't that hard." His guests accused him of buying a pie and putting it in the Pyrex pan (which is no small feat), until he showed them the photos we took on his phone as he was rolling out the dough.

Here are a few general tips that will make you a successful—and fearless—pie and tart baker:

Make-Ahead and Storage Tips
Tarts and pies can be made in stages. Doughs can be made ahead and refrigerated, well wrapped in plastic, for 2 days. They can be frozen for 1 month. Crusts can be baked in the morning and then filled and baked that day. Finished tarts or pies can be kept at room temperature unless there is cream in the filling, and then they should be refrigerated and brought out to take the chill off 10 to 20 minutes before serving. All tarts and pies are best eaten the day they are baked. That's when the crust is the flakiest and the filling is the freshest and most vibrant-tasting.

1. The method for mixing, rolling out, and baking a crust is virtually the same for both pies and tarts. The only real difference between the two is the pans that are used and how the dough is shaped into pans (for tart shells the dough is folded back onto the side wall to thicken and reinforce it).

2. Use refrigerated (cold) butter. Cut it up into small (1/2-inch or so) cubes—not thin, square pats—before adding to the flour.

3. If it's hot in my kitchen, sometimes I'll cut the butter into 1/2-inch pieces and pop them into the freezer for 10 minutes. You can also grate frozen butter with a cheese grater.

4. The water you add to the dough needs to be really cold. Put ice into it for a few minutes (straining the ice out before you use the water) or put a measuring cup with the water in the freezer for 10 minutes before adding it to the flour and butter.

5. Don't overmix dough when you add the butter or water. Follow the directions and watch the dough carefully. When you use a processor it can become overmixed in a matter of seconds.

6. Don't squeeze your dough like it's Play-Doh. You may find it anxiety-relieving, but you aren't helping the dough any. Unlike you, dough doesn't like being massaged, so use a light touch.

7. Don't be afraid to use a generous amount of flour to roll out your dough so it doesn't stick. Better too much than not enough (it doesn't get absorbed at that point). Brush off excess flour before and after rolling.

8. After you put the dough in the pan, put it in the fridge for at least an hour. Overnight is okay too. This does two things: it prevents shrinkage of the dough as it bakes and keeps it from toughening.

9. Save your dough scraps. During baking if a crack occurs you can patch it using the excess dough like Spackle, thinly spreading it on the warm crust and baking it a couple of minutes so it hardens and seals.

10. Defrost puff pastry in the refrigerator; it will defrost more evenly. All brands come cut in about the same size.

Purchased Pie and Tart Dough

Like any ingredient, there are good brands and bad brands of prepared dough. Avoid the pie shells in the supermarket freezer case. After trying many brands, I found them all to have an off flavor and they always cracked in many places and even shattered. My two favorite refrigerated doughs are Pillsbury and French Picnic. You just unroll the dough and form it into the pan. Puff pastry brands I like are Dufour, Pepperidge Farm, and Trader Joe's.

Basic Pie Dough

Makes enough dough for 1 (9-inch) pie with top crust or lattice

The ingredients for both this Basic Pie Dough and the Basic Tart Dough are the same (though proportions are different, as are the pans that are used and the way the doughs are shaped in the pans). I know that many very good pie bakers swear by shortening, because it makes for a flakier crust, but I prefer the taste of all butter and don't find it to be a huge sacrifice in texture.

Any kind of 9-inch pie pan can be used—metal, glass, or ceramic—as long as it's not "deep-dish," or you won't have enough filling. Though they don't conduct heat as well as metal pans and may take longer to cook, glass pie dishes are good for pies where the filling is baked in the raw crust, as in the apple pie, because you can see how much the crust is browning on the bottom.

Whenever a crust is baked without filling you have to fill it with something so it keeps its shape and doesn't shrink and fall down on the sides. With pies, you can line the raw dough in the pan with aluminum foil, poking with a fork all over so it stays in place. (For tarts, the foil-only technique doesn't work, you need to fill the pan with parchment or foil and weight it with raw rice, dry beans, or pie weights.) You can also use parchment paper and weights for pies, like I always do.

To make the dough in a food processor
Combine the flour, sugar, salt, and butter in the food processor bowl. Pressing the pulse button quickly, pulse the mixture until the butter is the size of small peas, 5 to 10 pulses. This will happen very quickly, do not overmix it. Add the 5 tablespoons of ice-cold water, then pulse just until the dough is crumbly. Stop the machine and gently squeeze about 1/3 cup of dough in your hand. If it comes together without any dry pieces, you've added enough water. If it's still floury, pulse in another tablespoon of water and test it again. Add a little more water if necessary or continue to mix until the dough forms small clumps. Do not process it to the point where it forms a ball.

WHAT YOU'LL NEED
Food processor or stand mixer

Rolling pin

9 1/2-inch pie pan

Parchment paper

Rice, dried beans, or pie weights

2 3/4 cups unbleached all-purpose flour

2 tablespoons granulated sugar

Pinch kosher salt

16 tablespoons (2 sticks) cold unsalted butter, cut into 1/2-inch cubes

About 5 tablespoons ice-cold water

FB: Oh no, here we go. I can't believe I'm actually making pie dough in a food processor that I may have used once or twice in my life. This is scary.

EL: Just breathe. Okay, keep pulsing the flour with the butter for three to five seconds until it looks like small peas. Add the ice water and pulse in several one-second increments until the mixture is crumbly. That's it. Now pick up some of the dough and squeeze it between your fingers.

FB: It kinda sticks together.

EL: That's what you're looking for. By squeezing it you're faking what's going to happen in the processor after you pulse it for a few seconds longer. Though many recipes say to let it form a ball on top of the blade, by that time, it's been overworked. That's the danger with making dough in a processor. Okay, pulse a few times more. Now look at the mixture. Notice how it's coming together in small clumps?

FB: Yeah, whew. Is it done?

EL: Yes. Now, dump the mixture out on the counter and, with your hands, form it into two disks, one a little bigger than the other. The smaller one we will use for the top of the pie.

FB: Like so?

EL: No, wait. Okay, here's the biggest mistake people make when they're working with pie dough for the first or even the second or third time. They get nervous that it's not right so they start massaging it. You want to form it into a disk but you don't want to work the bejeebies out of it.

Form the dough into 2 flat (1-inch-thick) disks—without treating it like Play-Doh and mashing it. One disk should use two-thirds of the dough, the other disk one-third. Wrap the disk in plastic and refrigerate for 1 hour or up to 2 days. The dough can also be frozen for 2 months. Make sure you let the dough warm up for about 15 minutes after taking it out of the fridge so that you can roll it easily. Defrost from the freezer overnight in the fridge.

To make the dough using a stand mixer

Put the flour, sugar, and salt in the bowl of the stand mixer. On low speed, using the paddle attachment, mix in the butter until it is the size of small peas. Add the 5 tablespoons of ice-cold water, then mix it in just until the dough is crumbly. Stop the machine and gently squeeze about 1/3 cup of dough in your hand. If it comes together without any dry pieces, you've added enough water. If it's still floury, stir in another tablespoon of water and test it again. Add a little more water if necessary or continue to mix until the dough forms small clumps. Do not mix it to the point where it forms a ball.

Form the dough into 2 flat (1-inch-thick) disks—without treating it like Play-Doh and mashing it. One disk should use two-thirds of the dough, the other disk one-third. Wrap the disks in plastic and refrigerate for 1 hour or up to 2 days. The dough can also be frozen for 2 months. Make sure you let the dough warm up for about 15 minutes after taking it out of the fridge so that you can roll it easily. Defrost overnight in the fridge.

To roll out the dough

Put the larger dough disk on a generously floured work surface—don't worry, the dough won't absorb any more flour at this point and it's more important that it doesn't stick. Sprinkle more flour on the top of the dough. Roll it into an evenly thick 14-inch circle, or one that's 2 inches wider than your pie pan. A quick and easy way to measure the size is to hold the pie pan over the dough and make sure the dough is about 2 inches wider than the top of pan. The important thing to keep in mind is that you're aiming for an evenly thick, as well as evenly round, circle. As you roll, try not to press the pin down at the outer edge, otherwise the center will be thick and the edge thin.

There are several ways to roll the dough, but a couple of them work for me. You can work from the center out and always roll away from your body, starting at the 12 noon position and then

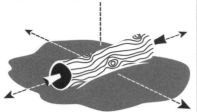

ROLL FROM THE CENTER OUT

CUT LATTICE STRIPS

PINCH TO CRIMP EDGES

rotating the dough a quarter turn each time. Or simply roll from the center, going to 12:00, then 3:00, 6:00, and 9:00. Whichever way you find you're comfortable with, pick up the dough occasionally to make sure it's not sticking to your work surface.

To line the pie pan with the dough
Make sure the dough isn't sticking to the work surface by running a large metal spatula underneath the dough. Transfer the dough to the pie pan by gently lifting up one end of the circle and loosely rolling it around the rolling pin and then unrolling it so it's centered over the pan. Press it into and along the inside bottom corner of the pie pan. Trim the dough around the edge of the pan, leaving a 1/4- to 1/2-inch edge hanging over the side. For a pie without a top crust, fold the edge under and crimp or make a decorative pattern (see illustration). Cover with plastic wrap and refrigerate the dough for at least 30 minutes or overnight.

For a double-crust pie
Roll the smaller disk into a 12-inch circle and place it on a baking sheet. Cover with plastic wrap and refrigerate the dough for 30 minutes or overnight before using it as a top crust (see Apple Pie, page 121).

For a lattice-top pie
Roll the smaller disk 1/4-inch thick and cut as directed in the recipe. Cover with plastic wrap and refrigerate the dough for 30 minutes or overnight.

To bake the pie crust
Preheat the oven to 375°F. Press foil onto the side and bottom of the dough-lined pan and loosely fold the excess foil over the pie edge. Using a fork, prick holes through the foil into dough all over the side and bottom. You can also use parchment paper and weights (see page 143 for more information). Bake until the edge of the dough is golden brown, 20 to 30 minutes. Remove the foil. Return the pan to the oven and bake until the crust is golden brown, about 10 minutes longer. Let cool to room temperature.

Apple Pie

Makes 1 pie, serving 8

Pies are perfect examples of baked things that get easier to make each time you do it. That said, your first time out will still be good. Since the apples take a long time to cook, it isn't necessary to bake the bottom crust before you put them in the dough-lined pan. By the time the apples are done the bottom crust will have browned. Using a Pyrex pie plate allows you to check the color of the crust before you remove it from the oven.

WHAT YOU'LL NEED

9-inch pie plate, preferably Pyrex (see headnote)

Rolling pin

Baking or cookie sheet

2 1/2 pounds Granny Smith apples (about 6)

Juice of 1/2 lemon

3/4 cup granulated sugar

3 tablespoons unbleached all-purpose flour

1/2 teaspoon ground cinnamon

1/8 teaspoon kosher salt

Basic Pie Dough (page 118) for a double-crust pie

1 tablespoon unsalted butter

Cinnamon sugar: 1 tablespoon granulated sugar stirred with 2 pinches ground cinnamon in a small bowl

1. Preheat the oven to 400°F.

2. Peel the apples. Core them by cutting down from the top along the sides of the core in 4 pieces, then slice the pieces thinly (about 1/8 inch). With your (clean) hands, toss the apples in a medium bowl with the lemon juice, sugar, flour, ground cinnamon, and salt. Set aside.

3. Roll out the larger dough disk and line the pie pan for the bottom crust. For the top crust, roll out the smaller dough disk into a 12-inch circle (see page 120).

4. Pile the apples in the dough-lined pan. Cut the butter into 8 pieces and scatter over the apples.

5. Place the top crust on top of the apples, then fold the edge of the bottom crust over the edge of the top crust. Press the edge together with your fingers. To make the pie picture-pretty, press around the pie edge with the tines of a fork or give it a ruffled edge by pinching the dough between your thumb and forefinger in 1-inch increments around the pie. Sprinkle the cinnamon sugar over the top of the pie. Cut 4 slits, each about 1 inch long, in a spoke pattern in the middle of the pie.

6. Place the pie in the top third of the oven. Put the baking sheet on the lower rack or on the oven floor to catch any dripping juices. Bake for 30 minutes. Reduce the oven temperature to 350°F and bake until the pie is nicely browned and the apple slices are soft when you insert a paring knife into one of the slits, about 45 minutes longer.

7. Let the pie cool for about 45 minutes so that the juices thicken before cutting and serving.

TOP LAYER
BOTTOM LAYER

Chocolate Pecan Pie

Makes 1 pie, serving 8 to 10

I love good pecan pie, but most versions are pretty sweet. I've found that adding chocolate to the nut filling cuts some of the sweetness and gives the pie another dimension of flavor.

Two steps need to be done ahead of time. It's important to toast the nuts so they retain their texture, and to bake the crust first before baking it with the filling. Otherwise it'll become soggy and never brown.

WHAT YOU'LL NEED
Saucepan and metal bowl, or double boiler if you have one

Rubber spatula

1 2/3 cups pecan pieces

2 1/2 ounces unsweetened chocolate

6 tablespoons (3/4 stick) unsalted butter

3 large eggs

2/3 cup granulated sugar

1/4 teaspoon kosher salt

3 tablespoons whole milk

1 disk Basic Pie Dough, made, formed, and baked as directed on pages 118–120

1. Preheat the oven to 350°F.

2. Spread the pecan pieces in one layer in a small baking pan and put in the (preheated) oven. Set a timer for 10 minutes and check the nuts to see if they're a light golden brown. If not, toast 2 minutes longer. Set aside to cool.

3. Melt the chocolate and butter by putting them in a heat-proof bowl set over a saucepan of simmering water, making sure the bowl does not touch the water. (You can use a double boiler if you have one.) Stir and scrape the side of the bowl occasionally with the rubber spatula until the chocolate is smooth and evenly melted. Remove from the heat. Let cool to room temperature.

4. In a medium bowl, whisk the eggs with the sugar and salt until combined. Whisk in the chocolate and then the milk until everything is well blended.

5. Scatter the pecan pieces over the baked pie crust and pour in the chocolate mixture.

6. Bake for 30 minutes, or until the pie is firm except for a 2-inch area in the center that should still be a little jiggly. It will firm up as it cools. Serve at room temperature—if you cut it when it's still warm it will fall apart.

Pumpkin Pie with Walnut–Brown Sugar Streusel

Makes 1 pie, serving 8

Over the years I have made thousands of pumpkin pies. When it came time for my own Thanksgiving dinner I would make it for others but I would steer towards the other desserts on the buffet to put on my plate. I had made so many it had lost its appeal. This recipe is bringing me around to pumpkin pie again. The streusel top gives it another dimension of texture and flavor.

I'm all for shortcuts, and canned pumpkin puree (not pumpkin pie filling, which has spices added) is one of the best.

WHAT YOU'LL NEED
Medium and small bowls

Whisk

2 large eggs

1/3 cup firmly packed light brown sugar

1/4 cup dark corn syrup

1 cup heavy cream

1 cup canned pumpkin puree

1 teaspoon ground cinnamon

1/2 teaspoon ground ginger

1/2 teaspoon kosher salt

1 teaspoon pure vanilla extract

1 disk Basic Pie Dough, made, formed, and baked as directed on pages 118–120

Walnut–Brown Sugar Streusel
2/3 cup walnuts

2 tablespoons firmly packed dark brown sugar

2 tablespoons unsalted butter, melted

1. Preheat the oven to 350°F.

2. In a medium bowl, whisk the eggs with the brown sugar until combined. Whisk in the corn syrup and then the cream, pumpkin puree, cinnamon, ginger, salt, and vanilla until everything is well blended. Pour the filling into the baked pie crust.

3. Bake the pie until all but a 2-inch area in the center of the filling is set, about 45 minutes.

While it's baking, make the streusel:
4. Chop the walnuts coarsely by hand. Transfer to a small bowl and stir in the brown sugar. Stir in the melted butter until well combined.

5. When the pie is in the last 5 minutes of baking, sprinkle the streusel in the center of the pie, leaving a 1-inch border around the edge. Return to the oven for 5 minutes to cook the streusel.

6. Let the pie cool to room temperature before serving. It will keep, refrigerated, for 2 to 3 days.

Lemon Meringue Pie

Makes 1 pie, serving 8

It's not easy to find a good old-fashioned lemon meringue pie these days, even though many people have told me it's their favorite, right up there with apple and pumpkin. Unfortunately, many commercial versions have brightly colored gloppy fillings, made with chemical-tasting store-bought lemon juice and rubbery meringue. It's a wonder people still love them, but I think it's because they have memories of the pie their mothers or grandmothers made with fresh lemon juice, a buttery crust, and light-as-air meringue.

WHAT YOU'LL NEED

Heat-proof rubber spatula

Electric stand mixer or handheld mixer and medium bowl

1 cup granulated sugar

1/3 cup cornstarch

1/4 teaspoon kosher salt

1 1/2 cups water

1/2 cup freshly squeezed lemon juice (from about 3 lemons)

3 large egg yolks (reserve 2 egg whites for the meringue)

2 tablespoons unsalted butter

1 disk Basic Pie Dough, made, formed, and baked as directed on pages 118–120

Meringue Topping

2 large egg whites (reserved)

1/4 teaspoon cream of tartar

1/4 cup granulated sugar

FB: Oh my, this is exciting. My mom is from the South and makes a great lemon meringue pie. I can't wait to show her my pie.

EL: (Laughing) Uh-oh, the pressure is on. We better start juicing those lemons. To cook the filling, use a medium saucepan because even though all the liquid will fit in here, you'll have more surface area in the larger pot, so the filling cooks faster and is easier to stir.

FB: Do I heat up the saucepan on the stove before I add the filling mixture?

EL: That's a really good question. The answer is no, because it's not like sautéing, where recipes say "heat the oil" first. In baking you put ingredients in cold. Here, if you put the egg mixture into a hot pot, you end up with scrambled eggs. Eggs need to cook gradually and gently, all the while being stirred, so you end up with a, luscious custard.

FB: That all makes sense.

EL: Now I know the recipe says "stirring constantly," but you don't have to worry for the first minute or so, because really the pan hasn't even heated up yet. You need to stir all the time so the mixture won't stick to the bottom of the pan, where it will curdle. You could make this in a double boiler if you want to be safe, but it takes a lot longer.

A few minutes later and the filling has thickened

EL: Now stir in the butter, and we'll transfer the filling to a bowl to cool down a little bit before putting it into the crust.

FB: (Licking some off the spoon). Oooh yum. Good as Mom's. Maybe even better!

1. In a medium bowl, whisk the sugar with the cornstarch and salt. Whisk in the water and lemon juice, then whisk in the egg yolks until combined.

2. Transfer the lemon mixture to a heavy-bottomed medium saucepan and cook over medium-low heat, stirring constantly with the rubber spatula, making sure you scrape the bottom of the pan and get into the corners. It will look like nothing is happening, but then after about 5 minutes the mixture will start to thicken. After a couple more minutes, as soon as it starts to boil, remove the pan from the heat. Stir in the butter.

3. Strain the lemon filling through a mesh sieve into a bowl and set aside, stirring occasionally until the filling has cooled to room temperature. (Once cool, the filling can be refrigerated for up to 4 hours.)

Meringue Topping

4. In the stand mixer with the wire whisk attachment, or using a handheld mixer and a medium bowl, whisk the egg whites and cream of tartar on medium speed until frothy. With the machine running, add the sugar in a slow, steady stream. Increase the speed to medium-high (high with a handheld mixer) and whip until the whites hold stiff glossy peaks (stop the mixer and lift the whisk to check or pull some out on a spatula). It should look like shiny marshmallow fluff.

5. Preheat the oven to 450°F.

6. Spread the cooled filling in the baked pie shell. Pile the meringue on top of the filling, and using the rubber spatula, spread it out so it covers the filling completely. Swirl and lift with the end of the spatula to create peaks. Bake the pie until the top is golden brown, about 5 minutes.

7. Let the pie cool completely before serving, about 15 minutes. You can leave it at room temperature for up to 6 hours.

Maple-Cinnamon Walnut Pie

Makes 1 pie, serving 8

My family, like most people's, has come to expect certain dishes at Thanksgiving. But sometimes, when I just want to tweak my relatives a little bit, I slip this walnut pie in with the pecan pies to see if anyone will notice. I'm never that surprised to see the walnut pie disappear first. The difference between the two pies, beyond the flavor of the nuts, is subtle, but I love how the cinnamon complements maple. Served with coffee ice cream, it's even better.

WHAT YOU'LL NEED
Medium bowl

Whisk

1 1/4 cups walnuts

3 large eggs

1/2 cup granulated sugar

1 teaspoon ground cinnamon

1/2 teaspoon kosher salt

1/2 cup pure maple syrup

1/2 cup dark corn syrup

4 tablespoons (1/2 stick) unsalted butter, melted

1 disk Basic Pie Dough, made, formed, and baked as directed on pages 118–120

1. Preheat the oven to 350°F.

2. Spread the walnuts in one layer in a small baking pan and put in the (preheated) oven. Set a timer for 10 minutes and check the nuts to see if they're a light golden brown. If not, toast 2 minutes longer. Let cool, then chop into 1/4-inch pieces and set aside.

3. In a medium bowl, whisk the eggs with the sugar, cinnamon, and salt until combined. Whisk in the maple syrup and corn syrup and then the melted butter until everything is well blended.

4. Scatter the chopped walnuts over the bottom of the baked pie crust. Pour the filling over the nuts.

5. Bake until the filling is set, about 50 minutes. Serve the pie warm or at room temperature.

Peach-Blueberry Streusel Pie

Makes 1 pie, serving 8

When I've got an abundance of summer fruit, it's time to make a pie, and this is a recipe I turn to often—I love the crunch of the streusel topping.

Peaches give off a lot of juice, so to keep your oven clean, put a pan or piece of foil on a rack underneath the pie to catch drips.

WHAT YOU'LL NEED
2 medium bowls

Crumble Topping
1 1/3 cups unbleached all-purpose flour

1/3 cup firmly packed brown sugar

3 tablespoons granulated sugar

1/3 cup sliced almonds

1/4 teaspoon salt

8 tablespoons (1 stick) unsalted butter, melted and cooled

Pie
6 medium peaches

1 1/4 cups blueberries

1/3 cup granulated sugar

1/4 cup cornstarch

1/4 teaspoon kosher salt

1 1/2 teaspoons lemon juice

1 disk Basic Pie Dough, made, formed, and baked as directed on pages 118–120

Crumble Topping

1. In a medium bowl, stir the flour, brown sugar, granulated sugar, almonds, and salt until evenly combined. Drizzle with the cooled melted butter and, with a spoon, carefully toss, being careful not to mix it too well—you want those clumpy streusel bits. Set aside.

2. Preheat the oven to 350°F.

Pie

3. Peel the peaches, halve, discard the pits, and slice into 1/4-inch-thick wedges. You should have about 4 cups. In a medium bowl, toss together the peaches, blueberries, sugar, cornstarch, salt, and lemon juice until everything is combined. Pile the peaches in the baked pie crust. Distribute the topping evenly over the fruit.

4. Bake until the juices are bubbling and thick, about 1 hour. Cool to warm or room temperature before serving.

Strawberry Rhubarb Pie

Makes 1 pie, serving 8

Without fail, I know that whenever I bring out a lattice-top pie or tart, it will elicit oohs and aahs from my guests and family. There's just something about that crisp and sugar-shiny crust, with its fruit filling peeking through, that puts other pies to shame in the appearance category. The best part is that it's relatively simple to make; I like to call it a big-bang-for-your-buck dessert.

Though many baking books will give you elaborate instructions on how to weave the lattice for pie crusts, you'll notice that I simply lay the dough strips down in rows one on top of the other. No weaving necessary, and it looks just as photogenic. Make sure, however, that you press the ends of the strips onto the edge of the bottom crust to anchor them so they don't pop up when they bake.

WHAT YOU'LL NEED
Rolling pin

Decorative wheel cutter (if you have one)

Baking or cookie sheet

Pastry brush

Basic Pie Dough; large disk made, formed, and baked as directed on pages 118–120; second disk refrigerated for the lattice

2 1/2 pints (about 2 1/4 pounds) strawberries

2 large stalks (about 12 ounces) rhubarb

2/3 cup plus 2 teaspoons granulated sugar

5 tablespoons cornstarch

Grated zest of 1 lemon

1 tablespoon heavy cream

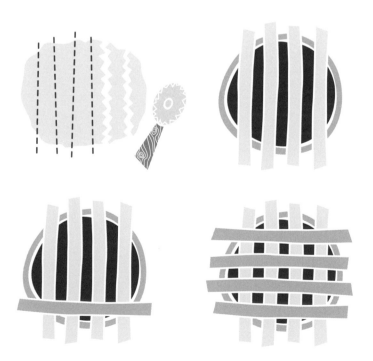

Our intrepid baker has already made the pie dough—two disks, one smaller and one larger— and lined the pie pan with the larger one, ready to bake it off.

EL: Now we're going to roll out the dough for the lattice.

FB: How do we make the lattice?

EL: You're going to roll out the smaller dough disk, cut it into strips, and refrigerate it while the bottom crust is baking.

FB: How big do I need to roll the dough?

EL: Unlike rolling the dough for the crust, all you need to do is roll it in a rough square or circle. It doesn't need to be round, or as thick either. An eighth of an inch will be fine.

A few minutes later ...

FB: So that's it. Now it says to cut it in strips.

EL: You can use a knife or this decorative wheel cutter. Which, once you try it, you'll want to go out and buy. They're also used for putting that zig-zag edge on ravioli and are sometimes called ravioli cutters.

FB: This is so cool. I feel like a professional. Love this little gadget.

1. Preheat the oven to 350°F.

2. Remove the smaller dough disk from the refrigerator and let sit at room temperature for 10 minutes or so to make it easier to roll out.

3. For the lattice top, roll the smaller disk so that it is 1/8 inch thick. It doesn't matter what shape you roll it, just so it's evenly thick. Using a sharp knife or decorative wheel cutter, cut it into 10 (3/4- to 1-inch-wide) strips. With a large metal spatula, transfer the lattice strips onto the baking sheet and refrigerate for at least 30 minutes. You can refrigerate them overnight, but cover with plastic wrap.

4. Remove and discard the stems from the strawberries. Cut the berries into 3/4-inch pieces. You should have about 4 cups. Transfer to a medium bowl.

5. Cut the rhubarb into 3/4-inch pieces to measure about 2 1/4 cups. Add to the bowl with the strawberries. Add the 2/3 cup sugar, the cornstarch, and lemon zest and stir until everything is evenly combined. Spread the fruit mixture evenly over the bottom of the baked pie crust.

6. Lay 5 of the lattice strips across the fruit filling and the other 5 strips across in the other direction to form a lattice pattern. Cut or press off extra overhanging dough and press the strips into the side of the dough shell to anchor them. Brush the strips with the cream and sprinkle with the remaining 2 teaspoons sugar.

7. Bake the pie until the filling is thick and bubbly, about 1 hour. Let cool and serve warm or at room temperature.

Basic Tart Dough

Makes 1 (9-inch) tart shell

As I mentioned in the pie section, I use basically the same dough for both my tarts and pies. The ingredients are identical, but the proportions a little different, as you need more dough for a pie. (The Basic Sugar Short Dough, page 142, is different entirely.) As a rule, I prefer the taste of butter and don't use shortening.

All the tarts are made in a 9-inch metal tart pan with a removable bottom. When it comes to unmolding tarts for presentation, I find them easier to work with, but a one-piece pan is fine too. It's important to note, though, that if you use a pan with a removable bottom, you always need to hold the tart by the side of the pan when moving it around. I also recommend you put it on a baking sheet to make it easier to transfer in and out of the oven. When forming the dough in a tart pan, the overhang is trimmed and then folded back to reinforce the side of the tart.

To bake a tart crust without a filling (cookbook recipes often refer to the technique as "blind baking"), the raw dough needs to be weighted down to prevent it from bubbling up and/or shrinking from the side of the pan. Line the dough with parchment and fill it with raw rice, dried beans, or pie weights (they can be reused many times). The crust is partially baked, the parchment is removed, weights and all, and then the crust finishes baking until it's golden brown.

WHAT YOU'LL NEED

Food processor or electric stand mixer

Rolling pin

9-inch tart pan, preferably with a removable bottom

Baking or cookie sheet

Parchment paper

Rice, dried beans, or pie weights

1 3/4 cups unbleached all-purpose flour

1 tablespoon granulated sugar

Pinch kosher salt

10 tablespoons (1 1/4 sticks) cold unsalted butter, cut into 1/2-inch pieces

About 4 tablespoons ice-cold water

PUT TART ON TOP OF CAN. LET RING DROP.

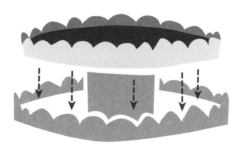

To make the tart dough in a food processor

Combine the flour, sugar, salt, and butter in the food processor bowl. Pressing the pulse button quickly, pulse the mixture until the butter is the size of small peas, 5 to 10 pulses. This will happen very quickly, so do not overmix it. Add the 4 tablespoons of ice-cold water, then pulse just until the dough is crumbly. Stop the machine and gently squeeze about 1/3 cup of dough in your hand. If it comes together without any dry pieces, you've added enough water. If it's still floury, pulse in another tablespoon of water and test it again. Add a little more water if necessary or continue to mix until the dough forms small clumps. Do not process it to the point where it forms a ball.

Form the dough into a flat (1-inch-thick) disk—without treating it like Play-Doh and mashing it. Wrap the disk in plastic and refrigerate for 1 hour or up to 2 days. The dough can also be frozen for 2 months. Make sure you let the dough warm up after taking it out of the fridge so that you can roll it easily, about 15 minutes. Defrost from the freezer overnight in the fridge.

To make the tart dough using a stand mixer

Put the flour, sugar, and salt in the bowl of the stand mixer. On low speed, using the paddle attachment, mix in the butter until it is the size of small peas. Add the 4 tablespoons of ice-cold water, then stir it in just until the dough is crumbly. Stop the machine and gently squeeze about 1/3 cup of dough in your hand. If it comes together without any dry pieces, you've added enough water. If it's still floury, stir in another tablespoon of water and test it again. Add a little more water if necessary or continue to mix until the dough forms small clumps. Do not mix it to the point where it forms a ball.

Form the dough into a flat (1-inch-thick) disk—without treating it like Play-Doh and mashing it. Wrap the disk in plastic and refrigerate for 1 hour or up to 2 days. The dough can also be frozen for 2 months. Make sure you let the dough warm up after taking it out of the fridge so that you can roll it easily, about 15 minutes. Defrost from the freezer overnight in the fridge.

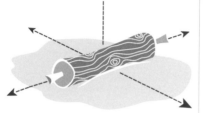

ROLL FROM THE CENTER OUT

To roll out the tart dough

Put the dough disk on a generously floured work surface. Don't worry, the dough won't absorb any more flour at this point and it's more important that it doesn't stick. Sprinkle more flour on top of the dough and working from the center out to the edge, roll the dough into a 12- to 13-inch circle. A quick and easy way to measure the size is to hold the tart pan over the dough and make sure the dough is about 2 inches wider than the pan. The important thing to keep in mind is that you're aiming for an evenly thick, as well as evenly round, circle. As you roll, try not to press the pin down at the outer edge, otherwise the center will be thick and the edges thin.

There are several ways to roll the dough, and a couple of them work for me. You can work from the center out and always roll away from your body, starting at the 12 noon position and then rotating the dough a quarter turn each time or simply roll from the center to 12:00, then 3:00, 6:00, and 9:00. Whichever way you find you're comfortable with, pick up the dough occasionally to make sure it's not sticking to your work surface.

To line the tart pan with the dough

Make sure the dough isn't sticking to the surface by running a large metal spatula underneath the dough. Transfer the dough to the tart pan by gently lifting it up and rolling it loosely around the rolling pin and then unrolling it so it's centered over the pan. Press it into and along the inside bottom corner of the pie pan. Trim the dough around the edge of the pan, leaving a 1/2- to 3/4-inch edge hanging over the side. Fold the overhang back onto the inside edge of the pan so that the side of the tart will be double thick. Lifting the pan by the side, put it on a baking sheet. Cover with plastic wrap and refrigerate for at least 30 minutes or overnight.

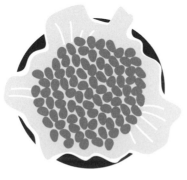

To bake the tart crust

Preheat the oven to 375°F. Press parchment paper into the dough-lined pan and fill completely with rice, dried beans, or pie weights. Make sure the parchment is against the crust and there isn't a gap between the parchment and the dough, especially in the corners. Cut off any excess parchment sticking up so it doesn't hit the top of the oven or another rack. Bake until the edges are golden brown, 20 to 30 minutes. Remove the parchment paper and rice. Return the pan to the oven and bake until the crust is golden brown all over, about 10 minutes more. Let cool to room temperature.

Banana Cream Tart

Makes 1 tart, serving 8

The best part of a banana pie for me has always been the textural contrast between the soft fruit and cream and the crust. That's why I prefer my bananas in a tart rather than a pie. There's a better ratio of crust to filling.

Make sure the bananas are completely covered by the custard so they don't turn brown.

WHAT YOU'LL NEED
Heat-proof rubber spatula

3 large egg yolks

1/3 cup granulated sugar

Large pinch kosher salt

2 tablespoons cornstarch

1/2 vanilla bean

1 1/2 cups whole milk

1 1/2 medium or 1 large banana

Basic Tart Dough, made, formed, and baked as directed on pages 130–132

Whipped Cream Topping
1/2 cup heavy cream

1/4 cup sour cream

1 tablespoon granulated sugar

1. In a medium bowl, whisk the egg yolks with the sugar and salt until smooth. Whisk in the cornstarch. Set aside.

2. Slit the bean half lengthwise and, while holding the bean on one end, scrape out the seeds with the back of a knife. Put the seeds, along with the scraped bean, in a medium saucepan with the milk.

3. Warm the milk over medium heat until it's steaming hot but not boiling. Gradually whisk the hot milk into the yolk mixture. Pour the liquid back into the saucepan. Over medium-low heat, stirring constantly with the rubber spatula and scraping the bottom of the pan so it doesn't stick, cook until the custard has a mayo-like consistency, about 5 minutes. You'll know the custard is done when it has thickened, it bubbles once or twice, and as you stir you can see the bottom of the pan.

4. Strain the custard through a medium-fine sieve into a bowl, discarding the vanilla bean. Press plastic wrap directly onto the surface of the custard so it doesn't form a skin. Refrigerate until cold, at least 1 hour, but overnight is fine.

5. Cut the banana lengthwise into quarters. Cut crosswise into 1/4-inch pieces. Fold the banana pieces into the custard. With the spatula, spread the custard into the baked tart crust.

Whipped Cream Topping
6. Using a whisk or handheld mixer, whip the cream and sour cream with the sugar until it forms softly mounded peaks.

7. Spread the topping over the top of the banana custard, leaving the crust exposed. Refrigerate until ready to serve. (If you make the tart a day ahead, add the topping on the day you plan to serve it.)

Coconut Rum Tart

Makes 1 tart, serving 8 to 10

I have a thing for macaroons. I love that they are chewy in the middle and crunchy on the outside. If you have a fondness for macaroons as I do, you'll love this tart. It's easy to prepare and tastes like one big coconut macaroon cookie in a crust.

WHAT YOU'LL NEED

Baking or cookie sheet

1 3/4 cups loosely packed sweetened shredded coconut

3 large egg yolks

1/2 cup granulated sugar

2 tablespoons dark rum

4 tablespoons (1/2 stick) unsalted butter, melted

1 cup heavy cream

Basic Tart Dough, made, formed, and baked as directed on pages 130–132

1. Preheat the oven to 350°F.

2. Spread the coconut in a single layer on the baking sheet. Bake for about 10 minutes, or until golden brown, stirring once or twice so that it browns evenly. Set aside.

3. In a medium bowl, whisk the egg yolks with the sugar until combined. Whisk in the rum, melted butter, and then the cream until everything is well blended.

4. Evenly spread the coconut in the baked crust. Pour in the egg-rum mixture.

5. Bake until the tart is set, about 20 minutes. Let cool to room temperature before serving.

Dried Cherry–Apricot Buttermilk Tart

Makes 1 tart, serving 8 to 10

Often we associate tarts only with fresh fruit, but this one is proof that dried fruits make good fillings too. With just a few easily obtained supermarket ingredients, you can make this tart year round, no matter the weather or where you live.

Make sure to cut the apricots (I use scissors) the same size as the cherries. The tart will be prettier and easier to eat. After you've taken the time to strew the fruit evenly over the bottom of the tart shell, slowly pour in the filling a little at a time. If you dump it all at once your nicely arranged fruit will all congregate in the middle.

WHAT YOU'LL NEED

Medium saucepan

Medium bowl

Whisk

1/2 cup dried apricot pieces

1/2 cup dried cherries

1/4 cup water

1 tablespoon brandy (optional)

Basic Tart Dough, made, formed, and baked as directed on pages 130–132

2 large eggs

1/3 cup granulated sugar

1 cup buttermilk or 1 cup whole milk mixed with 1 teaspoon lemon juice

Grated zest of 1 lemon

1. Preheat the oven to 350°F.

2. Cut the apricots into pieces the same size as the cherries. Put them in a medium saucepan with the cherries, water, and brandy (if using). Cook over medium heat until the fruit has plumped and the liquid has evaporated. Scatter the fruit evenly over the bottom of the baked tart crust.

3. In a medium bowl, whisk the eggs with the sugar until combined. Whisk in the buttermilk and lemon zest and pour over the fruit in the crust. Pour the filling as if you were watering a plant—a little at a time, letting it settle around the fruit and then adding more.

4. Bake for 15 minutes, or until the tart is firm except for a 2-inch area in the center that should still be a little jiggly. It will firm up as it cools. Serve at room temperature.

Fig-Walnut Marsala Tart

Makes 1 tart, serving 8 to 10

Figs and marsala—Italy's most famous fortified wine—make a perfect and classic combination, but you can substitute dark rum if you don't have or don't care for marsala. I usually serve this tart after an Italian dinner in the fall when figs are plentiful at the farmers' market, but you can use dried figs too.

WHAT YOU'LL NEED
Food processor

Rubber spatula

1 cup walnuts

1/2 cup granulated sugar

6 tablespoons (3/4 stick) unsalted butter, softened

2 large eggs

1 1/2 tablespoons marsala

Basic Tart Dough, made, formed, and baked as directed on pages 130–132

8 to 10 fresh figs

1. Preheat the oven to 350°F.

2. Spread the walnuts in one layer in a small baking pan and put in the (preheated) oven. Set a timer for 10 minutes and check to see if the nuts are a light golden brown. If not, toast 2 minutes longer. Set aside to cool.

3. In the food processor, process the walnuts with the sugar until they're finely ground and look like coarse sand. Add the butter and mix until smooth. Scrape down the side of the bowl with the rubber spatula. Mix in the eggs and then the marsala until combined.

4. Spread the filling into the baked tart crust. Cut the stems off the figs and halve them lengthwise. Arrange the figs flat side up, in circles on top of the filling. Press them gently into the filling so they are partially covered.

5. Bake until the filling is set, about 25 minutes. Let cool to room temperature before serving.

Lemon Blueberry Tart

Makes 1 tart, serving 8

While I'm known to like to serve whipped cream with almost everything, this tart doesn't need it. It's already velvety and rich, despite the fact that it has only 3 tablespoons of heavy cream. Lemon and blueberries are a favorite combination, the lemon enhancing the flavor of the berries.

WHAT YOU'LL NEED
Medium bowl

Whisk

1 1/4 cups blueberries

Basic Tart Dough, made, formed, and baked as directed on pages 130–132

2 large eggs

2/3 cup granulated sugar

1/3 cup whole milk

3 tablespoons heavy cream

2 teaspoons lemon juice

3 tablespoons unsalted butter, melted

Grated zest of 2 lemons

2 tablespoons unbleached all-purpose flour

1. Preheat the oven to 350°F.

2. Scatter the blueberries in the baked tart shell.

3. In a medium bowl, whisk the eggs and sugar together until well blended. Whisk in the milk, cream, and lemon juice. Whisk in the melted butter, lemon zest, and flour until everything is evenly combined. Pour the filling over the blueberries.

4. Bake until the filling is set, about 30 minutes. Serve the tart warm or at room temperature. It can be kept at room temperature for a few hours or refrigerated overnight covered with plastic wrap.

Nutty-Nut Chocolate Chip Tart

Makes 1 tart, serving 8

Chocolate chips and lots of nuts barely held together with a filling make this taste more like a candy bar in a crust than a tart. Serve it warm with a scoop of vanilla ice cream. If you want to reheat it, don't put it in the microwave or the crust will get soggy. Pop it into the oven for a few minutes instead.

WHAT YOU'LL NEED
Medium bowl

Whisk

1 cup sliced almonds

1/2 cup pecans

Basic Tart Dough, made, formed, and baked as directed on pages 130–132

1 cup bittersweet chocolate chips

1/2 cup milk chocolate chips

2 large eggs

1/3 cup firmly packed brown sugar

1/2 cup dark corn syrup

1/4 teaspoon kosher salt

3 tablespoons unsalted butter, melted

1. Preheat the oven to 350°F.

2. Spread the almonds and pecans separately in single layers in small baking pans and put in the (preheated) oven. Set a timer for 10 minutes and check the nuts to see if they're a light golden brown. If not, toast 2 minutes longer. Set aside to cool.

3. Coarsely chop the nuts into 1/4-inch pieces and scatter them over the bottom of the baked tart crust. Sprinkle the bittersweet and milk chocolate chips evenly over the nuts.

4. In a medium bowl, whisk the eggs with the brown sugar until combined, checking to make sure there aren't any clumps of sugar. Whisk in the corn syrup, salt, and melted butter until everything is well blended.

5. Pour the filling over the nuts and chocolate chips as if you were watering a plant—a little at a time, letting it settle around the nuts and then adding some more.

6. Bake until the filling is set, about 25 minutes. Let the tart cool to room temperature before serving.

Peach Custard Tart

Makes 1 tart, serving 8

Nectarines, peaches, and apricots can be used interchangeably in most any recipe, but peaches really should be peeled first. The easiest way to peel a lot of peaches is to dip them in hot water and then put them in a large bowl of ice water. The skins will slip off. But it's not worth the trouble for just a few. Instead I just use a paring knife. There are also serrated peelers, specifically designed for the task of peeling soft fruit.

The custard filling should not be completely set in the center when you take it from the oven. It'll firm up as the tart cools.

WHAT YOU'LL NEED
Medium bowl

Whisk

4 ripe peaches or nectarines

Basic Tart Dough, made, formed, and baked as directed on pages 130–132

2 large egg yolks

3/4 cup granulated sugar

3/4 cup sour cream

1/2 teaspoon pure vanilla extract

2 tablespoons unbleached all-purpose flour

Pinch kosher salt

1. Preheat the oven to 350°F.

2. Peel and pit the peaches and cut into 1-inch pieces. Arrange in a single layer in the bottom of the baked tart crust.

3. In a medium bowl, whisk the egg yolks and sugar together until well blended. Whisk in the sour cream and vanilla. Add the flour and salt and whisk until everything is evenly combined. Pour the filling over the peaches.

4. Bake until all but the very center of the tart is set, about 25 minutes. Let cool to room temperature before cutting into wedges.

Pineapple–Crème Fraîche Tart

Makes 1 tart, serving 8

For this recipe you'll need freshly cut pineapple; I know you can buy pineapple already cut in the produce department of most supermarkets these days, but it's really not that difficult to cut your own and it's certainly a lot cheaper. There is a detailed description of how to do it in the dialog on page 100 (Pineapple-Raspberry Upside Down Cake) and I suggest you give it a try. Once you have the baked crust and cut up the pineapple, this tart is quick to get into the oven.

WHAT YOU'LL NEED
Medium bowl

Whisk

1 1/2 cups fresh pineapple chunks cut into 1/2-inch pieces

Basic Tart Dough, made, formed, and baked as directed on pages 130–132

2 large egg yolks

1/2 cup granulated sugar

1 cup crème fraîche

2 tablespoons unbleached all-purpose flour

1. Preheat the oven to 350°F.

2. Scatter the pineapple chunks in the baked tart shell.

3. In a medium bowl, whisk the egg yolks and sugar together until well blended. Whisk in the crème fraîche. Add the flour and whisk until everything is evenly combined. Pour the filling over the pineapple pieces.

4. Bake the tart until all but a 1-inch circle in the center of the filling is set, about 20 minutes. Let the tart cool and serve at room temperature.

Turtle Tart

Makes 1 tart, serving 8

I've always loved the idea of turtle candy—nuts bound by caramel covered in chocolate—more than the actual confection. To me the proportions have always seemed way off, having too many nuts relative to chocolate or caramel. Besides that, a turtle is messy to eat, because with all the nuts it tends to fall apart when you bite into one. This tart answers all my concerns in one easy-to-eat, deliciously nutty, gooey-caramel, chocolaty treat.

WHAT YOU'LL NEED
Rubber spatula

1 cup walnuts

6 tablespoons (3/4 stick) unsalted butter

1/2 cup firmly packed brown sugar

1/2 cup granulated sugar

1/3 cup corn syrup

3/4 cup heavy cream

Basic Tart Dough, made, formed, and baked as directed on pages 130–132

4 ounces dark chocolate (58 to 62 percent cacao), chopped or broken into 1-inch pieces

1. Spread the walnuts in one layer in a small baking pan and put in the (preheated) oven. Set a timer for 10 minutes and check the nuts to see if they're a light golden brown. If not, toast 2 minutes longer. Set aside to cool.

2. In a medium saucepan, melt the butter over medium heat. Add the brown sugar, granulated sugar, and corn syrup. Turn up the heat to medium-high and bring to a boil. Boil, stirring occasionally, for 1 minute. Remove from the heat and whisk in 1/4 cup of the cream. Cool for 10 minutes. Pour into the baked crust.

3. Chop the walnuts into 1/4-inch pieces and scatter over the butterscotch layer. Pop the tart in the fridge while you make the chocolate layer.

4. In a small saucepan, heat the remaining 1/2 cup cream until bubbles appear around the edges. Remove the saucepan from the heat and add the chocolate. Let sit a couple of minutes, then stir with the rubber spatula until the chocolate is smooth and evenly melted. Cool for 5 minutes.

5. Spread the chocolate over the butterscotch. Refrigerate the tart for at least 1 hour to set before serving.

Basic Sugar Short Dough

Makes 1 (9-inch) tart shell

Unlike the basic pie and tart doughs, this crust is crumbly rather than flaky, more akin to a sugar cookie in texture. And this one doesn't need to be rolled out. It is pressed into the pan with your fingers, making it a great place to begin if you've not worked with dough before or don't have a rolling pin. You can use this dough for any of the recipes calling for the Basic Tart Dough as well as the recipes that follow.

WHAT YOU'LL NEED
Food processor or electric stand mixer

9-inch tart pan with removable bottom

Baking or cookie sheet

Parchment paper

Rice, dried beans, or pie weights

1 cup unbleached all-purpose flour

2 tablespoons granulated sugar

1/4 teaspoon kosher salt

6 tablespoons (3/4 stick) cold unsalted butter, cut into 1/2-inch cubes

1 large egg yolk

2 teaspoons water

1/4 teaspoon pure vanilla extract

Our Fearful Baker had really struggled with rolling out a regular pie dough.

FB: You mean I don't have to roll this one out? Oh, thank goodness.

EL: No, you're gonna love this. So now that you've got your dough, gather it into two pieces, one about three-fourths of the dough and the other one-fourth.

FB: Okay. Now what?

EL: Break off clumps of the larger piece of dough and spread them around the bottom of the pan.

FB: How big should the clumps be?

EL: About two inches, but it doesn't need to be that precise. You just want about six or eight pieces. Yeah, like that. Now, are you comfortable getting your fingers dirty or sticky?

FB: Uh, not really. You know me.

EL: Okay then put a piece of plastic wrap over the dough. Start pressing the dough evenly onto the bottom of the pan. That's it. Once you have the bottom pressed in, take the other dough—the quarter piece—and break off small pieces to press onto the side of the tart pan.

FB: Am I doing this right?

EL: You've got a little too much there, particularly where the side meets the bottom. Pinch off some of the excess so you have enough dough to go around.

FB: Ooh. This is way easier than that rolling.

EL: See, I told you you'd love making it. And it tastes really good, too.

To make the dough in a food processor

Put the flour, sugar, salt, and butter cubes in the food processor bowl. Pressing the pulse button quickly, pulse the mixture until the butter is the size of small peas, anywhere from 5 to 10 pulses. This will happen very quickly, do not overmix it. In a small bowl, whisk the egg yolk, water, and vanilla. Add it to the bowl and pulse until the dough comes together into several small clumps. Do not process to the point where it forms a ball.

To make the dough in a stand mixer

Put the flour, sugar, and salt in the bowl of the mixer. On low speed using the paddle attachment, mix in the butter until it is the size of small peas. In a small bowl, whisk the egg yolk, water, and vanilla. Add it to the bowl and mix until the dough comes together into several small clumps. Do not mix to the point where it forms a ball.

To line the tart pan with the dough

Turn the dough out onto a work surface and press the clumps together. Divide it into 2 pieces, one piece three-fourths of the dough and the other piece one-fourth. Separate the bigger piece into smaller 2-inch pieces and place them all over the bottom of the pan. Using your fingers, press them in an even layer covering the bottom of the pan. (You can also cover the dough with a piece of plastic wrap before you press it.) Take 1-inch sections of the smaller piece of dough and press them as evenly thick as possible onto the side of the pan. As you're doing that, make sure that where the side meets the bottom the dough is not too thick; otherwise you may not have enough dough to go all the way around. If that happens, pinch off any excess dough that extends over the edge or is in the corner and use it to finish the side. Transfer the pan to the baking sheet, holding it by the side and being careful to not press up on the bottom section, and refrigerate for 45 minutes.

To bake the tart shell

Preheat the oven to 350°F. Press parchment paper into the dough-lined pan and fill completely with rice, dried beans, or pie weights. Tear or cut off any excess parchment sticking up so it doesn't hit the top of the oven or an oven rack. Bake until the edge of the dough is golden brown, about 25 minutes. Remove the parchment paper and weights. Return the pan to the oven and bake until the crust is golden brown, 5 to 10 minutes longer. Let cool to room temperature.

Coffee Chiffon Cream Tart

Makes 1 tart, serving 8

If you've never worked with gelatin before, here—quickly—is what you're going to do: First, you want to soften the granules in water. After about 5 minutes, the gelatin will turn into something that looks like a gummy eraser. Don't fret. At that point you will add it to hot liquid and it will dissolve completely. Stick the mixture in the fridge to chill and set up and that's it, all there is to it.

Desserts containing gelatin taste best eaten within 2 days of when they're made; the longer they sit the more rubbery they become. Don't worry if you can see little speckles of dark coffee in the filling. You won't taste or feel them on your tongue.

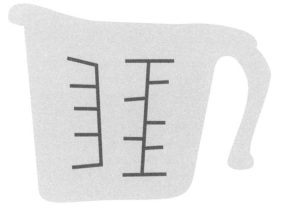

WHAT YOU'LL NEED

Pastry brush

Electric stand mixer or handheld mixer and medium bowl

Rubber spatula

2 ounces dark chocolate (58 to 62 percent cacao), chopped or broken into 1-inch pieces

Sugar Short Crust, made, formed, and baked as directed on pages 142–143

1 1/2 teaspoons gelatin

3 tablespoons water

1 cup hot coffee

2 teaspoons instant coffee granules

1/4 cup plus 1 tablespoon granulated sugar

1/4 teaspoon pure vanilla extract

1/4 teaspoon kosher salt

1 cup heavy cream

1 ounce bittersweet chocolate, chopped medium-fine, for garnish

EL: Okay, in a small bowl, sprinkle the gelatin over the water.

FB: Does the water need to be warm?

EL: No, it doesn't matter. Warm, cold, or room temp is fine. Just not hot water.

1. Melt the dark chocolate by putting it in a bowl set over a saucepan of simmering water, making sure the bowl does not touch the water. (You can use a double boiler if you have one.) Brush the chocolate over the bottom of the baked tart crust.

2. In a small bowl, sprinkle the gelatin over the water, stir it a couple of times, and let sit until the gelatin has softened, about 5 minutes.

3. In a medium bowl, whisk the hot coffee with the instant coffee granules, 1/4 cup of the sugar, the vanilla, and salt. Whisk in the softened gelatin. Refrigerate the mixture for about 30 minutes, or until it looks like Jell-O that's about half jelled. It's okay to gently stir it a little bit to check the consistency. If you've left it in too long and it's firm, break it up with the rubber spatula.

4. While the coffee gelatin is setting up, in the stand mixer fitted with the wire whisk, or using a handheld mixer and medium bowl, whip the cream with the remaining 1 tablespoon sugar until just before it forms softly mounded peaks—not pourable but not stiffly beaten either. Using the rubber spatula, fold the cream gently into the coffee mixture until it's evenly blended with no visible streaks.

5. Spread the coffee cream into the tart crust. Refrigerate the tart until the filling has firmed up, about 1 hour.

6. Garnish the tart by sprinkling the chopped bittersweet chocolate in a 1-inch border around the edge of the tart. Use a sharp knife to cut the tart into wedges for serving.

Double Strawberry Cream Tart

Makes 1 tart, serving 8

There are strawberry tarts and then there is this one. Not only is the sour cream filling topped with a layer of fresh strawberries, it hides a layer of fresh-cooked strawberry jam. If you or someone special loves strawberries—and have had your fill of shortcakes—try this tart.

Accidents are inevitable in the kitchen and I'm not just talking about burns or cuts. Overcook, undercook, whip too much or not enough, burn, melt, or drop on the floor, I've done them all. The key is how well you recover from or disguise your mistakes. Of course not all screwups can be rescued, and (sadly) sometimes you need to toss them, but the majority can be fixed so no one would ever have a clue.

WHAT YOU'LL NEED
Rubber spatula

2 pints (about 1 pound) strawberries

1/3 cup plus 1 1/2 tablespoons granulated sugar

Sugar Short Crust, made, formed, and baked as directed on pages 142–143

1 cup sour cream

1/4 teaspoon pure vanilla extract

Our FB has taken the tart shell she was baking out of the oven, removed the parchment containing the pie weights, and was putting it back in to brown the bottom.

EL: We've removed the parchment with the weights because the tart is browned on the side and now all you want to do is put it back in the oven for another five or ten minutes to finish the browning of the bottom.

FB: Oh, oww, oww, oww. (I picked the pan up from the bottom, causing the side of the tart to crack.)

EL: Did you burn yourself?

FB: No, I'm more worried about the tart. It broke.

EL: The tart shell will be fine, so don't worry. As long as you're okay. When you pick up a tart pan, make sure you hold it by the sides so you don't push the tart up from the bottom.

FB: What do I do about the crack in the crust?

EL: Never fear. You saved your dough scraps, so we'll just use it to patch the crust back together where it broke. You just spread and press it over the crack. If you don't have any dough left over you can make a simple paste of flour and water and kind of spackle it on with a small table knife or spatula. (This also works for cracks along the bottom of the tart.) And if the crust had really broken, I probably would have put it back in the pan as best I could and returned it to the oven on a baking sheet to finish browning. Then I would have layered the jam and cream and crumbled crust pieces in a bowl and called it a trifle tart or some such thing!

FB: This is actually kind of exciting, this mistake, I mean, and learning how to fix it. It's not all a lost cause, ever.

1. Remove the stems from all the strawberries. Cut half of them into 1/2-inch pieces (set the other half aside). Put the strawberry pieces in a small saucepan with the 1/3 cup sugar. Cook over medium heat, stirring occasionally, until it looks thick and jammy, about 10 minutes. Once the berries have cooked a bit, stir them frequently to prevent scorching. The mixture will be like jam with pieces of berries still visible. Cool to room temperature.

2. Use the rubber spatula to spread the berries into the baked tart crust.

3. In a small bowl, stir the sour cream with the remaining 1 1/2 tablespoons sugar and the vanilla. Using the rubber spatula, carefully spread it over the jam.

4. Slice the remaining strawberries 1/4 inch thick vertically through their stem ends. Arrange the slices prettily on top of the sour cream.

5. If you're not serving the tart right away, refrigerate it for up to 6 hours, but let it sit at room temperature for 30 minutes before serving.

Hazelnut Pear Tart

Makes 1 tart, serving 8

Pears and hazelnuts are a natural fall match—you've probably heard the saying, "What grows together goes together." Here a buttery filling of ground and toasted hazelnuts surrounds sweet pieces of ripe pear in a tart that is easy to put together.

WHAT YOU'LL NEED
Food processor

1 cup hazelnuts

1/2 cup granulated sugar

8 tablespoons (1 stick) unsalted butter, softened

2 tablespoons unbleached all-purpose flour

1/8 teaspoon kosher salt

2 large egg yolks

Sugar Short Crust, made, formed, and baked as directed on pages 142–143

1 ripe but firm pear

1. Preheat the oven to 350°F.

2. Spread the hazelnuts in one layer in a small baking pan and put in the (preheated) oven. Set a timer for 10 minutes and check the nuts to see if they're a light golden brown. If not, toast 2 minutes longer. Put the warm nuts in a colander and rub them with a clean kitchen towel to remove some of the skins. (If you don't have a colander, just rub them in the towel.) Don't worry about getting all the skins off—you just want to remove the loose pieces.

3. In the food processor, process the hazelnuts with the sugar until they're finely ground. Pulse in the butter, flour, and salt. Pulse in the egg yolks and process until everything is combined. Spread the filling evenly in the baked tart shell.

4. Stem and peel the pear. Cut around the core and discard it. Cut the pear into 3/4-inch pieces. Scatter the pear pieces over the tart and press slightly into the batter.

5. Bake the tart until it's set and a rich brown color, about 30 minutes.

6. Serve the tart warm or at room temperature.

Plum Almond Tart

Makes 1 tart, serving 8

Of all the stone fruits, I think plums
are the most neglected. People tend
to shy away from them in favor of the
more sweet-forward nectarines and
peaches, deeming plums too tart.
But bake them with a little sugar or
put them in a tart with a sweet and
creamy ground nut filling, as I've
done here, and they are transformed.
The filling is a classic French pastry
mixture called frangipane that is
made in the food processor. Often
I will double or triple the recipe and
put the extra frangipane in the freezer
for short-notice desserts.

WHAT YOU'LL NEED
Food processor

3/4 cup sliced almonds

**1/3 cup plus 1 tablespoon granulated
sugar**

**2 tablespoons unbleached all-purpose
flour**

**4 tablespoons (1/2 stick) unsalted butter,
softened**

Pinch kosher salt

1 large egg

Sugar Short Crust made, formed, and
baked as directed on pages 142–143

3 ripe purple plums

1. Preheat the oven to 350°F.

2. Spread the almonds in one layer in a small baking pan and put in
   the (preheated) oven. Set a timer for 10 minutes and check the
   nuts to see if they're a light golden brown. If not, toast 2 minutes
   longer. Set aside to cool.

3. In the food processor, process the almonds with the 1/3 cup sugar
   and the flour until they're finely ground and look like coarse
   sand. Pulse in the butter and salt. Add the egg and process until
   everything is combined. Spread the filling evenly in the baked
   tart shell.

4. Halve the plums and twist them to separate the halves. With
   a paring knife, pop out the pits. Slice the plums about 3/8 inch
   thick and, working from the outside in, arrange the slices
   in slightly overlapping circles around the tart. Sprinkle the
   remaining 1 tablespoon sugar over all.

5. Bake the tart until it's nutty brown and the filling looks almost
   set when you insert a small knife, about 35 minutes.

6. Serve the tart warm or at room temperature.

Better-Than-a-Candy-Bar Ice Cream Pie

Makes 1 pie, serving 12

When I'm trying to come up with new dessert ideas, I often look to the candy aisle of my grocery store for inspiration. Caramel and chocolate are a frequent combination there, so I thought I'd use those two ingredients with vanilla ice cream in an ice cream pie. It's a lot of bang for your buck—simple ingredients and maximum flavor.

It's easily prepared, but note that you need to allot adequate time since the pie has to freeze in between layerings. You can use purchased caramel sauce, but use a good-quality one.

WHAT YOU'LL NEED
Food processor

9-inch springform pan

Rubber spatula

5 ounces (1/3 of a 14.4-ounce package), or 9 graham crackers

4 tablespoons (1/2 stick) unsalted butter, melted

5 ounces milk chocolate, coarsely chopped

1/2 cup heavy cream

3 pints good-quality store-bought or homemade vanilla ice cream

1/2 cup cold Caramel Sauce (page 244) or good-quality store-bought

2 ounces dark chocolate (58 to 62 percent cacao), broken into pieces

1. Preheat the oven to 350°F.

2. Pulse the graham crackers in the food processor until they're finely ground. Transfer to a bowl and stir in the melted butter. Using your fingers or the bottom of a glass, evenly press the crumbs into the bottom of the springform pan. Bake the crust for 10 minutes. Let cool to room temperature.

3. Put the chopped milk chocolate in a bowl. Warm the cream in a saucepan over medium heat until it starts to bubble around the edge. Pour the hot cream over the chocolate. Shake the bowl a little to submerge all the chocolate pieces and cover the bowl for several minutes. (You can cover the bowl with anything that's handy, even a pot lid.) Whisk the cream with the chocolate until smooth. Let cool to room temperature.

4. Pour the chocolate cream onto the graham cracker crust. Freeze until firm, about 15 minutes.

5. Soften 1 1/2 pints of the ice cream in a microwave for 10 to 15 seconds, or until it's spreadable. If you don't have a microwave, put it in the refrigerator for 10 to 15 minutes. Spread the ice cream over the chocolate cream and return to the freezer until firm, about 30 minutes.

6. Spread the caramel sauce over the ice cream and return the pan to the freezer, again until the filling is firm, about 30 minutes.

7. Soften the remaining 1 1/2 pints ice cream in a microwave for 10 to 15 seconds, or until it's spreadable. Or, let sit at room temperature for 10 to 15 minutes. Spread the ice cream over the caramel sauce. Return to the freezer until firm, about 30 minutes.

8. Pulse the dark chocolate in the food processor until finely ground. Sprinkle over the top of the pie. Freeze for 2 hours, or until the pie is firm enough to slice into wedges for serving. It can be kept in the freezer for several days.

Chocolate Cream Pie

Makes 1 pie, serving 8

This is what I think of as a Gilded Lily dessert. It's basically my Dark Chocolate Pudding piled into a homemade graham cracker crust and topped with whipped cream. Even though the pie serves eight, it's so irresistible you could probably not keep four people from second pieces.

Rather than buying a graham cracker crust that's premade, it's not difficult and it's much tastier to make your own.

WHAT YOU'LL NEED

9-inch pie pan

Food processor

Heat-proof rubber spatula

5 ounces (1/3 of a 14.4-ounce package), or 9 graham crackers

4 tablespoons (1/2 stick) unsalted butter, melted

4 large egg yolks

1/3 cup granulated sugar

3 tablespoons cornstarch

2 cups whole milk

6 ounces dark chocolate (58 to 62 percent cacao), chopped or broken into 1-inch pieces

2 tablespoons unsalted butter, softened

Whipped Cream
1 1/2 cups heavy cream

3 tablespoons granulated sugar

1/2 teaspoon pure vanilla extract

1. Preheat the oven to 350°F.

2. Pulse the graham crackers in the food processor until finely ground. Transfer to a bowl and stir in the melted butter. With your fingers, evenly spread the crumbs onto the bottom and up the side of the pie pan. Use the flat bottom of a glass to firmly and evenly press the crumbs onto the bottom. Use a spoon to press the crumbs into the curve and up onto the side of the pan. Bake the crust for 10 minutes. Let cool to room temperature.

3. In a medium bowl, whisk the egg yolks with the sugar until smooth. Whisk in the cornstarch.

4. Warm the milk in a medium saucepan over medium heat until hot but not quite boiling. Gradually whisk the hot milk into the egg yolks. Pour the liquid back into the saucepan. Over medium-low heat, stirring constantly with a wooden spoon or rubber spatula and scraping the bottom of the pan so it doesn't stick, cook until the custard has a mayo-like consistency, about 5 minutes. You'll know the custard is done when it has thickened, it bubbles once or twice, and as you stir you can see the bottom of the pan. Remove the pan from the heat and whisk in the chocolate and softened butter until smooth. If you find that there are some lumps from the eggs, strain the custard through a medium-fine sieve.

5. With the rubber spatula, spread the chocolate cream into the crust. Place plastic wrap directly on the top of the cream so it doesn't form a skin. Refrigerate until cold, about 3 hours, but overnight is fine.

Whipped Cream

6. Using a whisk or handheld mixer, whip the cream, sugar, and vanilla until it forms softly mounded peaks. Spread over the top of the chocolate cream, leaving the crust exposed. Refrigerate until ready to serve. (If you make the pie a day ahead, put the whipped cream on the day you plan to serve it.)

Key Lime Pie

Makes 1 pie, serving 6 to 8

A Key lime pie is one of those iconic regional dishes that people have strong feelings about. With a nod to tradition, but with a wink to adaptation, I make my version with condensed milk (tradition) and a cookie crumb crust rather than flaky pie dough (adaptation). I find that good store-bought cookies make excellent crumb crusts and allow you to experiment with different flavors. One ingredient that cannot be tinkered with, however, is the Key lime juice. Because fresh Key limes are not common in most of the country, this is one time where bottled juice is acceptable.

WHAT YOU'LL NEED
Food processor

9-inch pie pan

36 Pepperidge Farm Bordeaux cookies (about 1 1/3 packages or 9 ounces—about 2 cups—of crumbs)

6 tablespoons (3/4 stick) unsalted butter, melted

5 large egg yolks

1 (14-ounce) can condensed milk

1/2 cup Key lime juice

FB: Why does the crust get put in the freezer?

EL: So the butter will harden more quickly and the crust will turn into one piece. Some recipes will tell you to bake the crust first before putting in the filling and baking the pie, but that's an unnecessary step.

FB: Okay, so here we go. It says to whisk the egg yolks with the milk and lime juice.

EL: Now, when you make a Key lime pie, don't ever try to substitute plain lime juice. Other than the fact that Key limes have a distinctive flavor, you can't call it a Key lime pie. But a lot of restaurants do. They'll put Key lime Pie on the menu and will use regular lime juice or even lemon juice. Sometimes they even add food coloring for an unnatural green color.

FB: I don't think I've ever seen Key lime juice in the store, not that I've looked for it.

EL: You can find it practically everywhere. Nellie & Joe's is one of the best-known companies that make it, but there are others as well. Nellie & Joe's just is the one I've always used.

1. Preheat the oven to 350°F.

2. Pulse the cookies in the food processor until they're like coarse sand. In a bowl, stir the crumbs with the butter until well mixed. With your fingers, evenly spread the crumbs onto the side and bottom of the pie pan. Use the flat bottom of a drinking glass to firmly and evenly press the crumbs onto the bottom. Use a spoon to press the crumbs into the curve and up onto the side of the pan.

3. Put the crust in the freezer to firm up while you make the pie filling.

4. In a medium bowl, whisk the egg yolks, condensed milk, and lime juice until evenly combined. Remove the crust from the freezer and pour in the filling. Bake the pie until the filling is set, about 15 minutes.

5. Let cool for 20 minutes then transfer to the refrigerator to chill for 2 to 3 hours. If you want to serve it sooner, you can put it in the freezer to chill thoroughly, but no longer than 45 minutes (you don't want it to freeze). The pie can be made 1 day ahead and kept, covered with plastic wrap, in the refrigerator.

6. Serve the pie sliced into wedges with generous dollops of whipped cream.

Coconut Cream Pie

I like to make press-in cookie and nut crusts. They're easy and fast. This one is made with thin chocolate wafer cookies. The Nabisco brand is the "Famous" one, but there are others as well.

The coconut gets toasted to bring out its flavor. Note that the coconut that goes into the filling is strained out (otherwise it gets soggy), and the rest is sprinkled on top for a textural garnish.

WHAT YOU'LL NEED
Food processor

9-inch pie pan

Baking or cookie sheet

Heat-proof rubber spatula

6 ounces chocolate wafer cookies (2/3 of a 9-ounce package)

4 tablespoons (1/2 stick) unsalted butter, melted

1 1/4 cups loosely packed sweetened shredded coconut

4 large egg yolks

1/2 cup granulated sugar

1/8 teaspoon kosher salt

3 tablespoons cornstarch

2 cups whole milk

2 tablespoons unsalted butter, softened

1/2 teaspoon pure vanilla extract

Whipped Cream
1 cup heavy cream

1 tablespoon granulated sugar

1. Preheat the oven to 350°F.

2. Pulse the wafer cookies in the food processor until finely ground. Transfer to a bowl and stir in the melted butter. (With your fingers, or the bottom of a glass, evenly spread the crumbs onto the side and bottom of the pie pan. Use the flat bottom of a drinking glass to firmly and evenly press the crumbs into the bottom. Use a spoon to press the crumbs into the curve and up the side of the pan. Bake the crust for 10 minutes.

3. Spread the coconut in a single layer on the baking sheet. Bake for about 10 minutes, until golden brown, stirring once or twice so that it browns evenly.

4. In a medium bowl, whisk the egg yolks with the sugar and salt until smooth. Whisk in the cornstarch.

5. Warm the milk and 1 cup coconut over medium heat until hot. Gradually whisk the hot milk into the egg yolks. Pour the liquid back into the saucepan. Over medium-low heat, stirring constantly with the heat-proof rubber spatula and scraping the bottom of the pan so it doesn't stick, cook until the custard has a mayo-like consistency, about 5 minutes. It's done when it bubbles, and as you stir you can see the bottom of the pan.

6. Whisk in the butter and vanilla. Strain the custard through a medium-fine sieve into a bowl, discarding the coconut. Press plastic wrap directly onto the surface. Refrigerate until cold, at least 1 hour, but overnight is fine.

7. Spread the custard into the crust.

Whipped Cream
8. Using a whisk or handheld mixer, whip the cream with the sugar until it forms softly mounded peaks. Spread over the top of the custard. Sprinkle the remaining 1/4 cup coconut in a 2-inch border around the edge of the pie. Refrigerate the pie 2 hours.

Apple Puff Pastry Galette

Makes 1 tart, serving 6 to 8

Everyone will think you slaved over this beautiful tart when you bring it to the table. Only you know how easy it is, with essentially two main ingredients: apples and purchased puff pastry. Since it tastes best warm out of the oven, I suggest you assemble it in the afternoon, stick it in the fridge, and then bake it right before or during dinner. Make sure the pastry turns a deep golden brown, otherwise the tart will be too doughy in the middle.

WHAT YOU'LL NEED
Rolling pin

Baking or cookie sheet

Parchment paper

1 sheet store-bought puff pastry (page 117), defrosted according to package directions

2 red apples, any kind except Red Delicious

2 tablespoons unsalted butter

2 tablespoons granulated sugar

1/8 teaspoon ground cinnamon

1. Preheat the oven to 400°F. Line the baking sheet with parchment.

2. Unfold the thawed sheet of puff pastry by carefully opening it to see if it's cold but pliable. If it starts to crack, let it defrost on the counter 5 minutes and test it again. Once it's fully flexible, unfold and check for any cracks along the fold. If there are any, simply push the edges back together and smooth them out.

3. Put the puff pastry on a lightly floured work surface and sprinkle with some more flour. With the rolling pin, roll the pastry into a 12-inch square. Put a 10- or 11-inch plate on top and, with a small sharp knife, use the plate as a template to cut out a circle. Place the pastry circle on the parchment-lined baking sheet and refrigerate while you prepare the apples.

4. Peel the apples and core each by cutting off the sides and discarding the rectangular piece of core. Slice lengthwise 1/8 inch thick.

5. Arrange the apple slices in the center of the pastry dough, leaving a 1-inch border around the edge. Cut the butter into small (1/4-inch) pieces and strew over the apples. Stir the sugar with the cinnamon in a small bowl and sprinkle over all.

6. Bake the galette until the puff pastry is a deep golden brown at the edges, about 25 minutes. Let cool for 5 minutes and serve warm.

Orange-Date Ricotta Tartlets

Makes 8 servings

These pretty little packages of puff pastry hold a delicious filling of ricotta and dates. You can use either whole-milk or skim ricotta, but if you can find one of the ricottas now being produced here in the U.S. by artisan cheese makers or any of the imported ricottas from Italy, they will be sweeter, cheesier, and less watery than the supermarket brands.

Even if you've pinched the edges of the puff pastry together well, they'll still have a tendency to pop open, which is okay.

WHAT YOU'LL NEED

Rolling pin

2 baking or cookie sheets

2 sheets store-bought puff pastry (page 117), defrosted according to package directions

1 cup ricotta cheese (see headnote)

1/4 cup granulated sugar

Grated zest of 2 oranges

1 tablespoon unbleached all-purpose flour

1/4 teaspoon kosher salt

1 large egg

16 pitted fresh dates, cut into 1/2-inch pieces

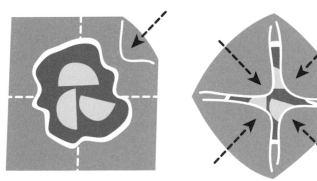

1. Preheat the oven to 400°F.

2. Unfold one of the thawed sheets of puff pastry by carefully opening it to see if it's cold but pliable. If it starts to crack, let it defrost on the counter 5 minutes and test it again. Once it's fully flexible, unfold and check for any cracks along the fold. If there are any, simply push the edges back together and smooth them out.

3. Roll one sheet of pastry out on a lightly floured surface into a 10-inch square. Cut into 4 (5-inch) squares and place on a baking sheet. Unfold the second sheet and repeat. Put the pastry back in the refrigerator to keep it cold. (You can also cut the squares, wrap them well with plastic and parchment between them, and freeze again for a week.) Defrost before filling.

4. In a medium bowl, stir the ricotta with the sugar, orange zest, flour, salt, and egg until well combined. Set aside.

5. Cut the dates into 1/2-inch pieces.

6. Place 2 tablespoons ricotta in the middle of each pastry square and top with 2 tablespoons dates. For each of the pastries, bring two opposite corners of a square together and tightly pinch them closed, repeating with the other two corners. Pinch the open corners closed.

7. Bake the pastry until golden brown, about 20 minutes. The pastries will probably open as they cook. Don't worry—they're pretty that way.

8. Serve the tartlets warm or at room temperature. They can be reheated, but taste best on the day they're made.

Fruit

As a professional pastry chef, I must confess that nothing inspires me more than a perfectly ripe piece of fruit. I love the smell of warm chocolate and the whiff of vanilla, but to me, the perfume of a ripe peach or a strawberry warm from the summer sun can't be beat.

I know I'm not the first chef or author to tell you to buy fresh, seasonal, and local fruit and vegetables, but here's a simple truth: no matter how good a baker you are, terrified or fearless, you'll never be able to turn unripe, out-of-season flavorless fruit into a good dessert. The difference between a local and freshly picked strawberry, peach, or plum in July and one flown in from halfway around the world in December is like night and day. So, my general rule is that the fruit should be good enough to stand alone and the cook's task is merely to not screw it up. That's not to say that you have to toss fruit that's a little past its prime; in fact, sometimes they make the best sauces, pie fillings, and preserves and jams (that's another book), but even then, it's imperative that the fruit is flavorful to begin with.

You'll see that I use fruit in other recipes throughout the book (I'm particularly a fan of dried fruit) but in this chapter it's fresh fruit that earns a starring role. The crusts, cakes, toppings, and sauces are merely supporting players or, in the case of the panna cotta and crème brûlée, the fruit takes what are wonderful but relatively simple desserts to another level of flavor.

Most of the desserts included in this chapter will be familiar to you: crumbles (crisps), cobblers, and shortcake. However, there are also a number of sautéed toppings for crepes, clafouti (which is kind of like a big pancake baked with fresh fruit), trifle cake layered with fresh fruit and cream, and whole fruit that is poached, roasted, baked, or sautéed. All these recipes are perfect for a novice baker. None requires much technical skill. You simply need a commitment to finding the best seasonal fruit available. To that end, see the next page for tips.

Make-Ahead and Storage Tips

Storage for fruit desserts depends on the individual recipe. As a rule, cake-based desserts with baked fruit can be kept at room temperature. Anything creamy or custard-based should be refrigerated.

2. If you're shopping at a grocery store, look for fruit that is labeled by origin (many Whole Foods and specialty grocers now stock locally grown produce and tell you that).

4. Use your senses when picking good fruit. While ripeness and sweetness indicators vary depending on the fruit, generally, pick it up in your hand, feel it for weight, give it a sniff test and gently squeeze without the clerk catching you.

1. Unless you have backyard fruit trees or friends with gardens or farms, your best source for fresh, ripe, delicious fruit is at a farmers' market.

3. No matter how good they look, pass up those raspberries in January.

Apple–Brown Butter Betty

Makes 8 servings

When I'm looking for a dessert to use up all those apples sitting in the fruit bowl, but don't have the time to make a pie, Betty comes to the rescue. Betties, which date back to colonial times, are simply dishes made of fruit, spiced and layered with buttered bread crumbs. The most well-known version is Apple Brown Betty, a homey dish made with apples and brown sugar. This recipe varies from the original in that I use regular sugar and make a brown butter to give the bread crumbs a slightly intriguing, nutty flavor.

In addition to being easy to throw together, Betties are a great way to make use of that day-old French bread sitting on your counter next to the apples in the fruit bowl (though fresh bread, toasted, works too). I like to layer the Betty in a pretty baking dish so I can serve it right at the table. If you have ramekins or small baking dishes, you can also make individual little Betties (decrease the cooking time to 25 to 35 minutes).

WHAT YOU'LL NEED

Food processor

9-inch square baking pan or dish

1 sweet or sour French bread baguette

14 tablespoons (1 3/4 sticks) unsalted butter

6 Granny Smith apples

1 cup golden raisins

3/4 cup chopped pitted dates

1/3 cup granulated sugar

2 tablespoons lemon juice

1 teaspoon ground cinnamon

1/4 teaspoon ground ginger

Pinch kosher salt

3/4 cup heavy cream

EL: Without realizing it, you've probably made brown butter before, just by leaving some in a pan for too long. Cooking it to the brown stage really brings out its flavor, but you want to catch it before it turns black and the milk solids have burned. What you're looking for is when the melted butter starts to cook and turns a nutty golden brown color.

FB: Yeah, I've made it, but never intentionally. Okay, so now the butter is melted.

1. Preheat the oven to 350°F.

2. If you have a day-old baguette you can skip this step. If the bread is fresh, slice the baguette in half lengthwise and toast in the (preheated) oven for 10 minutes. Let cool.

3. Slice the baguette crosswise into 1-inch pieces. Transfer to the food processor and pulse into coarse crumbs (pieces no bigger than 1/4 inch). You should have about 3 1/2 cups of crumbs.

4. Melt 8 tablespoons of the butter in a small saucepan or skillet over medium heat. After the foam subsides, let the butter continue to cook until it turns a pale golden brown. Remove from the heat and set aside for a couple of minutes so it can continue to cook and turn a rich golden brown.

5. In a medium bowl, stir the crumbs with the browned butter until evenly moist. Set aside.

6. Peel the apples and core by cutting from the top down the sides and discarding the rectangular piece of core. Slice lengthwise 1/4-inch thick. Transfer to a large skillet with the remaining 6 tablespoons butter, the raisins, dates, sugar, lemon juice, cinnamon, ginger, and salt. Cook over medium heat until the apples are soft, 15 to 20 minutes. Stir in the cream.

7. Evenly spread half of the cooked apples into the baking pan. Sprinkle half the bread crumbs over the apples. Make another layer with the remaining apples. Top with an even layer of bread crumbs. Bake until the Betty is golden brown, about 40 minutes.

8. Serve warm or at room temperature with vanilla ice cream or whipped cream.

Brown Butter Crepes

Makes about 12 crepes

One of my favorite spur-of-the-moment desserts is to serve crepes with lightly sautéed seasonal fruit, which is why you'll always be able to find a stash of crepes in my freezer. Once you learn the technique, they're super easy to make and no more difficult than your Sunday morning pancakes. You don't even need to make the brown butter as we do here; just use plain melted butter, though the little extra step of browning the butter adds a nice flavor note.

WHAT YOU'LL NEED
Small metal spatula or table knife for turning the crepes

3 tablespoons unsalted butter

1 cup unbleached all-purpose flour

1/2 cup confectioners' sugar

Large pinch kosher salt

2 large eggs

1 large egg yolk

1 1/2 cups whole or 2 percent milk

EL: Since you've never made crepes before, think of it like making a big, thin pancake. What you want to do first is measure out one ounce of the batter you just made into a little bowl or ladle, so you will be able to see what that amount looks like. For the rest of the crepes you can just pour the batter right into the pan from the measuring cup and you'll know how to eyeball the right amount.

FB: But how much is one ounce?

EL: It's two tablespoons. So now put your skillet on the burner and get it hot over medium heat. Just as when you're making pancakes, the pan has to be hot.

FB: Okay, I think it's hot enough.

EL: The tricky part, which really is not so tricky, is that as soon as you pour in the batter you need to pick up the pan and start rotating the pan to coat the bottom evenly with the batter.

FB: Like so?

EL: That's it, but you need to move it around a little faster so it's more even. The crepe is already starting to cook the second it hits the hot pan. Yeah, like that. Now put it back on the burner and, after a minute or two, with the spatula, lift up the edge of the crepe so you can check the bottom. Also, see how it's beginning to bubble a little and that the edge is starting to brown? If the bottom has browned, which it has, lift the edge with the spatula and, with your fingers, flip it over to cook the other side. The second side won't take more than a half-minute.

FB: What do I do with it when it's done?

EL: Turn it out onto the counter onto this piece of parchment paper. As the rest of them come out of the pan you can stack them, slightly overlapping.

FB: I did it!

EL: Everyone knows that with pancakes you don't serve the first one; crepes are the same way, and I consider the first one the cook's reward.

1. To make the brown butter, melt the butter in an 8-inch nonstick skillet over medium heat. After the foam subsides, let the butter continue to cook until it turns a pale golden brown. Remove from the heat and set aside. The butter will continue to cook and turn darker.

2. Over a medium bowl, sift the flour and sugar together in a sifter or in a fine strainer by gently tapping your hand against the edge. Add the salt (you can just leave it on top of the flour pile because it gets mixed in later).

3. In a medium bowl, whisk the whole eggs with the egg yolk and milk. Whisk the mixture into the bowl with the flour, then whisk in the brown butter (from the skillet) until everything is thoroughly combined. Transfer to a liquid measuring cup with a spout and either proceed to make the crepes or cover the cup with plastic wrap and refrigerate for up to 2 days.

4. Measure 2 tablespoons of batter into a small bowl. Place it and the small metal spatula or table knife near your cooktop. If you're making the crepes right away, heat the same skillet you used for the brown butter over medium heat (or start with a clean 8-inch nonstick skillet if the batter was made ahead). When the pan is hot, remove it from the heat and pour the 2 tablespoons of batter into the pan, quickly tilting and rotating the pan so the batter coats the bottom evenly. Put the pan back on the heat and cook until the batter bubbles and the edge begins to turn brown, about 1 minute. Using your spatula, peek at the underside first to see if it's lightly browned. If it is, lift up the edge of the crepe with the spatula and turn it over with your fingers. Cook the other side another 30 seconds, or until lightly browned. Flip the finished crepe out onto your work surface. Continue making crepes using up the remaining batter. The finished crepes can be stacked, slightly overlapping, once they're out of the pan. You should have at least 12 crepes. Once the crepes have cooled, stack them with parchment in between each and store tightly wrapped in the freezer for up to 2 months.

Brown Butter Crepes with Fruit Toppings

Makes 6 servings

If having to follow a precise recipe is what scares you away from baking, you'll find comfort in cooking fruit to use as a warm topping for crepes. The technique is really more of a guideline than an actual recipe. You simply add cut-up fruit, butter, and sugar to a warm skillet and cook for a few minutes until the fruit has warmed through, adding more sugar and lemon juice to taste. If there's too much liquid, turn up the heat and reduce it. That's all there is to it, once you've made the crepes of course. Just make sure your fruit is heated through, either straight out of the sauté pan or reheated. (The contrast of the warm fruit with cold ice cream is what turns each of these desserts into something special.)

Pear and Caramel Brown-Butter Crepes

If you have crepes in the freezer and buy the caramel sauce, this is a very quick dessert to prepare.

1. Spread about 2 teaspoons of the caramel sauce on each of the 12 crepes. Fold the crepes into quarters and place 2 on each of 6 dessert plates.

2. Stem, peel, and cut the pears in half. With a melon baller or small paring knife, cut out and remove the cores. Cut the pears in 1/2-inch pieces. Put the pears in a medium sauté pan or skillet with the butter, sugar, and lemon juice. Cook over medium heat until the pears are warmed through and the sugar and butter start to bubble, 3 to 5 minutes.

3. To serve, spoon the warm pears over the crepes and top with a scoop of vanilla ice cream. Drizzle a little more caramel sauce over all and serve while hot.

WHAT YOU'LL NEED
Melon baller or small knife

3/4 cup Caramel Sauce (page 244) or good-quality store-bought caramel sauce

12 Brown Butter Crepes (page 162)

3 ripe but firm pears (any kind)

2 tablespoons unsalted butter

3 tablespoons granulated sugar

1 teaspoon lemon juice

Good-quality store-bought vanilla ice cream

Small knife

Medium sauté pan or skillet

12 Brown Butter Crepes (page 162)

3 ripe but firm plums

3/4 cup orange juice

About 1/4 cup granulated sugar

6 tablespoons (3/4 stick) unsalted butter, softened

Good-quality store-bought ginger ice cream

Plum Crepes with Ginger Ice Cream

Ginger ice cream is spectacular with the plums, but good ol' vanilla will do.

1. Fold the crepes into quarters and place 2 on each of 6 dessert plates.

2. Halve the plums and twist them to separate the halves. With a paring knife, pop out the pits and cut the plums into 1-inch wedges.

3. In a medium sauté pan or skillet, heat the orange juice and about 3 tablespoons of the sugar over medium-high heat. When the juice is bubbling add the butter and cook until the butter has melted and begun to thicken slightly, 3 to 5 minutes. Gently stir in the plum pieces and cook for about 2 minutes, or until the fruit is heated through. Taste for sweetness and stir in more sugar if necessary. (This will depend on how sweet the orange juice is and how tart the plums are.)

4. Place a scoop of ice cream on each crepe. Top with a large spoonful of plums and sauce and serve while hot.

Medium sauté pan or skillet

12 Brown Butter Crepes (page 162)

3 tablespoons sliced almonds

6 ripe apricots

1/4 cup granulated sugar

2 tablespoons unsalted butter

2 tablespoons water

Good-quality store-bought vanilla ice cream

Apricot and Almond Brown-Butter Crepes

Fresh apricots have a short season. When you find them be sure to make this recipe.

1. Preheat the oven to 350°F.

2. Fold the crepes into quarters and place 2 on each of 6 dessert plates.

3. Spread the almonds in one layer in a small baking pan and put in the (preheated) oven. Set a timer for 10 minutes and check the nuts to see if they're a light golden brown. If not, toast 2 minutes longer. Set aside to cool.

4. Cut the apricots in half and pit them. Cut into 1-inch pieces. Put the apricots in a medium sauté pan or skillet with the sugar, butter, and water. Cook over medium-high heat until the sugar has melted and the apricots are soft, 3 to 5 minutes.

5. Place a scoop of ice cream on each crepe, then top with a large spoonful of apricots and sauce. Sprinkle with the toasted almonds and serve while hot.

Medium sauté pan or skillet

12 Brown Butter Crepes (page 162)

1 pint strawberries

3/4 cup orange juice

2 tablespoons Grand Marnier liqueur (optional)

About 3 tablespoons granulated sugar

Juice of 1/2 lemon

6 tablespoons (3/4 stick) unsalted butter, softened

1 pint raspberries

Good-quality store-bought vanilla ice cream

Red Berry Crepes

It's important here that before adding the berries you've thickened the juices to the right consistency, because they'll fall apart if cooked too long—they only need to be warmed through for no more than 2 minutes. The Grand Marnier leaves little alcohol taste; it's there purely to add a more complex orange flavor.

1. Fold the crepes into quarters and place 2 on each of 6 dessert plates.

2. Remove the green stems from the strawberries and cut into pieces the size of the raspberries.

3. In a medium sauté pan or skillet over medium-high heat, heat the orange juice, liqueur (if using), 2 tablespoons of the sugar, and the lemon juice. When the juice is bubbling, add the butter and cook until the butter has melted and begun to thicken slightly, 3 minutes. Gently stir in the strawberries and raspberries and cook for about 2 minutes, or until the fruit is heated through. Taste for sweetness and stir in more sugar if necessary. (This will depend on how sweet the orange juice is.)

4. Place a scoop of ice cream on each crepe. Top with a large spoonful of the berries and sauce and serve hot.

Baked Apples with Cinnamon-Honey Yogurt

Makes 6 servings

It may not be chic and it may not be complex, but sometimes a baked apple satisfies as no other dessert can. I like to serve them at dinner parties after a particularly indulgent meal and watch as people smile at the sight of something so familiar and comforting. Two things here make this baked apple a little more special than usual. One is the yogurt-with-honey sauce and the other is the syrup you make by reducing the cooking liquid.

I like thick Greek yogurt because it tastes extra creamy. You can use any kind of honey you prefer, but there are some wonderful artisan honeys worth seeking out that will add another flavor dimension.

WHAT YOU'LL NEED
Baking dish

3 Fuji apples

2 tablespoons unsalted butter

1/4 cup maple syrup

1/4 cup plus 1 tablespoon honey

1 cup apple juice

3/4 cup yogurt (or sour cream if you'd like)

1 teaspoon granulated sugar

1/2 teaspoon ground cinnamon

1. Preheat the oven to 350°F.

2. Cut the apples in half from top to bottom. With a small knife, cut out the cores. Place cut side up in the baking dish. If they won't lie flat, slice a thin piece off the bottom of each half. Cut the butter into small pieces and put inside the cut cores of the apples.

3. In a small bowl, stir the maple syrup with the 1/4 cup honey and the apple juice. Pour over the apples. Reserve the bowl to make the honey yogurt.

4. Bake the apples, basting every 10 minutes with the liquid, until they're tender and a small knife pierces them easily. Depending on the size of the apples, they may take as long as 50 minutes, but start checking after 35 minutes. Let cool slightly.

5. While the apples are baking, in the reserved bowl, whisk the remaining 1 tablespoon honey with the yogurt, sugar, and cinnamon.

6. Transfer the apples with a slotted spoon to 6 dessert plates. If your baking dish can go over direct heat, put it over medium-high heat and reduce the liquid until it's slightly syrupy. (If the dish is not for stovetop use, transfer the liquid to a small saucepan to reduce it.)

7. Serve each warm apple half topped with a spoonful of honey yogurt. Drizzle the syrup over the yogurt. The apples are best warm but can be reheated.

Black Forest Ice Cream Cake

Makes 1 cake, serving about 12

This is one of those no-brainer desserts that gets "oohs" and "aahs" from everyone you serve it to. It's also very adaptable. You can use any flavor of ice cream instead of the chocolate chip I've suggested here. Or you could simply add chopped chocolate to softened vanilla ice cream. You could also turn the whole dessert into a sundae.

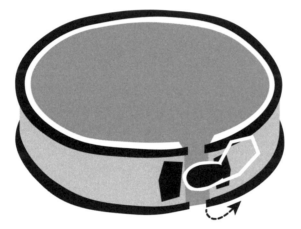

WHAT YOU'LL NEED
Food processor

9-inch springform pan

Rubber spatula

1 (9-ounce) package chocolate wafer cookies

3 tablespoons unsalted butter, melted

2 quarts good-quality store-bought chocolate chip ice cream

Cherry Topping
1 1/2 pounds ripe cherries, stemmed and pitted (see page 172)

1/3 cup granulated sugar

1 1/2 tablespoons cornstarch

1/3 cup water

1. Pulse the cookies in the food processor until they're like coarse sand (you should have about 2 cups.) In a bowl, stir the crumbs with the butter until well mixed. Using your fingers, evenly spread the crumbs onto the bottom of the springform pan and press flat with the bottom of a glass. Put the pan in the freezer for 30 minutes.

2. Soften the ice cream in a microwave for 10 to 15 seconds, until spreadable. If you don't have a microwave, let it sit in the refrigerator for 10 to 15 minutes. Mound the softened ice cream in the pan and then firmly press it on top of the crust. Spread out smoothly with the spatula. Pick the pan up a few inches and quickly drop it onto the counter to remove any air bubbles. Wrap in plastic wrap and return to the freezer for several hours, or until firm. The cake can be made up to a week before serving.

Cherry Topping

3. Put the pitted cherries, sugar, cornstarch, and water in a medium saucepan. Cook over medium heat, stirring frequently but gently and scraping the bottom of the pan with the rubber spatula to prevent sticking as the liquid comes to a low boil. After about 8 minutes, the cherries should have given off juice and thickened and you should still see some whole cherries in the thickened juice. Let cool. Refrigerate until cold, or let cool and transfer to a covered storage container and refrigerate for up to a week.

4. Just before serving, unmold the cake by unlatching the springform. If the cake is rock-hard when you take it out, let it sit for 10 minutes to soften a little. You can either cut the cake into wedges and serve each piece with cherry topping on the side, or, for a "wow" presentation, cover the whole cake with the topping before you cut and serve it at the table.

Blackberry Fool with Raspberry Sorbet

Makes 6 servings

This English dessert has been around since the 1700s, probably created as a way to use up leftover fruit. How it got its name is anyone's guess, but I'd like to think it's because it's foolishly easy to make, just pureed fruit folded into whipped cream.

WHAT YOU'LL NEED

Food processor

Rubber spatula

Electric stand mixer or handheld mixer and medium bowl

Small ice cream scoop (if you have one)

1 pint blackberries

1 cup heavy cream

3 tablespoons granulated sugar

1 pint good-quality store-bought raspberry sorbet

1. Puree half of the blackberries in the food processor. Using the rubber spatula or small ladle (it's faster with a ladle), push the berries through a medium sieve to strain out the seeds. Set aside.

2. Using the stand mixer with a wire whip attachment, or a handheld mixer and medium bowl, whip the cream on medium speed with the sugar until it forms softly mounded peaks. Fold in the berry puree with the rubber spatula. The cream can be made several hours before serving and kept covered in the refrigerator.

3. Spoon a scant 1/4 cup of berry cream into each of 6 parfait or dessert glasses. Top with 2 small scoops of sorbet. Spoon the remaining berry cream over the sorbet and garnish with the remaining blackberries. Serve immediately.

Cherry Puff Pastry Tart

Makes 1 tart, serving 6 or 8

The filling for this tart is one of my absolute favorites, and when cherries are in season I buy several pounds at a time so I can make it in quantity. Not only is the cherry filling good in tarts, pies, and turnovers, it's spectacular when simply spooned over ice cream or served alongside cake. Because it's so addictively delicious, the only problem I've encountered is making enough. That's why cherry pitters were invented (see the Cherry Clafouti dialog on page 172 for more on cherry pitters).

WHAT YOU'LL NEED

Cherry pitter (if you have one)

Baking or cookie sheet

Parchment paper

Rubber spatula

Pastry brush

1 1/4 pounds fresh cherries, stemmed and pitted (see headnote)

1/3 cup granulated sugar

1 1/2 tablespoons cornstarch

1/3 cup water

2 sheets store-bought puff pastry (page 117), defrosted according to the package directions

1 large egg, lightly beaten

1. Preheat the oven to 400°F. Line the baking sheet with parchment.

2. Put the pitted cherries, sugar, cornstarch, and water in a medium saucepan. Cook over medium heat, stirring frequently but gently and scraping the bottom of the pan with the rubber spatula to prevent sticking as the liquid comes to a low boil. After about 8 minutes, the cherries should have given off juice and thickened and you should still see some whole cherries in the thickened juice. Let cool. Refrigerate until cold or let cool and transfer to a covered storage container and refrigerate for up to a week.

3. Unfold 1 of the thawed sheets of puff pastry by carefully opening it to see if it's cold but pliable. If it starts to crack, let it defrost on the counter 5 minutes and test it again. Once it's flexible, unfold it and check for any cracks along the fold. If there are any, simply push the edges back together and smooth them out. Unfold the other pastry sheet.

4. Place 1 of the pastry sheets on the parchment-lined baking sheet. Brush the beaten egg in a 1-inch border along the edges of the pastry. Cut 4 (1-inch-wide) strips from the second piece. Place the strips along the egg-washed border to create a raised border. Save the remaining pastry for another use (see page 117 for some suggestions).

5. Spoon the cherry filling in the middle of the tart and spread out just to the raised border. Bake the tart for 15 minutes. Reduce the oven temperature to 350°F and rotate the pastry if it's not browning evenly. Bake for another 10 minutes, or until the pastry is a deep golden brown. Don't worry if the pastry seems very brown—you want to make sure the dough is cooked all the way through.

6. Let the tart cool for about 15 minutes so the filling sets up before cutting into 6 or 8 rectangles for serving.

Cherry Clafouti

Makes 6 servings

A clafouti is a rustic French dessert that really is just a big, fruit-filled, baked pancake. It is, however, much more delicious than that description makes it sound. Most recipes are pretty similar: eggs, sugar, and milk blended together, poured over fresh fruit (usually cherries, but also plums or pears), and baked until puffy and browned. In an effort to make this recipe a little different and yet still keep its simplicity, I've added cream to the batter for richness and mixed a little cardamom in with the confectioners' sugar topping. In this recipe I think it enhances the cherries.

It's nice to use a decorative baking dish so you can bring the warm clafouti right to the table, but really any round, square, or oval shallow dish will do, as long as it can hold 2 quarts.

WHAT YOU'LL NEED
Cherry pitter (if you have one)

8-inch baking dish

1 tablespoon plus 1/3 cup granulated sugar

1 1/4 pound fresh cherries, stemmed and pitted

3 large eggs

3/4 cup whole milk

3/4 cup heavy cream

2 teaspoons pure vanilla extract

1/2 cup unbleached all-purpose flour

1/4 teaspoon kosher salt

1 teaspoon confectioners' sugar

Pinch ground cardamom

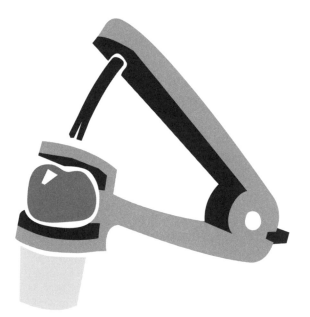

EL: Now you have to pit the cherries, and I'm going to let you use my handy-dandy cherry pitter.

FB: Wow, this works great. It's kind of like pitting olives, and I think I even have one of these at home.

EL: It's exactly like pitting olives, except this pitter has a little shield around it to keep the cherry juice from squirting everywhere. I bought it at a cookware store and they're pretty common. If you don't have one, though, you can cut the cherries in half, twist the sides in opposite directions, and pull out the pit with your fingers or the top of a paring knife.

FB: Now that sounds tedious.

EL: Sometimes you can go so fast with the pitter that you don't notice if the pit came out, so you need to either check the cherries at the end or make sure as you're going along.

FB: What if you don't pit them? Does anyone do that? Just leave them in I mean?

EL: Well, in France they often leave in the stems and the pits. They believe the pits give the cherries more flavor, and they may be right, but I'm not so sure.

FB: One good thing about that is that everyone knows to spit the pit rather than being caught by surprise with a random one.

EL: So it's an either-or situation. Make sure you remove them all or do as the French do and leave them all in. It's the cook's choice.

1. Preheat the oven to 375° F.

2. Grease the bottom and side of the baking dish with nonstick cooking spray or butter. Sprinkle the bottom of the dish evenly with the 1 tablespoon granulated sugar and rotate it to get some of the sugar onto the side. Scatter the pitted cherries evenly in the dish.

3. In a medium bowl, whisk the eggs, milk, cream, and vanilla. Whisk in the remaining 1/3 cup granulated sugar, the flour, and salt until everything is evenly combined. Strain the mixture through a mesh sieve (to eliminate any little lumps of flour) over the cherries. Bake until golden brown and puffy on the edges and the center is just firm and not jiggly, about 35 minutes. Let cool slightly.

4. Just before serving, in a small bowl or ramekin, stir the confectioners' sugar together with the cardamom. Transfer to a small fine sieve (like a tea strainer if you have one) and dust the sugar over the top of the clafouti. Using a big spoon, scoop the clafouti onto dessert plates. It's best served warm but will still taste good the next morning for breakfast.

Variation: Plum Clafouti
Prepare the clafouti as directed, except substitute 3 ripe plums for the cherries. Halve the plums and twist them to separate the halves. With a paring knife, pop out the pits and cut the plums into 1-inch pieces. Bake the clafouti in an 8-inch baking dish.

Lemon Crème Brûlée

Makes 6 servings

One of the most popular restaurant desserts—crème brûlée—strikes fear into the hearts of home cooks. It's actually easier to make than a cake or a pie (and the expression "easy as pie" never made sense to me). Making the custard is a two-step process, and you can refrigerate the baked ramekins for up to 3 days and then light the torch and "brûlée" them right before you're ready to put the desserts on the table. It dawned on me when we made crème brûlée at home with our Fearful Baker that it's the torch part that can be terrifying. Suddenly you have to turn into Rambo in the kitchen.

1. Heat the cream, milk, and lemon zest in a medium saucepan over medium-high heat until you can see bubbles beginning to surface around the edge of the pan. While you're heating the cream, whisk the egg yolks in a large bowl with the 6 tablespoons sugar until well combined.

2. Slowly pour the warm cream mixture into the yolks and sugar, stirring gently all the while with the whisk, making sure you scrape the side of the bowl. (You don't want to aerate the mixture but simply keep it moving so the eggs don't scramble when the warm liquid is added.) Strain the custard through a mesh sieve into a clean bowl. At this point you can bake the custards, or cool the custard mixture and refrigerate it for up to 3 days covered with plastic wrap.

3. Preheat the oven to 325°F and place a rack in the center.

4. Find a space near your oven to fill the roasting pan with water so you don't have to walk too far. Place the ramekins in the roasting pan. Transfer the custard to a glass measuring cup (or other container) with a spout, then evenly fill the ramekins to within 1/4 to 1/2 inch of the rims. Using very hot tap water (no need to bring a kettle of water to the boil), carefully—so that it's not splashed into the custards—pour the water into the roasting pan to come halfway up the ramekins. Cover the pan with aluminum foil and crimp the edges to seal well.

FB: Ooh. This whole torch idea is pretty scary.

EL: Not as scary as it seems. These butane or propane torches are great for home cooks. The big propane torch I use at the restaurant—the kind you buy at a hardware store—is even less scary to me, because you don't have to fill it with butane. When it's empty you buy a new canister.

FB: If you say so. Okay, show me what to do.

EL: Press the trigger. Hold the torch at a slight angle, so the flame is about one inch away from the surface of the custard, and move it slowly across the top. Don't let it hang out too long in any one spot or the sugar will burn. If you see it darkening, keep the torch moving. If you blacken the sugar it's gonna taste burned. What you're looking for is an even golden caramel color.

FB: Can you put the custards under a broiler instead? Seems like that would be easier.

EL: Some people do, but you have less control over the browning of the sugar, and if you leave them in too long it can curdle the custard.

FB: How far ahead can you brown the sugar?

EL: About thirty minutes. I like to do it right before I'm ready to serve them and sometimes get my guests to help me. Just make sure they haven't had too many drinks with dinner.

5. Moving carefully, transfer the roasting pan to the rack in the (preheated) oven (again you don't want any water in the custard).

6. The custards can take anywhere from 45 minutes to over 1 hour to cook, depending on the heat of your oven and the temperature of the custards when you put them in the oven. Lift the foil up halfway (if it tears you'll need to replace it). Look to see if when you gently shake the pan, the centers of the custards still jiggle a bit but don't seem loose or liquid. Start checking them every 7 minutes or so after 45 minutes.

7. Remove the foil and carefully transfer the pan from the oven to a countertop and let cool until you can pick up the ramekins with your fingers. Put them on a baking sheet or platter and refrigerate, uncovered, until cold, at least 2 hours and up to 2 days before serving. If you're storing them overnight, cover with plastic wrap.

8. No more than 30 minutes before you want to serve the custards, brûlée the sugar topping. (If it sits too long the shatteringly crisp topping you've worked so hard to achieve softens.) Sprinkle each of the custards with about 2 teaspoons of sugar, tapping and rotating each ramekin so you get as thin and (more importantly) as even a layer as possible.

9. Using your trusty torch, cook the sugar until it's golden, holding the torch 1 inch above the custard and continuously moving it back and forth and never letting it rest too long in one spot. Don't let the sugar burn. It may take you a few tries to get it right, but I guarantee your best ones will be the last couple you do, kind of like the pancake principle (the first are worst, last are best).

Honey-Roasted Pears with Chocolate Sauce and Barely Whipped Cream

Makes 6 servings

I believe there is nothing more sublime than a perfectly ripe pear, but finding one is not always easy. Pears require a lot of tender loving care before they reach the market and even more babying once you get them home to reach that state of ripe perfection. If I've gone to the trouble to get a pear to that point, I'll often simply slice it into a salad or serve it with some cheese and walnuts after dinner. One of the best ways I know to serve a slightly under-ripe pear is to roast it in the oven and baste it with a sauce. Most any kind of pear can be used, but they should be semi-ripe, not hard as rocks. Good candidates are Bartlett, Comice, and Anjou.

If I'm having company, I'll core the pears discreetly from the bottom end using a melon baller—it makes a nice presentation for guests. But for a casual family dinner I don't bother to core them. I let people use knife and fork to cut around the core.

1. Preheat the oven to 400°F.

2. Peel the pears. Leave on the stems if they have them. Cut a very thin slice off the bottom of each pear so it can stand upright in the dish without falling over.

3. Using the melon baller, cut out and discard the core: Hold the pear stem end down and from the bottom of the pear take out pieces of the core with the baller, working your way up but not all the way through to the stem. You can skip this step entirely if you'd like—see the headnote. You can also use a paring knife to carefully cut around the core and dig it out.

4. In a small bowl, stir the sugar, honey, and rum together. Pour into the baking dish. Roll the pears in the sauce to coat them. Stand them stem end up in the pan.

WHAT YOU'LL NEED

Melon baller (if you have one) or paring knife

9-inch square baking dish or similarly sized pan

Turkey baster (if you have one)

Electric stand mixer, or handheld mixer and medium bowl

6 pears, semi-ripe but not hard as rocks

1/2 cup granulated sugar

1/2 cup honey

3 tablespoons dark rum

Barely Whipped Cream
2/3 cup heavy cream

1 tablespoon granulated sugar

Chocolate Sauce
3 1/2 ounces dark chocolate (58 to 62 percent cacao), finely chopped

1/2 cup heavy cream

EL: So would you do this? I mean, would you go to the trouble of coring the pears, or would you leave in the cores and let your guests eat around them?

FB: Well, before I answer that, let me see how you do it.

EL: Do you have a melon baller at home?

5. Bake the pears for 15 minutes. Using a spoon (or a turkey baster), baste the pears with the sauce. Lay the pears on their sides and bake for another 15 minutes. Again, baste the pears with the sauce, turn them onto their other sides, and bake 10 minutes longer. The pears are done when they're soft if pierced with a small knife or bamboo skewer and are pale gold in color (discreetly poke the knife in the bottom, where the cut can't be seen). Depending on how ripe the pears are, they may need another 10 minutes or so, but keep an eye on the sauce and stir in a couple tablespoons of water if it seems to be getting dark.

6. Cradle the pears between 2 large spoons and transfer them to a platter or plate. Take care not to touch the sauce with your fingers—it's hot and sticky. If you added water to the sauce and it seems thin, reduce it over medium heat until it's syrupy. Cool the pears to room temperature, reserving the sauce in a smaller container. The pears and sauce can be kept at room temperature for 4 hours. They will keep for 4 days in the fridge, covered.

Barely Whipped Cream

7. Using the stand mixer with wire whip attachment, or a handheld mixer and medium bowl, whip the cream with the sugar on medium-high until it just holds its shape, about 2 minutes.

Chocolate Sauce

8. Put the chopped chocolate in a bowl. Warm the cream in a small saucepan over medium heat until it starts to bubble around the edges; then pour the warm cream over the chocolate. Shake the bowl a little to submerge all the chocolate pieces, then cover the bowl for several minutes. (You can cover the bowl with anything that's handy.)

9. Whisk the cream with the chocolate until it's smooth and you don't see any more chocolate pieces. The sauce will keep in the fridge for 2 weeks in a covered container.

10. To serve the pears, warm the honey sauce and the chocolate sauce in a microwave. If the pears have been refrigerated, warm them through as well. Spread about 2 tablespoons of the whipped cream in the center of each of 6 dessert plates and place a pear into the cream, stem end up. Spoon some of the reserved honey sauce over the pears along with a spoonful of the chocolate sauce. Serve extra chocolate sauce on the side.

FB: Surprisingly, I think I do. Somewhere…

EL: Take the melon baller and scoop out from the bottom end of the pear, where the core is, and go in further and further until you get two-thirds of the way to the top. You don't want to go all the way through; you just want to get out the part with the seeds.

FB: I would do that. The melon baller makes the coring pretty easy.

Key Lime Pudding Cakes

Makes 6 servings

Pudding cakes are little culinary marvels. Take what is basically a thin cake batter, fold in whipped egg whites, put the batter into a baking dish (or several ramekins as I do here), and voilà! As it bakes, the batter separates and forms a sponge cake on the top with a thick, kind of custardy pudding on the bottom. Lemon pudding cakes are common in the South, but I've swapped lemon for Key lime juice (you can buy the juice in bottles in many markets— see page 153).

To coat the insides of the ramekins with sugar, grease them with nonstick cooking spray or butter, put 1 tablespoon sugar in one, and then tilt and turn it around, tapping to coat all the inside surfaces. Tap the excess sugar into the next ramekin and repeat the process until all are dusted, adding more sugar as needed.

See Warm and Gooey Chocolate Cake (page 103) for more information on using an oven water bath.

WHAT YOU'LL NEED

6 (6-ounce) ramekins or custard cups

Electric stand mixer or a handheld mixer and medium bowl

Rubber spatula

9- by 13-inch baking pan that will hold the ramekins

2 tablespoons plus 1/2 cup granulated sugar

2 large eggs

3 tablespoons unsalted butter, at room temperature

1/4 cup unbleached all-purpose flour

1/8 teaspoon kosher salt

1 cup whole milk

1/4 cup Key lime juice

1/4 cup sliced almonds

1. Preheat the oven to 350°F and put the oven rack in the middle of the oven.

2. Grease the insides of the ramekins with nonstick cooking spray or butter and evenly coat with the 2 tablespoons sugar (see headnote). Separate the eggs into 2 bowls.

3. Using the stand mixer, or a handheld mixer and medium bowl, first on low speed and then gradually increasing the speed to medium, beat the butter and the 1/2 cup sugar together until smooth. Scrape down the side of the bowl with the rubber spatula. Beat in the egg yolks one at a time, mixing well after each addition, stopping once or twice to scrape down the side of the bowl. Reduce the speed to medium-low, add the flour and salt, and mix until everything is evenly combined. Mix in the milk, 1/3 cup at a time. Then, by hand, stir in the Key lime juice. The batter will be thin. Set aside while you whip the egg whites.

4. With a handheld or stand mixer, whisk the egg whites in a clean dry bowl on medium speed until frothy. Increase the speed to medium-high and whip until the whites hold a peak on the whisk or beaters (stop the mixer and lift to check).

5. Using the rubber spatula, gently fold the egg whites into the Key lime mixture. Using a measuring cup to scoop up the batter evenly, divide it among the ramekins so it comes to within 1/4 inch of the rims.

6. It's best to find a space near your oven to fill the baking pan with water so you don't have to walk too far. Place the ramekins in the baking pan and, using a container with a spout, slowly pour very hot tap water into the pan so that the water comes about half the way up the sides of the ramekins. Carefully transfer the baking pan to the oven. Bake the puddings until some begin to turn golden brown and have cracked slightly on the surface, about 40 minutes.

7. Remove the baking pan from the oven. Let cool until you can pick up the ramekins (15 minutes or so), then remove them from the water.

8. Spread the almonds in one layer in a small baking pan and put it in the still-warm oven. Set a timer for 10 minutes and check the nuts to see if they're a light golden brown. If not, toast 2 minutes longer. Set aside to cool.

9. Serve the cakes warm or at room temperature, the almonds scattered on top just before serving.

Nectarine and Blueberry Cobbler

Makes 6 to 8 servings

Sometimes you need a fruit dessert that you can throw together when you don't have a mixer or food processor, say, when you're staying at a vacation rental or with your bachelor son who has nothing in his kitchen. The fruit filling is versatile. You can substitute peaches for the nectarines (though they need to be peeled), raspberries for the blueberries, and in the winter you can make the cobbler with apples or pears.

WHAT YOU'LL NEED

2-quart baking dish (round, square, or oval)

Pastry blender (if you have one)

2-inch round cookie or biscuit cutter (if you have one)

Pastry brush (if you have one)

Fruit Filling

5 ripe nectarines (about 1 pound)

1 pint blueberries

1/2 cup granulated sugar

1/3 cup unbleached all-purpose flour

Cobbler Topping

1 1/4 cups unbleached all-purpose flour

7 teaspoons granulated sugar

1 teaspoon baking powder

1/8 teaspoon kosher salt

4 tablespoons (1/2 stick) cold unsalted butter

1 teaspoon pure vanilla extract

1/3 cup plus 1 tablespoon heavy cream

1. Preheat the oven to 350°F.

Fruit Filling

2. Cut the nectarines in half and remove the pits, then cut the halves into 3/4-inch pieces. In a medium bowl, gently stir the nectarine pieces and blueberries together with the sugar and flour. Put the fruit in the baking dish and set aside.

Cobbler Topping

3. In a medium bowl, stir the flour with 5 teaspoons of the sugar, the baking powder, and salt. Cut the butter into small (about 1/2-inch) cubes and bury the cubes in the flour. Using your thumbs and forefingers, pinch the butter into the flour until the small pieces are the size of small flakes or peas. Add the vanilla to the 1/3 cup cream and pour into the flour mixture. Still using your hands, stir in the cream and lightly press the mixture together until it forms a soft dough.

4. Turn the dough out onto a work surface that has been generously dusted with flour. Pat the dough gently into a circle that is about 1/2 inch thick. Using the round cookie cutter, cut the dough into circles. (You can re-pat the dough to use up the scraps.) If you don't have a cutter, pat the dough into a square and cut it into 2-inch pieces. Arrange the dough pieces on top of the fruit.

5. Brush the tops of the dough with the remaining 1 tablespoon cream and sprinkle with the remaining 2 teaspoons sugar. Bake until the cobbler is golden brown and you can see that the fruit is thick and bubbly underneath, about 40 minutes.

6. Serve warm or at room temperature with lightly whipped cream or vanilla ice cream.

Vanilla Bean Panna Cotta
with Strawberry-Cardamom Compote

Makes 8 servings

Other than tiramisu, I don't think there's a more popular Italian dessert on restaurant menus than panna cotta, nor one so perfect for a beginning baker. Not only do people love it, it's incredibly easy to make. Unlike custard, which contains eggs and is baked (making it prone to curdling), panna cotta is simply a mixture of cream, sugar, flavoring, and gelatin that sets in the refrigerator. Although panna cotta translates to "cooked cream," the cream is not really cooked at all, just heated to below the boiling point (what chefs call scalding) so that it can be infused with flavoring. Here we use vanilla beans, but I've also flavored panna cotta with toasted nuts, coffee beans, coconut, and spices like cinnamon and nutmeg. Once the still-warm liquid is infused, softened gelatin is stirred in to completely dissolve and disperse. Then the mixture is poured into molds or dessert cups and refrigerated.

WHAT YOU'LL NEED

8 (6-ounce) ramekins or custard cups set on a rimmed baking sheet or in a baking dish

3 cups heavy cream

1/2 cup whole milk

1 vanilla bean

1 envelope unflavored gelatin

3 tablespoons cool water

2/3 cup granulated sugar

Pinch kosher salt

Strawberry-Cardamom Compote

2 pints strawberries

2 tablespoons granulated sugar

1 teaspoon lemon juice

1/8 teaspoon ground cardamom

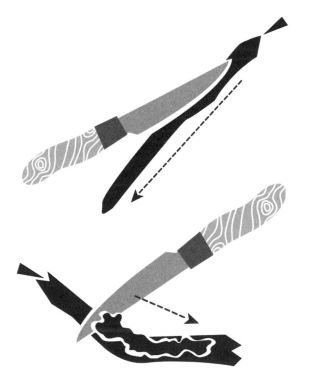

EL: I see you have the cream and milk heating. Let's deal with the vanilla bean.

FB: I've never really seen them whole. Can you buy them at any store?

EL: Most grocery and gourmet markets carry them. One problem with buying them in grocery stores is that unless the store has a good turnover, the vanilla beans may not be fresh, particularly the ones in the spice jars.

FB: How can you tell if a vanilla bean is fresh?

EL: If you can wrap it around your finger and it's supple, not brittle. That's why I like to buy them from a good online spice source or go to a market where I can do my "wrap" test or at least feel it.

FB: So, what do I do with the vanilla bean? I've only used extract.

EL: Using this paring knife, slit the pod lengthwise and then turn the knife over and, using the dull side—that's so you don't shred the pod—scrape out the tiny seeds and drop them into the cream in the pan on the stove.

FB: What do I do with the pod?

EL: Drop it in too. You're going to strain it out after the flavor has infused.

FB: Then toss it?

EL: No, you can use it again. Just rinse it, let it dry, and then wrap it in plastic to use later. After that you can bury the vanilla bean in a jar of sugar to make vanilla sugar. Even though vanilla beans are expensive, one pod can go a long way.

1. Put the cream and milk in a medium saucepan. Slice the vanilla bean lengthwise and, with the back (dull) edge of a knife, scrape out the seeds and add them, along with the vanilla bean, to the cream. Over medium heat, bring almost to the boil, or until little bubbles begin to surface at the inside edge of the pan. Remove from the heat and cover the pan with a lid or plastic wrap to let the vanilla bean steep in the cream mixture for 10 minutes.

2. While the cream is infusing, in a small bowl, sprinkle the gelatin over the water, stir it a couple of times, and let sit until the gelatin has softened, about 5 minutes.

3. Stir the sugar and salt into the cream mixture and then gently stir the softened gelatin into the cream. Be careful to stir gently—just until the gelatin is well distributed in the cream—because you don't want to create bubbles that would show up as little air pockets in the finished dish. Let cool until it's warm, stirring occasionally. Transfer to a container with a pouring spout, like a glass measuring cup. Pour into the ramekins.

4. Refrigerate until the cream has set, at least 4 hours. The panna cottas can be kept refrigerated, covered with plastic, for up to 2 days. (Any longer than 2 days and the panna cottas get rubbery.)

Strawberry-Cardamom Compote

5. Remove the green stems from the berries and cut off any white shoulders or tips (they're tasteless). Cut the berries into halves if they're small or quarters or eighths if they're large. Put them in a bowl. Just before serving or up to 30 minutes ahead, toss the berries with the sugar, lemon juice, and cardamom.

6. To serve, you can either unmold the panna cottas by running a small knife around the inside edges of the ramekins (or giving the bottoms of the ramekins a quick dip in hot water) or serve them as is, with the strawberry compote on the side or on top.

Peach-Blackberry Gratin

Makes 6 servings

With just five minutes of prep time and another couple minutes in the oven, a fruit gratin is one of the simplest ways I know to create a spur-of-the-moment dessert and to use up some of that fruit in the fruit bowl. Besides that, it's magical how even a little heat enhances the flavor and coaxes out the perfume of most any fruit.

WHAT YOU'LL NEED
9-inch baking dish (round, square, or oval)

3 large ripe peaches

1/2 pint raspberries

1/2 pint blackberries

1 1/4 cups sour cream

3 tablespoons heavy cream

1/2 cup firmly packed brown sugar

1. Preheat an oven broiler.

2. Peel, halve, and pit the peaches (I use a serrated or paring knife to peel peaches). Cut into 1-inch pieces.

3. Scatter the peaches over the bottom of the baking dish. Strew the raspberries and blackberries over and around the peaches.

4. In a small bowl, whisk the sour cream with the cream. With a large spoon, spread the mixture over the fruit to completely cover it. Sprinkle the brown sugar evenly over the cream.

5. Broil a few inches from the heat until the brown sugar is melted and bubbly, about 5 minutes. Serve hot.

Peach-Raspberry Crumble

Makes 6 to 8 servings

With juicy peaches, sweet berries, and a crisp, rich topping, I often turn to a fruit crumble in the summer. It's a great way to highlight beautiful fruit without having to go to much trouble. The recipe can be doubled or tripled and baked in a large dish to feed a crowd, or halved and served in individual gratins. You need the flour to thicken the peach juices.

WHAT YOU'LL NEED
2-quart baking dish

1 3/4 pounds ripe peaches (about 4 large)

1/2 pint raspberries

1/3 cup granulated sugar

1/4 cup unbleached all-purpose flour

Crumble Topping
10 tablespoons (1 1/4 sticks) unsalted butter

2/3 cup unbleached all-purpose flour

1/2 cup firmly packed brown sugar

3 tablespoons granulated sugar

1/2 cup slivered or sliced almonds

1. Preheat the oven to 350°F.

2. Peel, halve, and pit the peaches (I use a serrated or paring knife to peel peaches). Cut into 1-inch pieces. Toss gently in a medium bowl with the raspberries, sugar, and flour. Spread the fruit evenly in the baking dish.

Crumble Topping

3. Melt the butter and let it cool to room temperature. Transfer to a bowl and add the flour, brown sugar, granulated sugar, and almonds. Using your fingers or a fork, mix together. Distribute the topping evenly over the fruit.

4. Bake the crumble until the filling is thick and bubbly around the edges and the topping is golden, 35 to 40 minutes.

5. Let the crumble cool slightly before serving. It can be reheated.

Pecan Tea Cake with Blueberries and Sour Cream

Makes 1 cake, serving 8

This is a thin, dense, but moist cake, perfect after lunch or as an afternoon snack. Rather than serving it with whipped cream, I prefer the tang of sour cream along with the warm blueberry sauce.

WHAT YOU'LL NEED
9-inch round cake pan

Food processor

Rubber spatula

1 1/2 cups plus 3 tablespoons pecan pieces

6 large egg whites

1/2 cup plus 3 1/2 tablespoons granulated sugar

2/3 cup unbleached all-purpose flour

1 cup confectioners' sugar

1/4 teaspoon kosher salt

12 tablespoons (1 1/2 sticks) unsalted butter, melted and cooled to room temperature

1 1/2 pints blueberries

3 tablespoons water

3/4 cup sour cream

1. Preheat the oven to 350°F. Grease the bottom and side of the cake pan with nonstick cooking spray or butter and evenly coat with flour, tapping out the excess.

2. Spread all the pecan pieces in one layer in a small baking pan and put in the (preheated) oven. Set a timer for 10 minutes and check the nuts to see if they're a light golden brown. If not, toast 2 minutes longer. Set aside to cool.

3. In a medium bowl, whisk the egg whites with the 1/2 cup granulated sugar until the sugar is dissolved.

4. In the food processor, process all but 3 tablespoons of the toasted pecans with the flour, confectioners' sugar, and salt until the nuts are finely ground and look like coarse sand with a few larger visible pieces of pecans. Stir into the egg whites. Whisk in the melted butter. With the spatula, spread the batter in the prepared pan. Top with the remaining 3 tablespoons pecan pieces.

5. Bake the cake until golden brown and no longer glossy, 20 to 35 minutes. Let the cake cool in the pan.

6. While the cake is baking, put the blueberries in a small saucepan with 3 tablespoons of the remaining granulated sugar and the water. Cook over medium heat until the berries begin to pop and start to give off some juice, about 5 minutes. Set aside.

7. In a small bowl, whisk the sour cream with the remaining 1/2 tablespoon granulated sugar and set aside (can be made ahead and refrigerated for several hours or overnight in a covered container).

8. Turn the cake out onto a cake platter or plate and then turn it right side up. Serve at room temperature with the blueberries and sour cream.

Spice Cookie Napoleons with Apple Compote

Makes 8 servings

This elegant little dessert belies its humble supermarket origins. It begins with store-bought ginger cookies, which you layer with a homemade apple compote and whipped mascarpone flavored with vanilla bean. The mascarpone cream can be made before dinner (and the compote several days ahead) but the dessert should be assembled right before serving.

2 cups granulated sugar

1 cup orange juice

1 cup apple juice

2/3 cup white wine

1/2 cinnamon stick

2 large Granny Smith apples

Vanilla Mascarpone Cream
1/2 vanilla bean

2/3 cup mascarpone, softened

1/2 cup heavy cream

1 tablespoon granulated sugar

32 store-bought thin ginger cookies or Moravian cookies

1. Combine the sugar, orange and apple juices, white wine, and cinnamon stick in a medium saucepan. Bring to a boil over medium-heat and cook at a lively simmer until the liquid has reduced to 2 cups.

2. Meanwhile, peel the apples and, from the top, core them by cutting off the sides and removing the rectangular piece of core. Cut into 1/2-inch pieces. When the liquid has reduced, add the apples to the saucepan and cook, stirring frequently, until soft and translucent and the liquid is syrupy, about 15 minutes. Let cool to room temperature (add a tablespoon of water if it has thickened too much). The apple compote can be made 2 days ahead and refrigerated. Warm it to room temperature in a microwave or let sit out for an hour or so before serving.

Vanilla Mascarpone Cream

3. Slit the vanilla bean half lengthwise and, while holding the bean on one end, scrape out the seeds with the back of a knife into a medium bowl. Add the mascarpone, heavy cream, and sugar. With an electric mixer whip the cream until it forms softly mounded peaks. You can whisk it by hand with a wire whip, but the mixer is faster and easier.

4. To serve, spoon about 1 tablespoon of the mascarpone cream in the center of each of 8 dessert plates. Place 2 cookies side by side and slightly overlapping on the cream. (The cream acts like a glue to keep the cookies from sliding.) Spoon a tablespoon of the apples in the middle of the cookies and then top with a tablespoon of the cream. Layer with 2 more cookies in the same manner and then a tablespoon of cream. Finish with a tablespoon of apple compote.

Prosecco-Poached Peaches with Whipped Mascarpone Cream

Makes 6 servings

Learning how to poach fruit is a great place to begin if you're new to the dessert kitchen. The technique—if you even want to call it that—is easily mastered and little is required in the way of equipment, time, or ingredients. After you've done it a couple of times, I guarantee you won't even need to look at the recipe. While summertime for me is usually all about crisps, cobblers, and crumbles, poached fruit offers a simple but welcome change and is a nice contrast to all the smoky grilled meats coming off the barbecue.

Instead of Prosecco—Italian sparkling wine—you can use the same amount of champagne (but don't waste your vintage Dom Perignon) or Riesling. Sauternes would be good, though I would use a half bottle and an equal amount of water because it's so much richer.

WHAT YOU'LL NEED
Parchment paper

Electric stand mixer or handheld mixer and medium bowl

Large bowl that will hold a medium bowl

1 (750ml) bottle Prosecco

2 cups water

1/3 cup granulated sugar

1 cinnamon stick

6 ripe but firm peaches

Whipped Mascarpone Cream
1/2 cup heavy cream

1/4 cup mascarpone

3 tablespoons granulated sugar

1/2 teaspoon pure vanilla extract

3 tablespoons chopped pistachios for garnish

FB: So, could I use nectarines if I can't find good peaches?

EL: Yes, nectarines and peaches are interchangeable.

FB: Do you need to peel them?

EL: I never peel nectarines, but peaches I do, unless they're being poached, as they are here. Once the peaches are poached and cooled you can slip off the skins.

FB: It says to put parchment paper on top. How do I do that?

EL: You place it over the peaches and tuck it in around them. You can also use a towel, but I like parchment because I can throw it away. It keeps the peaches submerged in the liquid.

1. In a large saucepan, stir the Prosecco with the water, sugar, and cinnamon stick. Stir and bring to a boil over high heat to dissolve the sugar. Cut the peaches in half and remove the pits. Put the peaches in the hot liquid flat-side down. Tuck a piece of parchment paper or a dish towel on top of the peaches to keep them submerged in the liquid. Reduce the heat to maintain a simmer and cook for 10 minutes for medium-size peaches or 15 if the peaches are large.

2. While the peaches are poaching, prepare an ice bath by filling the large bowl half full of ice and add water to cover the ice.

3. Using a slotted spoon, gently transfer the peaches to the medium bowl. Pour the poaching liquid over the peaches. Nestle the bowl in the bowl of ice water. Let the peaches cool to room temperature.

4. Discard the skins from the peaches and refrigerate the fruit. Discard the cinnamon stick and return the poaching liquid to the saucepan. Bring to a simmer and reduce over high heat to 1 cup. Cool to room temperature. Both the peaches and the sauce can be refrigerated for up to 2 days.

Whipped Mascarpone Cream

5. Using the stand mixer with wire whip attachment, or a handheld mixer and medium bowl, whip the cream on medium speed with the mascarpone, sugar, and vanilla until it forms softly mounded peaks. The cream can be made several hours before serving, and kept covered in the refrigerator.

6. To serve, place 2 peach halves in each of 6 dessert bowls, top with dollops of whipped mascarpone cream, and spoon some sauce over the cream. Sprinkle with the chopped pistachios.

Red Berry Pavlova

Makes 6 to 8 servings

Although Australians and New Zealanders still argue over where this dish was created, there is no dispute that it was named for the Russian ballerina Anna Pavlova. Well, actually, it was named for her tutu, which the fluffy meringue shell resembled.

There are several kinds of meringues. Soft meringue, like the kind that tops pies, and hard meringue, which is used in cookies and as cake layers. This is a hard meringue, but instead of being brittle all the way through, it's baked until it's crisp on the outside and chewy-soft in the middle. Traditionally, pavlovas are served with passion fruit, kiwi, and berries. I use all berries and leave them on the tart side to contrast the sweetness of the meringue.

WHAT YOU'LL NEED
Baking or cookie sheet

Parchment paper

Electric stand mixer or handheld mixer and medium bowl

Rubber spatula

3 large egg whites

Pinch kosher salt

1 cup plus 1 tablespoon granulated sugar

1 teaspoon white or rice vinegar

1 teaspoon pure vanilla extract

1 pint strawberries

1/2 pint raspberries

1 cup heavy cream

1. Preheat the oven to 350°F. Line the baking sheet with parchment paper.

2. In the stand mixer with the wire whisk attachment, or using a handheld mixer and a medium bowl, whisk the egg whites and salt on medium speed until frothy. With the machine running, add the 1 cup sugar in a slow, steady stream. Increase the speed to medium-high and whip until the whites hold stiff glossy peaks on the whisk or beaters (stop the mixer and lift to check). On low speed, mix in the vinegar and vanilla.

3. Plop the whipped whites in a large mound in the center of the parchment-lined baking sheet using the rubber spatula. Spread it out into a 6-inch disk. Put the pan in the oven and immediately turn the oven temperature down to 300°F. Bake the meringue for 45 minutes. Turn off the heat but leave the pavlova in the oven with the door slightly ajar—leave it open as though you were broiling something or prop open with a wooden spoon—for 5 hours. You can leave it in the turned-off oven overnight if you want to make it the day before.

4. Remove the green stems from the strawberries, slice them, and, in a medium bowl, toss gently with the raspberries and remaining 1 tablespoon sugar (if the berries aren't particularly sweet add another tablespoon of sugar). Let the berries sit for about 15 minutes so they release some of their juices.

5. Using the stand mixer with wire whip attachment, or handheld mixer and medium bowl, whip the cream on medium speed until it forms softly mounded peaks. The cream can be made several hours before serving and kept covered in the refrigerator.

6. To serve, place the meringue disk on a platter. Spread on the whipped cream and spoon over the berries and their juices. Cut into wedges and serve right away.

Dried Cherry and Apricot Bread Pudding

Makes 6 to 8 servings

Bread pudding is the frugal housewife's time-honored way of making use of those day-old loaves. If I have the stale bread, great; if not I'll use a fresh loaf and toast it first in the preheated oven while I'm prepping all the other ingredients for the pudding. Not having leftover bread shouldn't stop you from making this comforting, old-fashioned dessert.

WHAT YOU'LL NEED

2-quart baking dish

1 piece French or Italian bread (about 12 inches long)

1 cup (6 ounces) dried apricots

1 cup (6 ounces) dried cherries

3/4 cup dark rum

1/2 cup water

4 large eggs

3 large egg yolks

3/4 cup granulated sugar

1/8 teaspoon kosher salt

1 teaspoon pure vanilla extract

2 1/2 cups heavy cream

1 1/2 cups whole milk

1. Preheat the oven to 350°F.

2. Slice the bread 1 inch thick and then tear or cut the slices into 1-inch pieces so that you end up with 5 cups. Set aside.

3. Cut the apricots into pieces the same size as the cherries (I like to use scissors to cut dried fruit).

4. Put the cherries and apricots in a small saucepan with the rum and water. Bring to a boil over medium heat, then turn off heat and let the fruit sit for 15 minutes to soften and plump. (If the rum ignites when it comes to the boil simply turn off the heat and cover the pot; the fire will go out.)

5. Strain the fruit, reserving the liquid. Scatter the fruit evenly over the bottom of the baking dish. Arrange the bread over the fruit.

6. Return the reserved liquid to the saucepan and reduce to 2 tablespoons over medium-high heat. Watch closely—once it starts boiling it reduces quickly.

7. In a medium bowl, whisk the rum reduction with the eggs, egg yolks, sugar, salt, and vanilla. Whisk in the cream and milk. Pour the egg mixture over the bread and fruit in the baking dish.

8. Bake for about 40 minutes, or until a small knife inserted in the middle comes out coated with a thick custard. Let cool slightly before serving.

Strawberry-Rhubarb Crumble

Makes 6 to 8 servings

If you grew up in the country, you're probably fairly familiar with rhubarb. This vegetable (yes, it's not a fruit) thrives in cold winters. In California we start seeing field-grown rhubarb in the markets in spring, but it can come in as late as September. The colors of the stalks vary from green to deep red and are no indication of quality. Hot-house rhubarb is generally bright red, while field-grown rhubarb is more green. Just look for stalks that are neither very thin nor very thick and are sturdy and crisp.

WHAT YOU'LL NEED
2-quart (or 9- by 13-inch) baking dish

Crumble Topping
10 tablespoons (1 1/4 sticks) unsalted butter

2/3 cup unbleached all-purpose flour

1/2 cup firmly packed brown sugar

3 tablespoons granulated sugar

Fruit Filling
2 1/2 pints (about 2 1/4 pounds) strawberries

2 large stalks rhubarb (about 12 ounces)

2/3 cup granulated sugar

3 tablespoons cornstarch

Grated zest of 1 lemon

Crumble Topping

1. Melt the butter and let it cool to room temperature. Put it in a bowl with the flour, brown sugar, and granulated sugar and mix together with your fingers or a fork. You can make the topping ahead of time and keep in a covered container in the fridge for up to 3 days.

2. Preheat the oven to 350°F.

Fruit Filling

3. Remove the green stems from the strawberries, cut into 3/4-inch pieces, and transfer to a medium bowl. You should have about 4 cups.

4. Cut the rhubarb into 3/4-inch pieces to measure about 2 1/4 cups. Add to the bowl with the strawberries. Add the sugar, cornstarch, and lemon zest and toss together until everything is evenly combined.

5. Spread the fruit evenly in the baking dish. Distribute the topping evenly over the fruit. Bake the crumble until the filling is thick and bubbly and the topping is golden, 35 to 40 minutes.

6. Let the crumble cool slightly before serving. It can be reheated.

Strawberry Shortcakes

Makes 6 servings

When you don't have access to a food processor or stand mixer but want to make pie dough or shortcake, you can go the low-tech route and use two knives or rub the fat and flour together with your fingers to "cut" the butter into the flour. Another alternative is a pastry blender, an inexpensive and undervalued tool our grandmothers used to use. It's made of several thin wires attached in a U-shape to a handle. You simply put the butter and flour into a bowl and use the pastry blender to press and cut the butter into little pieces that are coated with flour.

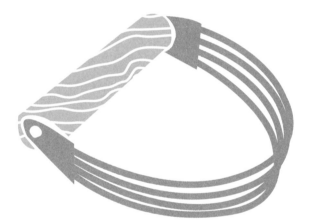

WHAT YOU'LL NEED
Baking or cookie sheet

Parchment paper

3-inch biscuit or cookie cutter (if you have one)

Electric stand mixer or a handheld mixer and medium bowl

Pastry blender

Shortcakes
1 1/2 cups unbleached all-purpose flour

3 tablespoons plus 1 teaspoon granulated sugar

2 teaspoons baking powder

1/4 teaspoon kosher salt

4 tablespoons (1/2 stick) cold unsalted butter

3/4 cup plus 1 tablespoon heavy cream

Strawberry Compote
2 1/2 pints (about 2 1/4 pounds) strawberries

1 cup granulated sugar

1/2 teaspoon kosher salt

Juice of 1 lemon

Whipped Cream
1 cup heavy cream

3 tablespoons granulated sugar

1/2 teaspoon pure vanilla extract

Shortcakes

1. Preheat the oven to 350°F. Line the baking sheet with parchment paper.

2. In a medium bowl, stir the flour with the 3 tablespoons sugar, the baking powder, and salt. Cut the butter into 1-inch pieces and scatter over the flour. Using your hands, rub the flour with the butter until the pieces are the size of small peas. Slowly pour in the 3/4 cup cream, stirring and tossing with a fork or your hands until the dough comes together.

3. On a lightly floured work surface, pat or roll out the dough until it is 1 inch thick. Cut into 3-inch circles using the round biscuit cutter or a straight-sided drinking glass. Cut as close as possible to minimize scraps. Piece scraps together and cut again until you have 6 shortcakes. Place on the parchment-lined baking sheet. Brush the tops with the remaining 1 tablespoon cream and sprinkle with the remaining 1 teaspoon sugar.

4. Bake the shortcakes until golden brown, about 25 minutes. Let cool on the baking sheet to room temperature.

Strawberry Compote

5. Remove the green stems from the strawberries and cut into quarters or sixths if they're large. Put them in a saucepan with the sugar and salt. Cook over medium-low heat for 1 minute. Turn the heat up to medium and continue to cook for 3 minutes. Remove the pan from heat and stir in the lemon juice. The compote can be prepared 1 to 2 hours ahead and kept covered at room temperature.

Whipped Cream

6. Using the stand mixer with wire whip attachment, or a handheld mixer and medium bowl, whip the cream on medium speed with the sugar and vanilla until it forms softly mounded peaks. The cream can be made several hours before serving and kept covered in the refrigerator. If it has thinned out you may need to rewhip it slightly before serving.

7. To serve, split the shortcakes in half horizontally and place a bottom half on each of 6 dessert plates. Spoon on the strawberry compote, then mound with dollops of the whipped cream. Place the shortcake tops on the cream.

Basic Trifle Cake

Makes 1 (9- by 13-inch) cake

This is not a cake designed to stand alone. It's a bit dry and bland on purpose—so that it can soak up juices and flavors when it's layered into a trifle and doesn't compete flavor-wise. It also won't fall apart as more tender cakes would.

WHAT YOU'LL NEED
9- by 13-inch cake pan

Electric stand mixer or handheld mixer and medium bowl

Rubber spatula

1 cup unbleached all-purpose flour

1 teaspoon baking powder

1/2 teaspoon kosher salt

1/2 cup whole milk

1 tablespoon unsalted butter

2 large eggs

3/4 cup granulated sugar

2 teaspoons pure vanilla extract

1. Preheat the oven to 350°F. Grease the bottom and side of the cake pan with nonstick cooking spray or butter and evenly coat with flour, tapping out excess. Line the bottom of the pan with parchment paper.

2. Over a bowl or piece of parchment, sift the flour and baking powder together in a sifter or in a fine strainer by gently tapping your hand against the edge. Add the salt (you can just leave it on top of the flour pile because it gets mixed in later). Set aside.

3. In a small saucepan, heat the milk with the butter until it's very hot but not boiling. Turn off the heat and let sit on the burner, stirring once or twice until the butter melts.

4. Using the stand mixer, or a handheld mixer and medium bowl, on medium-high speed, beat the eggs for 1 minute. Add the sugar and beat on high speed until the mixture has thickened and leaves a trail when you lift the beaters of the mixer. On low speed, stir in the hot milk and the vanilla, then the sifted flour mixture. Mix until everything is well blended. With the rubber spatula, spread the batter evenly in the prepared pan.

5. Bake until a bamboo skewer or toothpick inserted in the middle comes out clean, about 15 minutes. Cool the cake to room temperature.

6. Run a small knife around the inside edge of the pan, then remove the cake by flipping it over onto a platter or the counter.

Berry Trifle

Makes 8 to 10 servings

Make this in summertime when berries are plentiful.

WHAT YOU'LL NEED

Electric stand mixer or handheld mixer and medium bowl

2-quart glass bowl

2 pints blueberries

1/2 cup plus 2 tablespoons granulated sugar

2 cups heavy cream

1 teaspoon pure vanilla extract

Basic Trifle Cake (facing page)

1 pint raspberries

1. Put 1 pint of the blueberries and the 1/2 cup sugar in a small saucepan and cook over medium heat, stirring occasionally, until the blueberries start to give off juice and the sugar dissolves, about 5 minutes. Stir in the other pint of blueberries and remove the pan from the heat. Let cool to room temperature.

2. Using the stand mixer with wire whip attachment, or a handheld mixer and medium bowl, whip the cream on medium-high speed with the remaining 2 tablespoons sugar and the vanilla until it forms softly mounded peaks.

3. Cut the trifle cake into quarters, then cut each in half horizontally so you have 8 (6 1/2- by 4 1/2-inch) slabs of cake.

4. To assemble the trifle, spread 1/3 cup of the blueberry sauce in the bottom of the bowl. Top with a layer of cake, cutting or tearing it so it fits inside the bowl. Spread another 1/3 cup blueberry sauce over the cake. Spread half of the whipped cream on top of the blueberries. Distribute half of the raspberries over the cream.

5. Repeat layering the trifle with the remaining cake, blueberry sauce, cream, and finally the remaining raspberries. Refrigerate the trifle for 1 hour or overnight.

Apple–Crème Fraîche Trifle

Makes 10 to 12 servings

The British love trifles, an ethereal layered concoction of sponge cake, whipped cream, and berry jam. They like to include crème anglaise (rich custard) and a snockering amount of liquor in the dessert. I've eliminated the thin custard because I think it makes the trifle a trifle too soupy, and I prefer to omit the booze so you can focus on the fruit flavors. Trifles are the kind of dessert where you don't have to be that precise. Cake or ladyfingers, jam or sautéed fresh fruit, whipped cream or crème fraîche, no matter how you make it, you can't mess it up. In fact, it's a well-known chefs' secret that to disguise a failed cake you tear it to pieces, put it in a glass bowl with whipped cream, and call it a trifle. I also call a trifle a "cream dream."

There are large-footed glass bowls made just for trifles. Any glass bowl will do, as it shows off the layers. Actually any bowl will do, since you scoop out servings anyway, but glass is prettier.

WHAT YOU'LL NEED
2-quart glass bowl

6 red apples, any kind except Red Delicious

2/3 cup granulated sugar

1/2 teaspoon lemon juice

1 cinnamon stick

1/4 teaspoon kosher salt

1 cup water plus a little more if needed

Basic Trifle Cake (page 196)

3/4 cup Caramel Sauce (page 244) or good-quality store-bought caramel sauce, warmed but not hot

1 1/2 cups crème fraîche

Our Fearful Baker has already made the components for the trifle: the applesauce, cake, and caramel sauce.

FB: I've had trifles before, but I never thought they were all that special.

EL: That's probably because too many chefs don't think enough about all the layers and texture. You can use up ingredients, but the balance has to be right.

FB: How do I cut the cake? The recipe says to cut it horizontally. I don't get that.

EL: What I mean is once you've cut it into four rectangles, take your knife and cut it with the blade parallel to the cutting board.

FB: Like you were cutting a French roll for a sandwich?

EL: Exactly. What you'll end up with are what I call thin "slabs" of cake.

FB: How do I put it together?

EL: Simply start layering: cake, apples, caramel, cream, then cake, apples, caramel, and cream. Till they're used up.

FB: Well that's pretty easy. Except all those components.

EL: I understand, but it wasn't difficult and the good news is that you can make the components in advance.

FB: That's true.

1. Peel the apples and core from the top by cutting off the sides and removing the rectangular cores. Cut into 1/4-inch pieces.

2. Put the apples in a large saucepan with the sugar, lemon juice, cinnamon stick, salt, and 1/2 cup of the water. Cover the pan and cook over medium-high heat, stirring frequently for 15 minutes. Add another 1/2 cup water, reduce the heat to medium, and continue to cook (uncovered) until the fruit pieces have broken up, are soft, and look like chunky applesauce, 10 to 15 minutes longer. During cooking add a little water if the apples seem dry. If you add too much and the applesauce becomes thin, just cook a few minutes more with the cover off. The apples should be soft. Remove the cinnamon stick and let the applesauce cool to room temperature.

3. Cut the trifle cake into quarters, then cut each quarter in half horizontally so you have 8 (6 1/2- by 4 1/2-inch) slabs of cake.

4. To assemble the trifle, begin by spreading 1 cup of the applesauce in the bottom of the glass bowl. Top with a layer of cake, cutting or tearing it so it fits inside the bowl. Spread another 1 cup applesauce over the cake. Spoon and spread 1/4 cup caramel sauce over the applesauce and top with a 1/2 cup layer of the crème fraîche.

5. Repeat layering with the cake, applesauce, caramel sauce, and crème fraîche. You should have 3 layers of cake, 4 layers of applesauce. Refrigerate the trifle for 1 hour or overnight before serving.

Blackberry-Lime Cream Trifle

Makes 8 to 10 servings

Frozen blackberries are perfectly acceptable in this recipe and much cheaper than fresh since you need so many. Just be sure to buy a brand without any added sugar or syrup so you can add your own sugar to taste.

WHAT YOU'LL NEED
Food processor

Electric stand mixer or handheld mixer and medium bowl

2-quart glass bowl

1 1/2 pounds frozen no-sugar-added blackberries, defrosted and drained of liquid

About 1/2 cup granulated sugar

1 cup heavy cream

1/2 cup sour cream

Grated zest of 2 limes

Basic Trifle Cake (page 196)

1. Puree one-third of the blackberries in the food processor. Strain through a mesh strainer into a medium bowl. Stir in another third of the berries and 3 tablespoons of the sugar. Taste for sweetness and add more sugar if necessary. Set aside.

2. Using the stand mixer with wire whip attachment, or a handheld mixer and medium bowl, whip the cream and sour cream with 3 tablespoons of the sugar and the lime zest on medium-high speed until it forms softly mounded peaks.

3. Cut the trifle cake into quarters, then cut each in half horizontally so you have 8 (6 1/2- by 4 1/2-inch) slabs of cake.

4. To assemble the trifle, spread 1/2 cup of the pureed blackberries in the bottom of the bowl. Top with a layer of cake, cutting or tearing it so it fits inside the bowl. Spread another 1/2 cup of the pureed blackberries over the cake. Spread 1/2 cup of the whipped cream on top of the blackberries.

5. Repeat layering the trifle with the remaining cake, pureed blackberries, and cream, finishing with a layer of cream. Toss the remaining whole berries in a bowl with 2 tablespoons sugar (or more to taste). Spread over the final topping of cream. Refrigerate the trifle for 1 hour or overnight before serving.

Banana-Coffee Ice Cream Sundaes

Makes 4 servings

Similar to Bananas Foster—the quintessential New Orleans dessert made famous at Brennan's Restaurant—this is a nice dessert to serve after a rich and spicy dinner. I think coffee ice cream is a better match than vanilla. Choose the rum as you would for mojitos: dark over light for its richer, deeper flavor.

The recipe can be easily doubled to serve 8, but use a bigger pan or cook the bananas in 2 batches.

WHAT YOU'LL NEED
Ice cream scoop (if you have one)

1 cup orange juice

2 tablespoons dark rum

2 tablespoons granulated sugar

4 tablespoons (1/2 stick) unsalted butter, softened

2 large bananas, halved lengthwise and then cut into 1-inch pieces

2 tablespoons heavy cream

8 scoops good-quality store-bought coffee ice cream

1. Combine the orange juice, rum, and sugar in a large sauté pan or skillet and cook over medium heat until the liquid is reduced by almost half, 2 to 3 minutes. Add the butter and let it melt.

2. Add the bananas and cream and cook for a couple of minutes, until the bananas are warmed through.

3. Place 2 scoops of ice cream in each of 4 dessert bowls. Top with the bananas and sauce and serve immediately.

No Oven Required

If it's actually a fear of "baking" that gets in your way, then I think you'll find the recipes in this chapter, as opposed to say the Pies and Tarts or the Cakes chapters, to be a friendly way for you to ease yourself into dessert making.

Few require anything more difficult than melting chocolate or whipping cream, and they're also much more quickly put together, sometimes in just minutes from start to finish. One of the best things about not having the need for an oven is that you're relieved of the worry of "Is it done yet?" or "Did I overcook it?"

The recipes are divided into loose categories that include candies—truffles, bars, and barks—where the only real "technique" you need to learn is how to melt chocolate and puddings, mousses, and creams that sometimes need, in addition to melted chocolate, whipped cream and/or custard. And this is where I should mention that while this chapter is a No-Oven Zone, that does not mean it is also a No-Heat Required Zone. A number of the recipes call for sauces, such as butterscotch, or custards that need to be cooked on top of the stove. To keep true to the no-oven theme, I don't toast nuts used in this chapter but feel free to do so if you want.

The easiest recipes, and personal favorites of mine that I invariably turn to when I'm looking for something to make on short notice (or when I simply want to take it easy), are what I like to call "frozen assets." These are desserts that can be assembled with store-bought ice cream, sauce (which you can make yourself or buy), and fresh or pureed fruit.

Make-Ahead and Storage Tips

Most creams and custards will last a couple days in the refrigerator if they are well wrapped. Cream can pick up other odors from the fridge, so don't leave it uncovered.

For custards, make sure the ingredients are well whisked together before putting them in the saucepan. For the first couple of minutes, while the pan is heating, it's not necessary to stir more than a few times. Once the pan is hot you need to stir continually though not obsessively. (I wouldn't, however, get on the computer or do the laundry.) You're preventing the custard from sitting on the bottom of the pan so long that the eggs curdle. If you do get some lumps, after cooking push the custard through a strainer and you should be fine.

If you want to cool custard quickly, put the bowl of custard in an ice bath (a larger bowl filled with ice water) and stir it occasionally until it's cold. Afterward when you put the custard in the fridge, place a piece of plastic wrap directly onto the surface to prevent a skin from forming.

If ice cream is too hard to work with (to put in pans or molds), rather than letting it soften at room temperature on the counter, put the carton in the fridge for 10 minutes or zap it in the microwave for 10 seconds. Freezing times can vary a great deal depending on your freezer (whether it's a stand-alone, bottom or top compartment, and how full it is).

Chocolate that needs to harden can be left on the countertop, unless your kitchen is warm or humid. In that case put it in the freezer (which is drier than the fridge).

Dark Chocolate Truffles

Makes about 45 truffles

The technique for making chocolate truffles is straightforward and basically the same for the Orange Truffles and the two variations: The first step is to infuse cream with flavoring—orange peel, coffee beans, or mint leaves—then strain. Next, chocolate is melted in the cream, butter is stirred in, and the mixture is chilled. It is then scooped and rolled into irregularly shaped balls (which resemble the savory truffle), and finally rolled in cocoa powder. (For the Milk Chocolate Truffles on page 205, the cream is not flavored.)

A small, spring-loaded scoop (about 1 inch wide) is a good investment if you want to make a lot of truffles quickly.

Grated zest of 1 orange

1/3 cup heavy cream

8 ounces dark chocolate (58 to 62 percent cacao), chopped or broken into 1-inch pieces

3 tablespoons unsalted butter, softened

About 1/4 cup cocoa powder for dusting truffles

Orange Truffles

1. Put the orange zest and the cream in a small saucepan and heat over medium-high until bubbles begin to appear around the edge. Remove from the heat and let sit 15 minutes to infuse the cream with the orange. Strain the cream through a mesh sieve into a bowl and discard the orange zest. Return the cream to the saucepan and heat until hot. Remove the pan from the heat, add the chocolate, and let sit 5 minutes. Stir until smooth. Stir in the butter. Transfer the chocolate cream to a shallow dish or pie pan and refrigerate until it is firm enough to scoop, about 1 hour.

2. Put the cocoa in a shallow dish or pie pan.

3. With a teaspoon measure, scoop out the chocolate using a flat spoonful for each truffle. Between your palms, roll the chocolate pieces into balls, then toss the balls in the cocoa so they're completely coated. If at anytime they get warm and stick to your hands, put them back in the refrigerator for a bit to firm up.

4. The truffles will keep in a covered container in the fridge for 1 week and should be served cold.

Coffee Truffles

Follow the recipe for Orange Truffles, substituting 1/4 cup coffee beans for the orange zest in step 1.

Mint Truffles

Follow the recipe for Orange Truffles, substituting 1/4 cup loosely packed fresh mint leaves for the orange zest in step 1.

Milk Chocolate Truffles

Makes about 36 truffles

1/2 cup heavy cream

3 ounces dark chocolate (58 to 62 percent cacao), chopped or broken into 1-inch pieces

6 ounces milk chocolate, chopped or broken into 1-inch pieces

3 tablespoons unsalted butter, softened

About 1/3 cup cocoa powder for dusting the truffles

1. Heat the cream over medium-high heat until bubbles begin to appear around the edge. Turn off the heat and add the dark and milk chocolates; let sit 5 minutes. Stir until the chocolate is melted, then stir in the butter.

2. Put the cocoa powder in a shallow dish or pie pan.

3. With a teaspoon measure, scoop out the chocolate using a flat spoonful for each truffle. Between your palms, roll the chocolate pieces into balls, then toss the balls in the cocoa so they're coated with the powder. If at anytime they get warm and stick to your hands, put them back in the refrigerator for a bit to firm up.

4. The truffles will keep in a covered container in the fridge for 1 week and should be served cold.

Bittersweet Chocolate Nut Clusters

Makes about 30 pieces

Can you think of anything better than a lot of crunchy, nutty goodness surrounded by chocolate? I didn't think so. Neither can I.

Be careful when melting chocolate not to overheat it, otherwise it will develop a speckled white "bloom" when it cools. The bloom doesn't affect the taste of the candy, just its appearance. The chocolate doesn't need to get very hot to melt.

Cocoa nibs are small shaved pieces from the edible part of roasted cocoa beans. I use them for their crunch and a boost of chocolate flavor.

WHAT YOU'LL NEED
Saucepan and metal bowl, or double boiler if you have one

Rubber spatula

Baking or cookie sheet

Parchment paper

7 ounces dark chocolate (58 to 62 percent cacao), chopped or broken into 1-inch pieces

2/3 cup dry-roasted peanuts

2/3 cup dried cherries

1/4 cup cocoa nibs or small chocolate chips

1 1/4 cups puffed wheat cereal

1. Melt the chocolate by putting it in a heat-proof bowl set over a saucepan of simmering water, making sure the bowl does not touch the water. (You can use a double boiler if you have one.) Stir and scrape the side of the bowl occasionally with the rubber spatula until the chocolate is smooth and evenly melted.

2. Remove the bowl from the heat and stir in the nuts, dried cherries, cocoa nibs, and puffed wheat.

3. Line the baking sheet with parchment paper. Place tablespoon mounds of the chocolate mixture on the parchment-lined baking sheet and let them sit until they harden, about 1 hour. Store at room temperature in a covered container for up to 1 week.

Almond Sundaes
with Espresso–White Chocolate Sauce

Makes 6 servings

Having this ridiculously easy to make sauce in the refrigerator when you need a quick dessert is like having money in the bank. The sauce, along with others in this book, keeps for weeks in the fridge, ready to be pulled out on a moment's notice and turned into the makings of an impromptu sundae.

WHAT YOU'LL NEED
1/2 cup sliced almonds

Good-quality store-bought chocolate ice cream

Good-quality store-bought vanilla ice cream

Espresso–White Chocolate Sauce
1/3 cup heavy cream

1 tablespoon brewed espresso or strong coffee

5 ounces white chocolate, chopped or broken into 1-inch pieces

Put 1 scoop of each flavor of ice cream into each of 6 bowls and top with some of the sauce (see below). Don't be stingy lest your guests complain. Sprinkle over the almonds.

Espresso–White Chocolate Sauce
In a small saucepan, heat the cream with the espresso. Place the chocolate in a bowl and pour the hot cream over. Stir a couple of times and cover. Let sit 5 minutes so that the cream can melt the chocolate. Gently whisk until smooth.

> **FB:** I have to admit that I always stop by the bakery on the way home if I need a dessert.

> **EL:** That's why this sauce is so great. A lot of times, I'm not afraid to say, I use store-bought ingredients, like ice cream, to put into a sundae or cookie sandwiches. If you make the sauce, or the cookies, you can still call it a homemade dessert.

> **FB:** Okay, so the cream is starting to bubble around the edge of the saucepan. I just pour it over the chocolate?

> **EL:** That's it. Remove the pan from the heat and pour it over the chocolate. Put the lid on, and then whisk it in five minutes and the chocolate will have melted.

Chocolate–Peanut Butter Bites

Makes about 64 (1-inch) squares

Use whatever kind of nut you like, or a mixture, if you're not big on peanuts.

WHAT YOU'LL NEED

8-inch square baking pan

Saucepan and metal bowl, or double boiler if you have one

Rubber spatula

16 ounces dark chocolate (58 to 62 percent cacao), chopped or broken into 1-inch pieces

1 cup cornflakes, or other flaked cereal

1 cup dry-roasted peanuts

1/2 cup smooth peanut butter

1/4 teaspoon kosher salt

FB: It's funny that you mention using a double boiler. Just a couple of weeks ago I was preparing to cook something and the recipe called for one and I had to phone my mom to ask what it was.

EL: The French call it a "bain-marie" (which translates as "Mary's bath")—a much prettier name I might add. A double boiler is a two-part saucepan, one that fits snugly inside the other. You put water in the bottom and the ingredient to be cooked in the top and bring the water to a boil. We use makeshift double boilers all the time in the pastry kitchen for those tasks where you want a gentle heat, say for melting chocolate as in this recipe, or cooking custards.

FB: What if I don't have one? How do I make one?

EL: All you need is a metal bowl that can fit over a tall saucepan. You need to make sure that when you add the water, it doesn't touch the bottom of the bowl, which would defeat the purpose of diffusing the heat.

1. Spritz the bottom and sides of the baking pan lightly with nonstick cooking spray. This is so that the plastic wrap will adhere to the pan, so don't obsess about coating it well. Line the pan with a piece of plastic wrap, making sure it evenly runs up the sides of the pan and pressing it neatly into the corners so that the plastic doesn't get folded up into the chocolate mixture.

2. Melt the chocolate by putting it in the bowl set over a saucepan of simmering water, making sure the bowl does not touch the water. (You can use a double boiler if you have one.) Stir and scrape the side of the bowl occasionally with the rubber spatula until the chocolate is smooth and evenly melted.

3. In a large bowl, crush the cornflakes with your hands to break them up slightly. Stir in the peanuts, peanut butter, and salt. Using the rubber spatula, pour in the melted chocolate and stir so that all the peanuts are coated with chocolate and everything looks well combined.

4. Again using the rubber spatula, spread the chocolate mixture in the pan, and, with a light touch, smooth the top so that it's even.

5. Let the pan sit at room temperature for at least 3 hours or until firmed up. Using the sides of the plastic wrap as handles, lift the whole chocolate square out of the pan. Peel off the plastic and place it on a cutting surface. With a sharp knife, cut the chocolate into even 1-inch squares. If you want a really professional look, or if you're the kind of person who straightens hanging pictures in other people's homes, use a ruler so your squares are perfect.

6. These little bites can be kept in a covered container at room temperature for several weeks, but only if you hide them.

Hedgehogs

Makes 81 (1-inch) squares

Hedgehogs are an Australian concoction of chocolate, caramel, shortbread, and nuts, all mixed up together, spread into a pan to set, and cut into bars. Straightforward and absolutely delicious.

When I first tested this recipe I used Scottish shortbread, but found that the pieces were so thick there was barely enough chocolate to hold them together. Besides that, the imports made these simple treats way too expensive. The ideal shortbread cookie turned out to be from Pepperidge Farm, the well-known supermarket brand—perfect size and price.

WHAT YOU'LL NEED

9-inch square cake pan

Saucepan and metal bowl, or double boiler if you have one

Rubber spatula

36 Pepperidge Farm Chessman cookies (1 1/2 packages) or other shortbread cookie of the same thickness (about 1/4 inch)

2/3 cup Caramel Sauce (page 244), or good-quality store-bought caramel sauce

1/2 cup confectioners' sugar

7 ounces dark chocolate (58 to 62 percent cacao), chopped or broken into 1-inch pieces

7 tablespoons unsalted butter

2/3 cup sliced almonds, chopped

1. Grease the bottom and sides of the cake pan with nonstick cooking spray or butter. This is just so that the plastic wrap will adhere to the pan, so don't obsess about coating it well. Line the pan with a piece of plastic wrap, making sure it evenly runs up the sides of the pan and pressing it neatly into the corners so that the plastic doesn't get folded up into the cookie mixture.

2. Arrange an even layer of cookies in the pan (about 20 cookies), cutting them as necessary so they fit to the edges of the pan. Spread the caramel sauce over the cookies, completely covering them. Chop the remaining 16 cookies into about 1/4-inch crumbles and set aside.

3. Over a bowl or onto a piece of parchment, sift the confectioners' sugar in a fine strainer by gently tapping your hand against the edge.

4. Melt the chocolate and butter by putting them in the metal bowl set over a saucepan of simmering water, making sure the bowl does not touch the water. (You can use a double boiler if you have one.) Stir and scrape the side of the bowl occasionally with the rubber spatula until the chocolate is smooth and evenly melted.

5. Remove bowl from the saucepan and add the sifted sugar to the chocolate. Stir until everything is well blended. Add the almonds and cookie crumbles and stir with the rubber spatula so they're well coated with the chocolate.

6. Spread the chocolate mixture evenly over the caramel sauce in the pan. Refrigerate until firm, about 1 hour.

7. To serve, using the sides of the plastic wrap as handles, lift the whole square out of the pan. Peel off the plastic and put it on a cutting surface. With a super-sharp, thin-bladed knife, cut the chocolate into even 1-inch squares. If you want a really professional look, use a ruler so your squares are perfect. Keep refrigerated until serving time.

Chocolate Bark

Makes about 24 pieces

Chocolate bark—squares or irregular pieces of good-quality dark chocolate studded with dried fruit, nuts, or candies—can be found in many high-end market and candy shops. I doubt you'll be surprised to hear that it's much cheaper to make your own, but you may not realize how easy it is. Melt some chocolate, stir in a combination of nuts (or nuts and marshmallows as in one of the recipes that follow), spread the mixture out onto a baking sheet, and let it harden. Don't feel limited to the two recipes here; you can experiment with other ingredients, including different chocolates. Chocolate bark makes a great gift. If you like 70 percent chocolate, you can substitute it.

WHAT YOU'LL NEED

Saucepan and metal bowl, or double boiler if you have one

Rubber spatula

Baking or cookie sheet

Parchment paper

Offset spatula if you have one

Chocolate Nut Bark
8 ounces dark chocolate (58 to 62 percent cacao), chopped or broken into 1-inch pieces

1 cup whole natural almonds

Rocky Road Bark
2/3 cup hazelnuts (or any nut you prefer)

12 ounces dark chocolate (58 to 62 percent cacao), chopped or broken into 1-inch pieces

2/3 cup mini marshmallows

Chocolate Nut Bark

1. Melt the chocolate by putting it in a heat-proof bowl set over a saucepan of simmering water, making sure the bowl does not touch the water. (You can use a double boiler if you have one.) Stir and scrape the side of the bowl occasionally with the rubber spatula until the chocolate is smooth and evenly melted. Stir in the almonds.

2. Line the baking sheet with parchment paper. Using a spatula (offset works well if you have one), spread the chocolate and almonds on the parchment in a slab that is about 3/8 inch thick.

3. Refrigerate the chocolate until hard, about 1 hour. Break into pieces and keep in a covered container in the fridge for up to 2 weeks or at (cool) room temperature for 1 week.

Rocky Road Bark

1. If you're using hazelnuts, put them in a colander and rub them with a clean kitchen towel to remove some of the skins. (If you don't have a colander, just rub them in the towel.) Don't worry about getting all the skins—you just want to remove the loose pieces. Chop the nuts into 1/4-inch pieces and set aside.

2. Melt the chocolate by putting it in a heat-proof bowl set over a saucepan of simmering water, making sure the bowl does not touch the water. (You can use a double boiler if you have one.) Stir and scrape the side of the bowl occasionally with the rubber spatula until the chocolate is smooth and evenly melted. Remove the pan from the heat and stir in half the marshmallows and half the hazelnuts. Let cool to room temperature.

3. Line the baking sheet with parchment paper. Using a spatula (an offset spatula works well if you have one) spread the chocolate and hazelnuts on the parchment in a slab that is about 3/8 inch thick. Press the remaining marshmallows and hazelnuts into the chocolate.

4. Let the chocolate sit at room temperature until hard, 2 to 3 hours. Break into pieces and keep in a covered container in the fridge for up to 2 weeks or at (cool) room temperature for 1 week.

Honey Fruit Bites

Makes about 28 (1-inch) balls

I like to give these as holiday gifts to friends who aren't into chocolate. Use a good-quality honey for maximum flavor.

WHAT YOU'LL NEED
Food processor

1 cup prunes, pitted

1 cup dried cherries

2 tablespoons honey

1 cup sliced almonds

1. In a food processor, chop the prunes and cherries so you have medium to small pieces (about 1/4 inch), taking care to not turn them into a paste. Put the fruit in a bowl and stir in the honey.

2. By hand, chop the almonds into (1/4-inch) pieces.

3. Form the mixture into 1-inch balls and press the almonds around them. Store at room temperature.

Crunchy Peanut Butter Clusters

Makes about 24 pieces

With apologies to Mrs. See, I think this is one of the best nonchocolate candies around. It's simply peanut butter combined with wheat bran cereal. It may not sound sexy, but if you love peanuts this will become a favorite.

Natural peanut butter has less sugar added and is my preference. These confections are best eaten within two days of being made.

WHAT YOU'LL NEED
Baking or cookie sheet

Parchment paper

2 cups wheat or multi-grain flakes or shredded wheat cereal

1/2 cup corn syrup

1/4 cup granulated sugar

1/4 cup firmly packed light brown sugar

1/2 cup peanut butter, preferably natural

1/2 teaspoon pure vanilla extract

1/8 teaspoon salt

1. Put the cereal in a medium bowl. If you're using shredded wheat, crush it with your hands to break it up a little.

2. Combine the corn syrup, granulated sugar, and brown sugar in a small saucepan and bring to a boil over medium heat, stirring occasionally. Remove the pan from heat and stir in the peanut butter, vanilla, and salt. Pour the peanut butter mixture over the cereal and stir so everything is well coated.

3. Line the baking sheet with parchment paper. Place 1-inch mounds of the mixture on the parchment and let them sit until they firm up, about 45 minutes. Store at room temperature in a covered container for up to 1 week.

No-Cook Fudge

Makes 64 (1-inch) pieces

Most of the time, fudge is way too sweet for me. Not this one. The cream cheese adds to the creamy texture without adding any additional sweetness. Make it with or without the nuts as you prefer.

When measuring the confectioners' sugar, simply pour it from the box (or bag) into the measuring cup. Do not pack it down.

WHAT YOU'LL NEED

Electric stand mixer or handheld mixer and medium bowl

Rubber spatula

Saucepan and metal bowl, or double boiler if you have one

8-inch square baking pan

6 ounces cream cheese, softened

3 tablespoons warm water

4 cups confectioners' sugar

Large pinch kosher salt

6 ounces unsweetened chocolate, chopped or broken into 1-inch pieces

1 1/4 cups pecan pieces

1. Line the pan with foil, leaving an overhang on 2 sides.

2. Using the stand mixer, or a handheld mixer and medium bowl, first on low speed and then gradually increasing the speed to medium, beat the cream cheese, water, and sugar together until smooth. Scrape down the side of the bowl with the rubber spatula. Add the salt.

3. Melt the chocolate by putting it in a heat-proof bowl set over a saucepan of simmering water, making sure the bowl does not touch the water. (You can use a double boiler if you have one.) Stir and scrape the side of the bowl occasionally with the rubber spatula until the chocolate is smooth and evenly melted.

4. While the chocolate is still warm, stir it by hand into the cream cheese. Add the pecan pieces and stir until combined.

5. Spread the mixture into the prepared pan and chill for 2 hours, or until set. Using the overhanging foil for "handles," lift the fudge out of the pan. Cut the fudge into even 1-inch squares. Store in a covered container at room temperature for 2 days or refrigerate for up to 2 weeks.

Nonpareils

Makes about 36 pieces

We've all seen them, those teeny tiny, white or colored, poppy seed–sized sugar balls on candy, but how many of us know they're called "nonpareils"? In some countries they're called "hundreds and thousands," I'm guessing because of how many can fit in a jar, although I've never counted. In France, the chocolate candy disks that are sprinkled with them are called "nonpareils," which means "without equal." A delicious little candy, welcome as a gift or an after-dinner sweet bite.

White nonpareils are common in the baking section of most supermarkets as well as gourmet shops. Colored nonpareils can be used.

WHAT YOU'LL NEED
Saucepan and metal bowl, or double boiler if you have one

Rubber spatula

Baking or cookie sheet

Parchment paper

8 ounces dark chocolate (58 to 62 percent cacao), chopped or broken into 1-inch pieces

1/2 teaspoon unsalted butter

1/4 cup white nonpareils

1. Melt the chocolate and butter by putting them in a heat-proof bowl set over a saucepan of simmering water, making sure the bowl does not touch the water. (You can use a double boiler if you have one.) Stir and scrape the side of the bowl with the rubber spatula until the chocolate is smooth and evenly melted. Let cool to room temperature.

2. Line the baking sheet with parchment paper. Using a teaspoon measure, drop the chocolate in circles 1 inch apart. Generously sprinkle the chocolate drops with the nonpareils and let sit until the chocolate has hardened, about 1 hour.

3. Remove the nonpareils from the paper with a small spatula. Store in a covered container at room temperature for up to 1 week.

Dark Chocolate Pudding

Makes 6 servings

For most of my childhood, I thought all puddings were instant and came out of a powdered mix in a box, so the first time I prepared this recipe was a revelation. It was made entirely on the stovetop in just a few minutes—almost instant—and had a depth of flavor that amazed me. That was a long time ago, and the recipe has become one of my classics, though now I substitute good-quality chocolate for the supermarket brand I used to use, which makes it a very grown-up dessert, suitable in my book for even the fanciest of dinner parties.

WHAT YOU'LL NEED

Heat-proof rubber spatula

4 ounces dark chocolate (58 to 62 percent cacao), broken or chopped into 1/2-inch pieces

1 tablespoon unsalted butter

1 teaspoon pure vanilla extract

1/8 teaspoon kosher salt

1 large egg

1/2 cup granulated sugar

3 tablespoons Dutch-processed cocoa

2 tablespoons cornstarch

1 1/2 cups heavy cream

1 cup whole or 2 percent milk

Whipped Cream (page 240)

FB: Should I get out a double boiler for this recipe?

EL: You don't need a double boiler, or have to whip egg whites, or use a strainer. You cook all the ingredients, in one pot on the stovetop, let it cool, then eat it.

FB: That's it?

EL: Well, you do have to make sure to stir it.

FB: Constantly? With a whisk?

EL: You can actually walk away from the stove for a minute, in the beginning while the pan is starting to heat up. What you want to do, because the base mixture has egg and cornstarch and can get lumpy, is leisurely stir back and forth with a spatula so that you thoroughly scrape and reach all the surfaces of the bottom of the saucepan, including the corners. With a whisk, you really can't do that.

1. Put the chocolate, butter, vanilla extract, and salt in a bowl and set the bowl near your cooktop (but not too near the heat source—you don't want to melt the chocolate).

2. In a medium bowl, whisk the egg until it's foamy and then whisk in the sugar until you don't see any pieces of egg or sugar. Whisk in the cocoa and cornstarch so everything is well combined, but don't worry if there are a few lumps, because they will smooth out eventually. Whisk in the cream and milk.

3. Transfer the mixture to a medium saucepan and, over medium heat, use the spatula to stir the mixture while it cooks to a point where bubbles are just breaking the surface. Maintain the heat, and constantly (but not obsessively) move the spatula back and forth, making sure it reaches both the bottom as well as the corners of the pan. If it starts to sputter violently, turn down the heat. After about 10 minutes of total cooking time, you'll begin to be able to see a clear trail on the bottom of the pan as you scrape, indicating that the pudding is ready.

4. Remove the saucepan from the heat and add the chocolate and butter. Still using the spatula, stir all the ingredients together until they're melted and the mixture is all one color with no streaks.

5. Transfer the pudding to a bowl and place a piece of plastic wrap directly on the surface so that it doesn't form a skin. Refrigerate until thoroughly chilled, at least 2 hours. (If you want to chill it more quickly, put the bowl in a large bowl of ice water.)

6. To serve, place large spoonfuls of the pudding into each of 6 bowls and top with dollops of whipped cream.

Chocolate Mousse

Makes 6 servings

Mousse is a French word for "froth" or "foam." Chocolate mousses range from light and airy to dense and creamy, as in this version. It only has three ingredients (one of which is water), making for possibly the shortest ingredients list in the book.

If you fold too much cream (which is cold) at one time into chocolate that is hot, you'll end up with mini-chocolate chips, which isn't a bad thing if you like chips. Make sure that you under-whip the cream, stopping just before it dollops.

WHAT YOU'LL NEED
Saucepan and metal bowl, or double boiler if you have one

Rubber spatula

Electric stand mixer or handheld mixer and medium bowl

13 ounces dark chocolate (58 to 62 percent cacao), chopped or broken into 1-inch pieces

1/2 cup plus 1 tablespoon water

2 1/4 cups heavy cream

Whipped Cream (page 240)

1. Melt the chocolate with the water by putting them in a heat-proof bowl set over a saucepan of simmering water, making sure the bowl does not touch the water (You can use a double boiler if you have one.) Stir and scrape the side of the bowl occasionally with the rubber spatula until the chocolate is smooth and evenly melted. Set the bowl aside to cool to room temperature.

2. In the stand mixer fitted with the wire whisk, or using a handheld mixer and medium bowl, whip the cream to a point somewhere between pourable and softly mounded peaks.

3. Using the rubber spatula, very gently fold one-third of the cream into the chocolate until it's well blended; a few white streaks are okay. Fold in another third of the cream, then the final third, blending well after the final addition. Pour the mousse into each of 6 pretty dessert bowls or glasses.

4. Cover the bowls with plastic wrap and refrigerate until serving, at least 1 hour or up to overnight. Serve with dollops of whipped cream.

Lemon Cream with Smashed Berries

Makes 6 servings

If you're a fan of all things lemon, then this is a recipe you need to add to your repertoire. In essence, it's a lemon curd—a thick custardy mixture of eggs, sugar, and lemon juice cooked on the stove top—that's been lightened with whipped cream. Here it's served with berries that have been smashed lightly with sugar, but the lemon cream is so versatile that you can also serve it with cake (Lemon Angel Food Cake, page 88) and cookies (Thin Crispy Ginger Cookies, page 58).

You must stir the lemon curd constantly until it thickens, but take your time and do it over medium-low heat so it doesn't curdle or stick to the bottom of the pan. It takes only 5 minutes or so.

WHAT YOU'LL NEED
Heat-proof rubber spatula

Electric stand mixer or handheld mixer and medium bowl

4 large egg yolks

2 large eggs

About 3/4 cup granulated sugar

1/2 cup lemon juice

1 cup heavy cream

1 pint strawberries

1 pint raspberries

1. In a medium bowl, whisk the yolks and whole eggs with 1/2 cup of the sugar and the lemon juice until smooth. Transfer to a medium saucepan and cook over medium-low heat, stirring continuously with the heat-proof rubber spatula or wooden spoon, for about 5 minutes, or until the mixture thickens to a mayo-like consistency. (If the mixture gets lumpy at any point, switch to a whisk and whisk until it's smoothed out.)

2. Strain the lemon curd through a mesh sieve into a bowl and place plastic wrap directly on the surface to prevent a skin from forming. Refrigerate until cold, about 1 hour.

3. Using the stand mixer, or a handheld mixer and medium bowl, whip the cream on medium-high speed with 2 tablespoons sugar until it forms softly mounded peaks. Using the rubber spatula, fold the whipped cream into the chilled lemon curd.

4. Remove the green stems from the strawberries and cut in half if they're large. Put them in a medium bowl with 2 tablespoons sugar and, with the back of a spoon, smash them a bit to break them up. Stir in the raspberries, smashing and breaking them up a little too. Taste for sweetness and add more sugar if necessary.

5. Spoon the lemon cream into glasses and top with the smashed berries.

Frozen Chocolate Mousse Cake
with Chocolate-Covered Pretzels

Makes 1 cake, serving 10 to 12

It may sound odd, chocolate with pretzels, but it's one of those great sweet-salty combinations. Add the crunchy pretzels to the unctuously smooth chocolate mousse and what you have is another level of contrast. This frozen treat makes a memorable do-ahead dessert. Try not to eat all the chocolate pretzels before you can get them on top of the cake—they make a yummy snack.

Though there are several steps to this recipe, none are difficult. Make sure that when you whisk the yolks in the double boiler, do it constantly. But don't worry, it's only for a short time, 3 minutes or so until the mixture has thickened.

Chocolate Mousse Cake

1. Melt the chocolate by putting it in a heat-proof bowl set over a saucepan of simmering water, making sure the bowl does not touch the water. (You can use a double boiler if you have one.) Stir and scrape the side of the bowl occasionally with the rubber spatula until the chocolate is smooth and evenly melted.

2. In the second heat-proof bowl, whisk the egg yolks with the coffee, sugar, and liqueur until blended. Put over the saucepan of simmering water and whisk continuously until the mixture has thickened, about 3 minutes. Transfer to the bowl of the stand mixer (or a medium bowl if you're using a handheld mixer) and whip on medium speed until the eggs have cooled and thickened. On low speed, stir in the melted chocolate.

WHAT YOU'LL NEED
Saucepan and 2 metal bowls, or double boiler if you have one

Rubber spatula

Electric stand mixer or handheld mixer and medium bowl

9-inch springform pan

4 ounces dark chocolate (58 to 62 percent cacao), chopped or broken into 1-inch pieces

5 large egg yolks

1/4 cup brewed coffee

1/4 cup granulated sugar

2 tablespoons orange flavored liqueur (such as Grand Marnier or Cointreau)

1 1/2 cups heavy cream

1/4 cup sour cream

Chocolate-Covered Pretzels

WHAT YOU'LL NEED
Saucepan and metal bowl, or double boiler if you have one

Rubber spatula

Baking or cookie sheet

Parchment paper

4 ounces dark chocolate (58 to 62 percent cacao), chopped or broken into 1-inch pieces

3 ounces milk chocolate, coarsely chopped

1 1/2 cups skinny pretzel sticks (about 3-inches long, 1/8-inch thick; measure by standing them up in 1-cup and 1/2-cup measuring cups)

3. In a clean bowl, whip the heavy cream with the sour cream on medium-high until it forms softly mounded peaks. Using the rubber spatula, fold the cream into the chocolate mixture.

4. Arrange half the chocolate-covered pretzels (see below) in the bottom of a springform pan. Spread the chocolate-cream mixture over the pretzels. Freeze until hard, about 4 hours (overnight is okay too).

5. To remove the mousse cake from the pan, run a small knife around the inside edge of the pan. Release the latch and then remove the ring. To serve, place the remaining chocolate-covered pretzels on top and cut into wedges.

Chocolate-Covered Pretzels

1. Melt the dark and milk chocolates in a heat-proof bowl set over (but not touching) a saucepan of simmering water (or use a double boiler if you have one). Stir and scrape the side of the bowl occasionally with the rubber spatula until the chocolate is smooth and evenly melted. Remove the bowl from the heat, add the pretzels, and stir so they're well coated with the chocolate. Break up some of the pretzels as you stir.

2. Line the baking sheet with parchment and spread out the pretzels. Let them sit until the chocolate is set, about 30 minutes. The pretzels can be made 1 day ahead and kept at room temperature in a covered container.

Brownie–Brown Sugar Parfaits

Makes 6 servings

Parfaits are a welcome change from the cakes, tarts, and pies we so often turn to when we make dessert. They're kind of quaint—you don't see them much on menus anymore. I happen to make them a lot, both at home as well as at the restaurants. I find them really versatile—they can be layered with ice cream, custard, or whipped cream and all kinds of fruit, cake, or cookies. If you have or can find parfait glasses—tall, narrow, footed glass dishes— they will look particularly elegant. But whatever you use, make sure it is glass so the layers can be seen.

The brown-sugar custard is essentially a pastry cream sweetened with brown sugar and lightened with whipped cream. Once it's done it can be kept in the fridge for a few hours before you're ready to assemble the parfaits.

WHAT YOU'LL NEED

Heat-proof rubber spatula

Electric stand mixer or handheld mixer and medium bowl

6 parfait glasses, wineglasses, or dessert bowls

4 large egg yolks

1/3 cup granulated sugar

1/3 cup firmly packed light brown sugar

3/4 cup evaporated milk

1 tablespoon plus 1 1/2 teaspoons cornstarch

1 teaspoon pure vanilla extract

1 1/2 cups heavy cream

3 cups of 1/2-inch pieces of brownies or soft chocolate cookies

About 2/3 cup Caramel Sauce (page 244), or good-quality store-bought caramel sauce

1 cup chopped pecans

FB: Let me get all my things ready to put these parfaits together. Okay, I have the custard, the caramel sauce—which I made, thank you very much—the brownies, and the nuts, which I toasted.

EL: You need some glasses to put it in.

1. In a medium bowl, whisk the egg yolks with the granulated sugar and brown sugar. Whisk in the evaporated milk, then the cornstarch and vanilla.

2. Cook the egg mixture in a medium saucepan over medium-low heat, stirring constantly and scraping the bottom with the heat-proof rubber spatula, until it thickens to a mayonnaise-like consistency, about 5 minutes. (If the mixture gets lumpy at any point, remove the pan from the heat, switch to a whisk, and whisk until it's smoothed out.) Transfer the brown sugar custard to a medium bowl and place plastic wrap directly on the surface to prevent a skin from forming. Refrigerate until cold, about 45 minutes.

3. Using the stand mixer with wire whip attachment, or handheld mixer and medium bowl, whip the cream on medium-high speed until it forms softly mounded peaks. You want the cream somewhere just past the pourable stage and soft peak. It should just begin to hold its shape.

4. If the custard has become really thick, stir it with the rubber spatula. Fold the cream into the cooled custard.

5. Put 3 pieces of brownies, a generous 2 teaspoons of caramel, and 2 teaspoons pecan pieces into the bottom of each of the 6 parfait glasses. Spoon on 1/3 cup of the custard. Top with 3 more brownie pieces and then drizzle with 2 teaspoons of caramel sauce and sprinkle on 2 teaspoons pecans. Make another layer of the custard, brownie pieces, caramel, and pecans.

6. Cover each glass with plastic wrap and refrigerate for at least 30 minutes or up to overnight.

Caramelized Apple–Rice Pudding Parfaits

Makes 8 servings

I was probably one of the few kids who never ate rice pudding growing up—
not because I didn't like it, it simply was something my mother never made.
However, when I was a young culinary student, the first time I ate rice pudding
I loved it and also realized what a terrific and versatile vehicle it is. Just like
risotto, rice pudding is kind of like a culinary canvas: it absorbs other flavors.
I tried making pudding with regular rice and didn't like it. Then, when I used
Arborio rice, the rice used in risotto, I had one of those "aha" moments:
the natural creaminess from the starch inherent in Arborio rice enhances the
texture of rice pudding. What is it that makes rice pudding so delectable? Not
the rice itself, but all the sweet cream you fold into it. As well as all the other
ingredients, like fresh or dried fruit, that you add. Just like risotto, only sweet.

WHAT YOU'LL NEED
Rubber spatula

8 parfait or wineglasses

6 tablespoons (3/4 stick) unsalted butter

1 cup Arborio rice

2 cups heavy cream, plus up to additional
1/2 cup if needed

4 cups whole milk

1/2 cup plus 6 tablespoons granulated
sugar

1/4 teaspoon kosher salt

4 red apples (any kind except
Red Delicious)

Ground cinnamon for garnish, optional

REMOVING THE CORE FROM AN APPLE

FB: Why are we using
Arborio rice?

EL: Because it's a thicker grain
that absorbs more liquid
and also releases a lot of its
own starch, making it
naturally creamier.

FB: I love risotto though I've
never made it.

EL: Rice pudding is like risotto only it's lightly sweetened. Measure the sugar out ahead of time—as you should always do with all your ingredients. You put the sugar in after the rice is done, and I can't tell you how many times at the restaurant we made this dessert and someone forgot to put in the sugar. If you have it there already measured out, you won't be likely to forget it.

FB: How do you know when it's done?

EL: You just have to taste it. See if the rice kernel is hard in the middle, or if you can bite through with only a little resistance.

FB: Do you think Fearful Bakers will pass this recipe by? Say "Oh, Arborio rice, that sounds hard"?

EL: Hopefully they'll just say "Arborio rice, mmmm rice pudding."

1. In a medium saucepan, melt 2 tablespoons of the butter over medium heat. Stir in the rice and cook, stirring frequently with the rubber spatula, until lightly toasted, about 1 minute. Add the 2 cups cream and the milk and bring to a boil over high heat. Reduce the heat a little and simmer, stirring occasionally in the beginning and then more frequently after the mixture thickens and scraping the bottom of the pan to prevent the rice from scorching. The rice is done when it's tender and the cream has thickened, about 25 minutes (bite into a few kernels to be sure).

2. Stir in the 1/2 cup granulated sugar and the salt. Transfer the rice pudding to a bowl and refrigerate until cold, at least 1 hour. You can make the rice a day or two ahead and keep it refrigerated in a covered container. (If the pudding gets too thick when chilled and seems gluey, stir in some more cream, a tablespoon at a time. You want it to be creamy.)

3. Peel the apples and core them by cutting off the sides and removing the rectangular piece of core. Cut the apples into 1/2- by 1/4-inch-thick pieces and put in a large skillet with the remaining 4 tablespoons butter and 6 tablespoons sugar. Cook over medium heat until the apples are soft, 15 to 20 minutes depending on the variety of apple. If the apples are not golden brown by the time they are soft, increase the heat to medium-high or high and cook until they've colored and the juice has evaporated. Let the apples cool to room temperature before assembling the parfaits, or refrigerate them in a covered container for up to 3 days.

4. To assemble the parfaits, in the bottom of each of the 8 glasses, layer 1/4 cup rice and 1 tablespoon apples, then another 1/4 cup rice. Top with 1 tablespoon apples and sprinkle each with a little cinnamon, if you like. The parfaits can be made up to 8 hours ahead and kept, covered with plastic wrap, in the refrigerator.

Lemon Prosecco Sabayon
with Raspberries and Blackberries

Makes 8 servings

Whenever I have unexpected guests and am stuck for a dessert—admittedly this doesn't happen often in my house—I usually turn to sabayon, but not just by default. Sabayon is luscious unto itself, and I've made it many times for big fancy dinners too. What is sabayon? It's the French version of Italian zabaglione, a frothy mixture of egg yolks and sugar whipped over low heat with some sort of wine until it has the thickened texture of whipped cream. In Italy the alcohol is classically marsala, but in France many kinds of wine are used. The reason I like making sabayon for spur-of-the-moment desserts is that I always have eggs and sugar of course, and usually wine and cream. It's also perfect for a Fearful Baker. The only thing you need to be careful of is to not overheat the eggs so that they scramble.

I've made sabayon not only with Prosecco (an Italian sparkling wine), but champagne, sauternes, gewürztraminer, Riesling, and even apple cider for my friends who don't drink alcohol. Whatever you choose, you won't need much, so a half-bottle, or split, would do. If you open a large bottle, either serve it at dinner or put a stopper (there are some designed just for sparkling wine) on it and have it the next day.

EL: This recipe, you're gonna love. Once you get the hang of it, you'll want to use it for everything. What I do so I can keep track of how many eggs I've separated—say the phone rings or you get interrupted—is to put the shells for each one back in the carton so I can count them.

FB: Great tip. I've had that happen to me where I forgot how many I've added. Just curious, what do you do with the egg whites?

EL: I will make an egg-white omelet in the morning. Got to have something healthy during the day.

1. Fill the large bowl half full with ice and add just enough water to cover the ice. (This is for cooling down the bowl of sabayon.)

2. In a medium heat-proof bowl, whisk the egg yolks with the sugar and salt until well blended. Whisk in the Prosecco. Set the bowl over (but not touching) a saucepan of simmering water (or use a double boiler if you have one). Whisking constantly and making sure you whisk the side and bottom of the bowl simultaneously so the eggs don't scramble—be careful, this goes very quickly— cook the eggs until the mixture has thickened and there are no visible bubbles, 2 to 3 minutes. Immediately put the bowl into the ice bath and give it a few whisks to begin cooling it down.

3. Let the sabayon cool to room temperature, whisking frequently. Remove the bowl from the ice bath and set aside while you whip the cream.

4. In the stand mixer fitted with the wire whisk, or using a handheld mixer and a medium bowl, whip the cream until it just forms softly mounded peaks.

5. Add the lemon zest, and using the rubber spatula, fold the whipped cream into the cooled bowl of sabayon. If you notice any lumps of cream you can use a whisk to blend them in. Cover the bowl with plastic and refrigerate until serving.

6. To serve, put a mixture of berries into each of 8 dessert bowls or wineglasses. Top each with a large spoonful of sabayon.

Mandarin Orange Bavarian Cream

Makes 8 servings

While it may be classically French in its origins, this ethereal dessert made of custard, whipped cream, flavorings (orange here), and gelatin is not difficult to make. The only thing you need to be aware of is that the gelatin needs to have set up enough so when you fold in the whipped cream the mixture stays thick. While the custard is in the fridge chilling, make sure that you occasionally stir the firmer (colder) outside parts into the middle so it sets up evenly. In summer you can use berries instead of oranges.

WHAT YOU'LL NEED
Heat-proof rubber spatula

Electric stand mixer or handheld mixer and medium bowl

8 parfait glasses, wineglasses, or dessert bowls

Mesh sieve

7 satsuma mandarins or navel oranges, peeled

1/4 cup water

1 1/2 teaspoons powdered gelatin (note that this is less than a package)

5 large egg yolks

1/3 cup granulated sugar

1/4 teaspoon kosher salt

1 1/2 cups whole milk

1/4 cup orange-flavored liqueur (such as Cointreau or Grand Marnier)

1/2 teaspoon pure vanilla extract

3/4 cup heavy cream

1. Pull the mandarins into segments or cut the navel oranges into segments (see page 86).

2. Put the water in a small bowl and stir in the gelatin. Set aside to soften while you cook the custard.

3. In a medium bowl, whisk the egg yolks with the sugar and salt until well blended.

4. In a medium saucepan, warm the milk over medium heat until it starts to bubble around the edges. Slowly whisk the milk into the bowl with the egg yolks. Return the milk-egg mixture to the saucepan and cook over medium-low heat, stirring continually with the heat-proof rubber spatula, until the custard thickens slightly and coats the spatula when you lift it up, 5 to 8 minutes. (It should have the consistency of heavy cream.)

5. Remove the pan from the heat. If there are any firm pieces of egg, strain the custard through a mesh sieve into a clean bowl. Whisk in the softened gelatin, liqueur, and vanilla. Refrigerate the custard for 30 minutes. Stir it gently with the rubber spatula to evenly mix in the setting parts. Put it back in the fridge for 45 minutes, or until the custard is cold. Continue to stir occasionally to make sure it's smooth without lumps.

6. In the stand mixer fitted with the wire whisk, or using a handheld mixer and a medium bowl, whip the cream until it forms softly mounded peaks. With the rubber spatula, fold the cream into the custard until it's evenly blended. Switch to a whisk to gently smooth out any lumps.

7. Divide half of the orange segments among the 8 glasses. Spoon half of the cream over the fruit, then top with the remaining oranges and cream.

Fudgsicle Bars
with Caramel and Spanish Peanuts

Makes 9 bars

This is a childhood favorite reinvented for grown-up tastes. You've got the texture of a Fudgsicle but with the flavor of rich dark chocolate, salty peanuts, and sweet caramel, all combined in a dessert pretty enough to make people think it came out of a professional kitchen.

It's important that the Fudgsicle bars soften at room temperature for 5 minutes before serving, otherwise they'll be too hard to cut into. The flavor comes forward when the dessert warms a little. Don't forgo the ice-water bath. You need to cool the custard quickly to keep it from overcooking.

WHAT YOU'LL NEED

9- by 9-inch baking pan

Heat-proof rubber spatula

6 large egg yolks

1/2 cup granulated sugar

Large pinch kosher salt

4 cups heavy cream

4 ounces dark chocolate (58 to 62 percent cacao), chopped or broken into 1-inch pieces

2 tablespoons instant coffee granules

1/2 cup Spanish peanuts

1 1/2 cups Caramel Sauce (page 244), or good-quality store-bought caramel sauce

1. Line the baking pan with foil, leaving a 2-inch overhang on 2 sides. Set aside. Fill a large bowl half full of ice and cover the ice with water. Set aside.

2. In a medium bowl that will fit into the large bowl of ice water, whisk the yolks with the sugar and salt until well blended.

3. In a large saucepan, warm the cream over medium heat until it starts to bubble around the edges. Remove from heat and stir in the chocolate and coffee until smooth. Slowly pour the chocolate cream into the bowl with the egg yolks. Return the chocolate cream to the saucepan (reserving the bowl) and cook over medium-low heat, stirring continually with the heat-proof rubber spatula, until the chocolate custard thickens slightly and coats and clings to the spatula when you lift it up out of the pot, about 5 minutes.

4. Pour the custard back into the reserved bowl. Put the bowl in the ice bath. Stirring occasionally, let the custard cool to room temperature, about 15 minutes.

5. Pour the custard into the foil-lined baking pan. Freeze until firm, 3 to 4 hours.

6. Put the peanuts in a colander and rub them with a clean kitchen towel to remove some of the skins. (If you don't have a colander, just rub them in the towel.) Don't worry about getting all the skins—you just want to remove the loose pieces. Chop the peanuts into 1/4-inch or smaller pieces.

7. To serve, holding the foil, lift the Fudgsicles out of the pan. Peel back the foil. Cut the firm fudge into 3-inch squares. Place a piece on each plate. Let sit for 5 minutes to soften. Top with some caramel sauce and peanuts.

Grape Granita with Vanilla Mascarpone Cream

Makes 8 servings

Italian granitas are a more rustic version of sorbet. They're both frozen desserts made from flavorful liquid—usually fruit juice—combined with sugar, but where sorbets are smooth textured from their constant stirring in an ice cream machine, granitas are coarsely grained from their occasional stirring by hand.

Welch's grape juice is perfectly delicious and another example of how supermarket ingredients can be turned into super desserts. If you have access to freshly squeezed Concord grape juice, so much the better.

WHAT YOU'LL NEED
9-inch baking pan

4 cups Concord grape juice

3 tablespoons granulated sugar

1/2 teaspoon kosher salt

Vanilla Mascarpone Cream
1/2 vanilla bean

2/3 cup mascarpone, softened

1/2 cup heavy cream

1 tablespoon granulated sugar

1 teaspoon grated lemon zest

1. In a medium bowl, whisk the grape juice with the sugar and salt until the sugar is dissolved. Pour into the pan and put the pan in the freezer. After 30 minutes, use a fork to scrape the mixture and break it up into pieces. Continue scraping every 20 minutes or so for 1 hour longer, until it has flaky ice crystals and a light, feathery texture. The total freezing time will be about 1 1/2 hours.

Vanilla Mascarpone Cream

2. Slit the bean half lengthwise and, while holding the bean on one end, scrape out the seeds with the back of a knife into a medium bowl. Add the mascarpone, cream, sugar, and lemon zest. With a rotary beater or an electric mixer, whip the mixture until it forms softly mounded peaks. You can whisk it by hand with a wire whip, but the mixer is faster and easier.

3. To serve, scoop some granita into each of 8 glasses and dollop each serving with a spoonful of the mascarpone cream.

Mango-Raspberry Yogurt Terrine

Makes 8 to 10 servings

Here's a way to turn store-bought ingredients into a dessert that will impress even your snobbiest friends. Not only is the combination of sweet-tart sorbet and creamy frozen yogurt luscious, layering the terrine makes a striking presentation.

WHAT YOU'LL NEED
9- by 5-inch loaf pan

2 pints good-quality store-bought frozen vanilla yogurt

1 pint good-quality store-bought raspberry sorbet

1 pint good-quality store-bought mango sorbet

1 ripe mango, peeled, seeded, and cut into 1/4-inch pieces

1. Grease the loaf pan with nonstick cooking spray or butter and line with plastic wrap or foil, making sure to press it into the corners and leaving an overhang of plastic or foil on a couple of sides.

2. Partially defrost one of the pints of frozen yogurt in the microwave for 10 seconds. Spread the yogurt in the prepared pan. Soften the raspberry sorbet in the microwave and spread it over the vanilla yogurt. Return the pan to the freezer to harden, about 30 minutes.

3. Repeat the softening and layering process with the remaining frozen yogurt and then the mango sorbet. Cover with plastic wrap and freeze until the terrine is hard, at least 2 hours or overnight.

4. To serve, using the overhang of plastic or foil, lift the terrine out of the pan and put it on a cutting board. Peel off the plastic wrap or foil and cut the loaf into 8 to 10 slices. Place the slices on dessert plates. Top each serving with a spoonful of mango pieces and serve immediately.

Milk Chocolate Affogato

Makes 6 servings

In Italy, if you order an *affogato*, you'll get a shot of espresso poured over vanilla ice cream or gelato. The name comes from *affogare*, which means "to drown." Here, I've added chocolate to take the bitter edge off and enhance the coffee flavor, technically making it a *mocha affogato*. Use decaf coffee if you don't want the caffeine.

WHAT YOU'LL NEED
Ice cream scoop (if you have one)

1 cup heavy cream

6 ounces milk chocolate, finely chopped

6 tablespoons freshly brewed room-temperature coffee (regular or decaf)

1 pint good-quality store-bought vanilla ice cream

1. In a small saucepan, bring the cream just to a boil and turn off the heat. Add the chocolate, stir until smooth, and then stir in the coffee.

2. Put 2 scoops of ice cream in each of 6 dessert bowls. Top with a spoonful of the chocolate coffee sauce.

Butterscotch Peach Split

Makes 6 servings

One summer weekend I was inspired by some stellar farmers' market peaches to make something a little out of the ordinary for summer. I've never been a fan of banana splits, but I thought, "Where is it written that a banana split has to contain bananas? Why not make a peach split, and while I'm into changing things, how about using homemade butterscotch, dried cherries, real whipped cream, and macadamias?" Answer to self: "Yum."

WHAT YOU'LL NEED
Serrated peeler (if you have one)

Ice cream scoop (if you have one)

8 tablespoons (1 stick) unsalted butter

1/2 cup firmly packed light brown sugar

3 tablespoons granulated sugar

1/4 cup plus 2 tablespoons light corn syrup

1/4 cup heavy cream

3 tablespoons macadamia nuts

3 large ripe peaches

Good-quality store-bought vanilla ice cream

Whipped Cream (page 240)

1/3 cup dried cherries

1. In a medium saucepan, melt the butter. Stir in the brown sugar, granulated sugar, and corn syrup. Bring to a boil over medium heat and boil for 2 minutes, stirring occasionally. Remove the pan from the heat and stir in the cream. Bring back to a boil and stir in the macadamia nuts. The butterscotch sauce can be made several days ahead and refrigerated, but add the nuts just before you rewarm the sauce for serving.

2. Peel the peaches with the serrated peeler or paring knife. Cut them in half and remove the pits.

3. To serve, put a peach half cut-side up in each of 6 dessert bowls or plates (take a little slice off the rounded side so the peach will stay stable). Top with a scoop of ice cream and spoon over some warm butterscotch sauce. Dollop on some whipped cream and sprinkle with dried cherries.

Brown Sugar–Honey Blackberry Sundae

Makes 6 servings

Like all sundaes, this is truly a last-minute dessert. It takes only minutes to pull together. Err on the side of caution when cooking the sauce — it's done when it has the consistency of maple syrup. If it's reduced too much it will turn to taffy when it hits the cold ice cream.

WHAT YOU'LL NEED
Ice cream scoop (if you have one)

1 cup firmly packed light brown sugar

1/4 cup honey

1/2 cup water

3 tablespoons unsalted butter

1 pint good-quality store-bought vanilla ice cream

1 pint blackberries

1. Stir the brown sugar with the honey and water in a medium saucepan. Bring to a boil over medium heat. Reduce the heat to medium-low (so it doesn't boil over) and cook, stirring occasionally, until it has the consistency of maple syrup. Remove the pan from the heat and stir in the butter. Cool slightly before serving or refrigerate for up to 1 week and reheat.

2. Place 2 scoops of ice cream in each of 6 dessert bowls. Spoon the sauce over the ice cream and top with the blackberries.

Plum Melba Sundaes

Makes 6 servings

Because plums are the dominant flavor in this simply prepared summer dessert, it's crucial that they're ripe and sweet and of the best quality. The array of plum varieties can be mind-boggling, particularly if you shop the farmers' market, but I find red plums to be the best choice here. This is true particularly early in the season, when red plums have a nicer balance of sweet to tart compared to the black plum varieties. It may sound heretical to use frozen raspberries when you can buy fresh, but I think they're a better value (and have more consistent flavor) if all you're doing is pureeing them for a sauce.

WHAT YOU'LL NEED
Food processor

6 parfait glasses, wineglasses, or dessert bowls

12 ounces frozen raspberries (no sugar added), defrosted

3 to 4 tablespoons granulated sugar

4 ripe red plums

1/2 cup hazelnuts

Good-quality store-bought vanilla ice cream

1. Puree the raspberries in the food processor. Strain the puree through a mesh sieve, discarding the seeds. Stir in 3 tablespoons sugar, then taste for sweetness and add another tablespoon if necessary.

2. Halve the plums and, with a paring knife, pop out the pits. Cut into 1/2-inch pieces.

3. Rub the hazelnuts in a dish towel to remove any loose skin. By hand with a sharp knife, chop the hazelnuts into 1/4-inch pieces.

4. To serve, divide half of the chopped plums among the 6 parfait glasses and top each with 1 tablespoon raspberry sauce. Cover with a scoop of ice cream, the remaining plums, and raspberry sauce. Sprinkle the nuts over the tops.

Best Dessert Sauces

These three recipes are the most popular dessert sauces. At least one of them will complement any dessert you make, and they have the miraculous ability to disguise any imperfections in your desserts.

Your guests will never notice a not-so-perfect pie or tart when warm chocolate or caramel sauce is poured over it, or softly mounded whipped cream is dolloped on top. These sauces are a dessert maker's secret arsenal. If you're late getting home from work and pick up a cake from your favorite bakery, add one or more of these to turn it into your own creation.

Two of the recipes—chocolate sauce and whipped cream—are easy to make. Caramel sauce does require a bit more attention, but once you make it a couple of times it will become a staple in your baking repertoire and you'll find yourself making it at the last minute to serve over ice cream.

All three recipes require only a few ingredients: cream, sugar, and/or chocolate, and I suggest you always keep chocolate and sugar in your cupboard as I do, leaving only the cream to be picked up at the store.

I consider these three recipes the "three musketeers" of dessert sauces, used alone or together, and you'll find that I often suggest serving them alongside many of the desserts in this book.

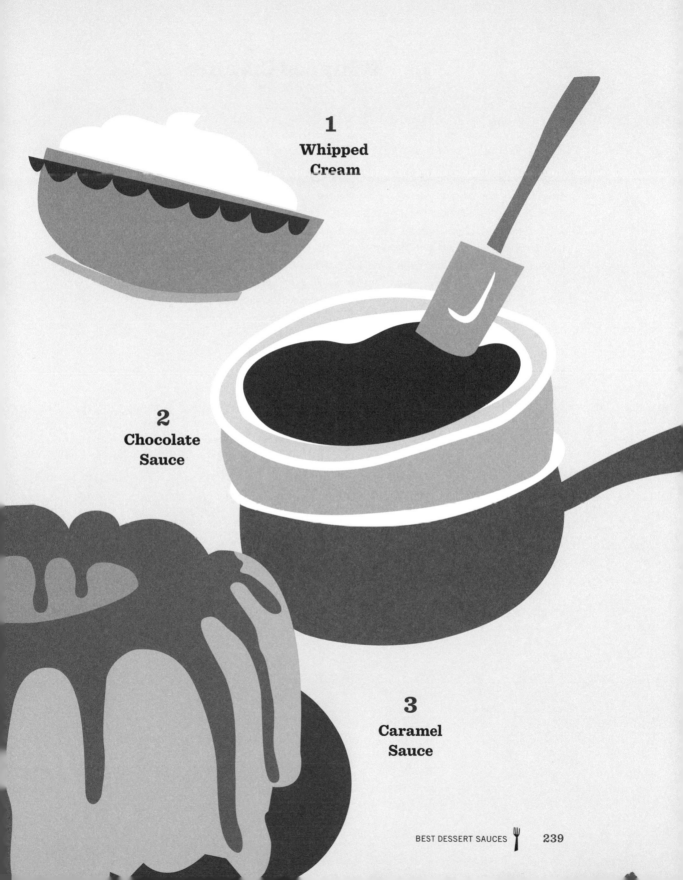

1
Whipped Cream

2
Chocolate Sauce

3
Caramel Sauce

Whipped Cream

Makes 2 cups

I can't think of a dessert that whipped cream doesn't enhance. It is often called Chantilly Cream on dessert menus (pronounced shan-*tee,* not shan-*tilly,* the L's are silent). That's just the fancy-sounding French word for sweetened whipped cream. Its creamy lusciousness makes it the ideal complement to both warm and cold fruit desserts, flaky pies and tarts, layer cakes and pound cakes. And even though it may seem contradictory, whipped cream actually seems to cut the richness of chocolate. Add a little sour cream (as in the Banana Cream Tart on page 133) or crème fraîche to whipped cream to give it tang and complexity.

I'm pretty picky when it comes to whipped cream and feel strongly that it shouldn't be over-whipped. If it's really over-whipped it will be on its way to butter. Properly whipped, it should hold a smooth mound when dolloped off the end of a spoon. The silky texture isn't just a visual thing—perfectly whipped cream tastes of butterfat, has a better mouthfeel, and is more delicious. If you whip cream by hand with a whisk, there's less chance that you will over-whip it, and in fact many pastry chefs will serve only "hand-whipped" cream. I'm not one of them and like the ease of using a mixer. Just watch it carefully and stop when the cream is thick and soft.

1. Combine all of the ingredients and whisk until soft peaks form.

2. Refrigerate the bowl covered tightly with plastic wrap, until ready to serve.

WHAT YOU'LL NEED
Bowl and whisk, rotary beater, or electric mixer

1 cup heavy (whipping) cream

3 tablespoons granulated sugar

1/2 teaspoon pure vanilla extract

Basic Tips for

Whipped Cream 101

Although I've given you one, it's not necessary to follow a precise recipe when making whipped cream. You want a touch of sweetness but not so much that it makes the whole dessert too sweet. Add more or less sugar to my basic recipe as you prefer.

You can use either heavy cream or heavy whipping cream, but avoid ultra-pasteurized if you can. Ultra-pasteurized cream is heated to a higher temperature to lengthen its shelf life, but the taste is not clean nor does it hold a whip well. It also goes from under-whipped to over-whipped in seconds.

Many recipes call for confectioners' sugar, but I prefer to use granulated because confectioners' has cornstarch added to prevent it from lumping and you can taste it in the finished cream.

Flavor the cream with pure vanilla extract or a scraped out vanilla bean (see pages 182–183 for illustrations on how to do this).

I never bother to chill the bowl or beaters in the fridge beforehand unless it's a hot, humid day in the middle of summer.

If I'm serving the cream as an accompaniment to dessert, I'll often splurge on organic or artisan cream because you'll be able to taste the difference. It's not worth the expense if the cream is an ingredient in the dessert.

If I have only a cup or so of cream to whip, I use an old-fashioned rotary beater, sometimes called an egg beater. It's faster than by hand with a whisk and you don't have to haul out the mixer.

If you have over-whipped the cream, fold in some un-whipped cream and it will bring it back. (This trick won't work if you have whipped it so far that it looks like butter.)

You can whip cream several hours before you need it. Put the bowl in the fridge, well wrapped with plastic (cream can absorb odors). Just give the cream a few whisks if it has separated and it will come back.

Replace half the cream with mascarpone to make it creamier or crème fraîche to give it tang.

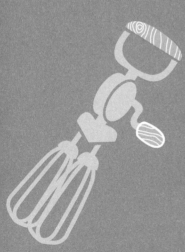

Chocolate Sauce

Makes about 2 cups

Chocolate sauce is all about the chocolate, so find a dark chocolate brand you like and use it. While the dessert recipes in this book call for chocolate that has 58 to 62 percent cacao, for sauce you can use a higher percentage, around 70 percent, if that's more to your taste. If you do, the sauce may turn out thicker, in which case just add a couple extra tablespoons of cream. Chocolate sauce is embarrassingly easy to make when you consider how much flavor it delivers. Bring cream to a low boil, add chopped chocolate, and that's it. I even use it as a base for my husband Peter's hot chocolate. The sauce can be reheated either in the microwave or a double boiler.

I like to make the sauce in quantity just to have it around. It goes with so many desserts and can even turn a bowl of store-bought vanilla ice cream into something special. Besides, I hate seeing the disappointed faces of my friends if I have to tell them they can only have a little drizzle. This recipe is double the amount of the one served with the Honey-Roasted Pears (page 176) and can be tripled. In addition to the pears, the sauce is wonderful with Coffee-Orange Angel Food Cake (page 90), Vanilla Pound Cake (page 108), and Coconut Rum Tart (page 134), just to name a few. I am sure you will find more.

WHAT YOU'LL NEED
Medium saucepan

Spoon or heat-proof rubber spatula

7 ounces dark chocolate (58 to 62 percent cacao), chopped or broken into 1-inch pieces

1 cup heavy cream

1. Put the chopped chocolate in a bowl. Warm the cream in a medium saucepan over medium heat until it starts to bubble around the edge. Pour the warm cream over the chocolate. Shake the bowl a little to submerge all the chocolate pieces, then cover the bowl for several minutes.

2. Whisk the cream with the chocolate until it's smooth and you don't see any more chocolate pieces. The sauce will keep in the fridge for 2 weeks in a covered container.

Caramel Sauce

Makes 1 3/4 cups

If I could only have one dessert sauce this—without a doubt—would be it. Caramel sauce is the most complex tasting sauce I know and it goes with every flavor in the pastry kitchen: apples, nuts, berries, stone fruit, chocolate, coffee, and pineapple. It is a staple in my kitchen. I use it to dress up store-bought ice cream, serve it alongside cake, and layer it into parfaits. Frankly, no commercial caramel sauce compares to one that's homemade. There are a few good specialty ones out there, but they are expensive. Making it at home is inexpensive—sugar, water, and cream. That's it. It keeps for weeks in the fridge and can be reheated in the microwave or double boiler.

I know a lot of cooks who are afraid to make caramel. It can be tricky business for sure. Lest I scare you off, let me reassure you that if you follow these instructions carefully, you'll soon be making it all the time.

If your first try is a light tan and the sauce is thin even after it's cooled, next time cook the caramel a little bit further. On the other hand, if the caramel has a bitter aftertaste, next time cook it a little less.

A pastry chef trick to easily clean a pot you have just made caramel in is to fill it half full of water and bring it to a boil. The hot water will dissolve any hard caramel pieces that stick to the side. Another trick, on the off chance you do burn your caramel and you want to get rid of it, is to add a couple cups of water, carefully at first, just as when you add the cream, to dilute it. Let it cool some and then it can be poured down the sink.

WHAT YOU'LL NEED

Medium saucepan

Pastry brush

Wooden spoon or heat-proof rubber spatula

Oven mitts

1 1/2 cups granulated sugar

1/2 cup water

1 cup heavy cream

EL: Now that you have your ingredients measured, put the measuring cup with the cream next to the stovetop so you can quickly add it to the caramel to stop the caramel from cooking.

FB: Okay. Got it right here. So the recipe says to put the sugar and water in a medium saucepan, stir them together, and cook over medium heat until the sugar is dissolved and the water looks clear, 2 to 3 minutes.

EL: Yes, there are two phases in making caramel. First you want the sugar to dissolve. I like to start it out on medium heat. If you turn it too high to begin with, then you might find it cooks unevenly before the sugar is dissolved and it will look cloudy in areas and clear in others. If that happens, it can crystallize, which is how you make rock candy. Then you'll have to throw it out and start over.

1. In the medium saucepan, whisk the sugar with the water so there are no sugar clumps. Cook over medium heat until the sugar is dissolved and the water looks clear, 2 to 3 minutes. Turn the heat up to medium-high and brush down the side of the saucepan with the pastry brush dipped in water. (This prevents any sugar from sticking to the side of the pan and forming crystals.) Have the cream in a measuring cup with a spout right near your stovetop where you can reach it.

2. With the heat still at medium-high, continue to cook. Do not stir the caramel anymore at this point. After about 15 minutes, you'll notice the bubbles getting bigger and slower just before the caramel begins to turn color.

3. As soon as the caramel turns a medium tan color, remove the pan from the heat. The bubbles will subside a little, so it will be easier for you to check the color.* Watch carefully and as soon as it turns a dark tan, slowly pour in a couple of tablespoons of the cream. Stand back a little and be careful—the cream will cause the hot caramel to bubble up. Stir the cream into the caramel with the heat-proof spatula. Once the caramel stops sputtering, stir in more cream. Continue to pour in the remaining cream but stop again at any time if it sputters.

4. Let the caramel sauce cool to room temperature. Refrigerate in a covered container for up to 3 weeks. If there is any hard caramel sticking to the pan, fill it with water and bring it to a boil. Allow to cool before cleaning the pan.

* If, at the point where you are going to add the cream, the caramel seems too dark, add water instead of cream so you can pour it down the drain and start over.

Breakfast

If it's true that we're a fast food nation, then it's doubly true that we're a fast food breakfast nation — that is, if we eat breakfast at all. Many of my friends, and particularly chef colleagues, start their day with nothing more than coffee (and are starving by ten o'clock).

I'm always amazed at how people who turn down a simple fresh fruit dessert after dinner will run into the nearest coffee shop in the morning, order a mocha latte, and say "Oh by the way, how about one of those cheese and prune Danishes?" I won't name names.

I don't understand wasting your daily calorie allotment on baked goods or sweets that have no redeeming quality other than that they satisfy an urge or taste for sugar in the morning. I have to ask why, since it's so much better for you and, believe it or not, easy to make your own breakfast treats? But I know that what may seem easy to me, a professional pastry chef, might seem really intimidating to others.

Let me reassure you that the recipes in this chapter were all chosen because they are meant to be prepared without complicated techniques, special equipment, or hard-to-find ingredients. All the familiar favorites are included—scones, muffins, coffee cakes—and I guarantee they are better than anything you can buy.

Baked goods for breakfast can really be considered weekend treats, but I don't think you should limit yourself there. A homemade pastry for breakfast is a good way to start a Wednesday or any other workday. All the recipes in this chapter can be made from scratch in the morning for a Sunday brunch without a huge time commitment. Others can be baked ahead of time and eaten on the run for a weekday breakfast—particularly the quick breads, which I like to toast and smear with butter or jam. Some of the recipes, like the scones, can be prepared to a point and refrigerated, ready to be baked right before you want to eat or serve them.

If you're new to baking and want to start with something that will give you a boost of confidence, try one of the breakfast treats in this chapter. Anyone you make them for—including yourself—will be grateful. Here are a few do-ahead tips before we get started:

- A time-saving trick for muffins and scones is to measure out the wet and dry ingredients into separate bowls at night and then stir them together in the morning right before popping them into the oven.

- All coffee cakes can be made the night before, cut into pieces, and reheated in a 300°F oven.

- Sticky buns and cinnamon rolls can be assembled the night before, refrigerated, and baked in the morning (let them sit at room temperature while the oven is preheating).

Apple Turnovers

Makes 8 turnovers

Tastier than a greasy doughnut from the neighborhood coffee shop (and much better for you), these apple turnovers are the ultimate eat-on-the-run breakfast. Made with fresh apples and store-bought puff pastry, they're undeniably easy, not to mention delicious.

I will often make a lot of this apple filling and freeze it just to have it on hand. Most red apple varieties, except Red Delicious, have the right combination of sweet-tart flavor and juiciness.

WHAT YOU'LL NEED

2 baking sheets

Parchment paper

Pastry brush

4 red apples, any kind except Red Delicious

3 tablespoons granulated sugar

1 tablespoon freshly squeezed lemon juice

1/4 teaspoon kosher salt

2 sheets store-bought puff pastry (see page 117), defrosted according to the package directions

1 large egg, slightly beaten for the egg wash

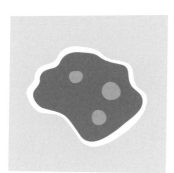

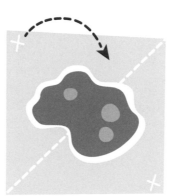

1. Peel the apples and core them from the top by cutting off the sides and removing the rectangular pieces of core. Cut the apples into 1/2- by 1/4-inch-thick pieces.

2. Combine the apples, sugar, lemon juice, and salt in a large skillet and cook over medium-high heat, stirring occasionally, until they're soft and starting to break apart, 15 to 20 minutes. If they brown too much before they're soft, decrease the heat to medium. Add a little water if they look too dry. Since the apples won't cook in the turnovers, you want them to be thoroughly soft. Bite into one piece if you're not sure. If you're going to make the turnovers right away, set the pan aside and let the apples cool to room temperature; or refrigerate for up to 2 days in a covered container.

3. Preheat the oven to 375°F.

4. When you're ready to assemble the turnovers, line the 2 baking sheets with parchment paper. Unfold one of the thawed sheets of puff pastry by carefully opening it to see if it's cold but pliable. If it starts to crack, let it defrost on the counter for 5 minutes and test it again. Once it's fully flexible, unfold it and check for any cracks along the seam. If there are any, simply push the edges back together and smooth them out. Place the puff pastry onto a lightly floured work surface and cut it into 4 equal squares.

5. Place 2 tablespoons of apple filling in the center of each pastry square. Brush the outer 1/2-inch edge of the squares with the egg wash. Fold one of the points of the square over the filling to meet an opposite point to form a triangle. Press the 2 sides of each of the triangles with the tines of a fork to seal them. (If the pastry tears, don't worry, just press it together lightly.) Repeat folding the remaining 3 turnovers. Cut 3 small (1-inch) slits in the middle of each triangle and place the turnovers on one of the baking sheets.

6. Using the second piece of puff pastry, make 4 more turnovers.

7. Bake the turnovers until golden brown, about 25 minutes.

Almond–Dried Cherry Coffee Cake

Makes 1 cake, serving about 12

This coffee cake is a favorite of mine, mostly because of the streusel top. You'll notice I add streusel to a lot of my quick-bread and muffin recipes to give them more texture. I love the contrast between the soft cake and crunchy topping. Here, once you've mixed the dry ingredients, you reserve 3/4 cup to combine with oil for the topping, saving you the extra step of having to make streusel.

WHAT YOU'LL NEED
9-inch square baking pan

Rubber spatula

1 cup sliced almonds

2 cups unbleached all-purpose flour

1 cup granulated sugar

3/4 cup firmly packed brown sugar

1/4 cup white cornmeal

2 teaspoons ground cinnamon

1/2 teaspoon kosher salt

1 teaspoon baking powder

1 large egg

1 cup buttermilk or 1 cup whole milk mixed with 1 teaspoon lemon juice

1/2 cup dried tart cherries

3/4 cup vegetable oil

1. Preheat the oven to 350°F. Grease the bottom and side of the baking pan with nonstick cooking spray or butter.

2. Spread the almonds in one layer in a small baking pan and put in the (preheated) oven. Set a timer for 10 minutes and check the nuts to see if they're a light golden brown. If not, toast 2 minutes longer. Set aside to cool.

3. In a medium bowl, whisk the flour, granulated sugar, brown sugar, cornmeal, cinnamon, and salt. Stir in the almonds. Transfer 3/4 cup of the mixture to a small bowl and set it aside.

4. Stir the baking powder into the remaining flour mixture. Stir in the egg and buttermilk until well blended.

5. Using the spatula, spread the batter into the prepared pan and sprinkle with the cherries, pressing them lightly into the batter.

6. Stir the vegetable oil into the reserved mixture in the small bowl and sprinkle it on the top.

7. Bake the cake until a bamboo skewer or toothpick inserted in the middle comes out clean, about 35 minutes. Let the coffee cake cool in the pan before cutting.

Almond Morning Bread (Bostock)

Makes 6 servings

In France they call this *bostock*. I don't know how it got its name, but I'm sure the concept was a clever baker's way of trying to make use of leftover brioche. It's rich, eggy bread spread with almond paste, sprinkled with toasted almonds, then baked until it is puffy and golden. It's deceptively plain but undeniably good.

You can make the almond paste 2 or 3 days ahead; let it soften to room temperature and spread it on the bread just before you're going to toast it. The bread can be fresh or one or two days old.

WHAT YOU'LL NEED
Food processor

Rubber spatula

Baking or cookie sheet

2/3 cup plus 3/4 cup sliced almonds

1/2 cup granulated sugar

1 large egg

1 teaspoon pure vanilla extract

2 tablespoons unsalted butter, softened

2 tablespoons unbleached all-purpose flour

Pinch kosher salt

6 slices challah, brioche, or other rich (eggy) sandwich bread

4 tablespoons (1/2 stick) unsalted butter, melted

1. Preheat the oven to 350°F.

2. Spread the 2/3 cup almonds in one layer in a small baking pan and put in the (preheated) oven. Set a timer for 10 minutes and check the nuts to see if they're a light golden brown. If not, toast 2 minutes longer. Let cool.

3. In the food processor, process the toasted almonds with the sugar until they're finely ground and look like coarse sand. Add the egg, vanilla, and softened butter and process until everything is well blended. Mix in the flour and salt. With the spatula, scrape the almond paste into a bowl.

4. Brush both sides of the bread slices with some melted butter and then spread some almond paste on one side of each slice. Arrange the bread on the baking sheet and sprinkle the 3/4 cup untoasted sliced almonds over the tops.

5. Bake for 15 minutes, or until golden brown. Serve hot.

Basic Tips for:

Muffins

It's hard to screw up a muffin if you follow a few simple rules. Besides, they're delicious and always welcome for breakfast, brunch, coffee breaks, bake sales, potlucks, scout meetings—well, you get the idea.

Muffins are supposed to be light and crumbly. If they're not, it's because they were overmixed. Stop stirring a few seconds before you think you're done, mixing just until no dry streaks are visible.

I prefer nonstick muffin tins and spray them with baking spray as added insurance that the muffins will release easily. I also like them because the muffins get a crust. For that reason, avoid silicone muffin pans altogether. Muffins baked in paper liners make a nice presentation.

If you use frozen fruit, don't defrost it first.

Scones

The next time you are tempted to grab a scone at Starbucks on the way to work, consider making your own instead. Seriously, they're not at all difficult and they taste better and fresher than anything you could buy. One of the best parts is that you can make the dough the night before, put it in the fridge, and before you take your shower put them in the oven. Brush on the glaze and there you go!

The trick to light and fluffy scones is to mix the ingredients together until they're barely combined. And I mean just that. Contrary to most recipes and our natural inclinations to be thorough, in this case you still want visible streaks (but not clumps) of flour.

Maple-Oatmeal Scones

Makes 8 scones

More than a few of our bakers asked, "What are old-fashioned oats?" Not a silly question when you look at the array of oat cereals on grocery shelves. The classic round box with the Quaker on the label is the most familiar brand. "Old-fashioned" oats are labeled that way to distinguish them from the instant or quick-cooking variety. If you were to substitute instant oats when old-fashioned are specified, they'd turn to mush in your finished product. And regarding ingredients, make sure you use real maple syrup. Imitations lack the flavor of the real thing.

WHAT YOU'LL NEED

Baking or cookie sheet

Parchment paper

1/4 cup plus 5 teaspoons real maple syrup

1/4 cup buttermilk or 1/4 cup whole milk mixed with 1/4 teaspoon lemon juice

1 1/2 cups unbleached all-purpose flour

1 cup old-fashioned oats

2 tablespoons firmly packed brown sugar

1 1/4 teaspoons baking powder

1/2 teaspoon baking soda

1/2 teaspoon kosher salt

10 tablespoons (1 1/4 sticks) cold unsalted butter

1/3 cup confectioners' sugar

1. Preheat the oven to 375°F. Line the baking sheet with parchment paper.

2. In a small bowl, stir the 1/4 cup maple syrup with the buttermilk. Set aside.

3. In a medium bowl, whisk the flour with the oats, brown sugar, baking powder, baking soda, and salt.

4. Cut the butter into 1/2-inch cubes. Add to the bowl with the flour and, using your fingers, a fork, or a pastry blender, break up the butter until it's about the size of cornflakes and is mixed with the dry ingredients. Add the buttermilk mixture and stir until combined.

5. Turn the dough out onto a floured work surface. Sprinkle with flour and press into an evenly thick 8-inch circle. If it sticks, don't be afraid to sprinkle with more flour. Cut into 8 wedges and arrange on the parchment-lined baking sheet.

6. Bake the scones until they're golden brown, about 15 minutes.

7. While the scones are baking, make a glaze by whisking the remaining 5 teaspoons maple syrup with the confectioners' sugar. Remove the scones from the oven and brush with the glaze. Serve warm or at room temperature.

FB: Now this recipe is much more technical than the last one (our FB had just made a crumble).

EL: Maybe, but it's not hard. Once you learn how to make this recipe, you can make any scone in the world. The sky is the scone limit.

Apple-Cinnamon Scones

Makes 12 scones

WHAT YOU'LL NEED

Baking or cookie sheet

Parchment paper

1 medium apple

3/4 cup heavy cream

1 large egg

1/2 teaspoon pure vanilla extract

1 3/4 cups unbleached all-purpose flour

4 tablespoons granulated sugar

2 1/2 teaspoons baking powder

1/2 teaspoon plus large pinch ground cinnamon

1/2 teaspoon kosher salt

6 tablespoons (3/4 stick) cold unsalted butter

1. Preheat the oven to 350°F. Line the baking sheet with parchment paper.

2. Peel the apple and core it from the top by cutting off the sides and removing the rectangular piece of core. Cut into small (1/4-inch) pieces. In a small bowl, whisk the cream with the egg and vanilla extract and then stir in the apple pieces.

3. In a medium bowl, whisk the flour with 3 tablespoons of the sugar, the baking powder, cinnamon, and salt.

4. Cut the butter into 1/2-inch cubes. Add to the bowl with the flour and, using your fingers, a fork, or a pastry blender, break up the butter until it's about the size and thickness of cornflakes and is mixed with the dry ingredients. Add the apples and cream and stir until combined.

5. Turn the dough out onto on a floured work surface. Sprinkle with flour and press into an evenly thick 8-inch circle. Cut into 12 wedges and arrange on the parchment-lined baking sheet. Stir together the remaining 1 tablespoon sugar and pinch cinnamon and sprinkle on the scones.

6. Bake the scones until golden brown, about 25 minutes.

Golden Raisin–Lime Scones

Makes 12 scones

WHAT YOU'LL NEED

Baking or cookie sheet

Parchment paper

2 cups unbleached all-purpose flour

1/4 cup plus 2 tablespoons granulated sugar

Grated zest of 2 limes

1 tablespoon baking powder

1/4 teaspoon kosher salt

8 tablespoons (1 stick) cold unsalted butter

1/2 cup golden raisins

3/4 cup buttermilk or 3/4 cup whole milk mixed with 1 teaspoon lemon juice

1. Preheat the oven to 375°F. Line the baking sheet with parchment paper.

2. In a medium bowl, whisk the flour with the 1/4 cup sugar, the zest, baking powder, and salt.

3. Cut the butter into 1/2-inch pieces. Add to the bowl with the flour and, using your fingers, a fork, or a pastry blender, break up the butter until it's about the size and thickness of cornflakes and is mixed with the dry ingredients. Add the raisins and buttermilk and stir until combined.

4. Turn the dough out onto a floured work surface. Sprinkle with flour and press into an evenly thick 12-inch circle. Cut into 12 wedges and arrange on the parchment-lined baking sheet. Sprinkle the tops with the remaining 2 tablespoons sugar.

5. Bake the scones until golden brown, about 25 minutes.

Bran Muffins

Makes 12 muffins

I love bran muffins, but too often the ones you buy are heavy and overly sweetened. I think you'll find these muffins sweet, light, and moist. If you grind the bran in the processor the night before, the rest of the recipe can be quickly put together by hand, a good thing in the morning, when you don't want to get out the mixer.

Wheat bran comes in several forms. There are the unprocessed flakes (which look like sawdust), the pebbly cereal (think Grape-Nuts), and the thread-like cereal, such as All-Bran, which is what you want here.

WHAT YOU'LL NEED
Standard 12-cup muffin pan

Food processor

3 cups bran cereal (All-Bran or Bran Flakes)

1 1/4 cups unbleached all-purpose flour

3/4 cup granulated sugar

1 1/4 teaspoons baking soda

1/4 teaspoon kosher salt

1 large egg

1/4 cup vegetable oil

1 cup buttermilk or 1 cup whole milk mixed with 1 teaspoon lemon juice

1. Preheat the oven to 400°F. Butter the cups of the muffin pan, spritz with nonstick cooking spray, or fill with paper liners.

2. In the food processor, pulse the bran cereal until finely ground.

3. Stir the ground bran in a medium bowl with the flour, sugar, baking soda, and salt.

4. In a small bowl, whisk the egg with the oil and buttermilk. Using a rubber spatula or large spoon, stir the egg mixture into the bran mixture until evenly combined and no dry pieces are visible. Mix until everything is barely blended—to keep the muffins light it's important not to overmix the batter.

5. Spoon the batter into the prepared muffin cups, filling them equally. Bake until a bamboo skewer or toothpick inserted into the middles of the muffins comes out clean, about 15 minutes. Let cool in the pan for 5 minutes and then use a small paring knife to pop them out of the cups.

Apple Muffins

Makes 12 muffins

WHAT YOU'LL NEED
Standard 12-cup muffin pan

2 medium apples

8 tablespoons (1 stick) unsalted butter, softened

2/3 cup granulated sugar

1/4 cup firmly packed brown sugar

1 large egg

1/4 cup whole or 2 percent milk

1 3/4 cups unbleached all-purpose flour

2 1/4 teaspoons baking powder

1/2 teaspoon ground cinnamon

1/2 teaspoon kosher salt

1. Preheat the oven to 350°F. Butter the cups of the muffin pan, spritz with nonstick cooking spray, or fill with paper liners.

2. Peel the apples and core them from the top by cutting off the sides and removing the rectangular pieces of core. Cut them into small (1/4-inch) pieces (you should have about 2 cups).

3. In a medium bowl, mix the butter with the granulated sugar and brown sugar until smooth. Stir in the egg and milk until combined. Stir in the apple pieces, flour, baking powder, cinnamon, and salt. Mix until everything is barely blended—to keep the muffins light it's important not to overmix the batter.

4. Spoon the batter into the prepared muffin cups, filling them equally. Bake until a bamboo skewer or toothpick inserted into the middles of the muffins comes out clean, about 18 minutes. Let cool in the pan for 5 minutes and then use a small paring knife to pop them out of the cups.

Blueberry Streusel Muffins

Makes 12 muffins

WHAT YOU'LL NEED
Standard 12-cup muffin pan

2/3 cup granulated sugar

6 tablespoons unsalted butter, softened

Zest of 2 lemons

2 large eggs

2/3 cup sour cream

3 cups blueberries

2 cups unbleached all-purpose flour

2 teaspoons baking powder

1/4 teaspoon kosher salt

Streusel Topping
1/4 cup unbleached all-purpose flour

1/4 cup firmly packed light brown sugar

2 tablespoons unsalted butter, softened

1. Preheat the oven to 375°F. Butter the cups of the muffin pan, spritz with nonstick cooking spray, or fill with paper liners.

2. In a medium bowl with a wooden spoon, mix the sugar with the butter and lemon zest until well combined. Stir in the eggs and sour cream. Add the blueberries, flour, baking powder, and salt and mix until everything is evenly combined and no dry streaks are visible. Mix until everything is barely blended—to keep the muffins light it's important to not overmix the batter.

Streusel Topping

3. In a medium bowl, stir the flour with the brown sugar. Add the softened butter in pieces and combine with a fork until the topping is in coarse crumbs.

4. Spoon the batter into the prepared muffin cups, filling them equally. Sprinkle the streusel evenly over the tops.

5. Bake until a bamboo skewer or toothpick inserted into the middles of the muffins comes out clean and the tops are golden brown, about 25 minutes. Let the muffins cool in the pan for 5 minutes and then use a small paring knife to pop them out of the cups.

Raspberry Corn Muffins

Makes 12 muffins

WHAT YOU'LL NEED
Standard 12-cup muffin pan

1 cup cornmeal

1 1/4 cups unbleached all-purpose flour

1/2 cup granulated sugar

2 teaspoons baking powder

1 1/2 teaspoons baking soda

1/2 teaspoon kosher salt

2 large eggs

3/4 cup buttermilk or 3/4 cup whole milk mixed with 1 teaspoon lemon juice

12 tablespoons (1 1/2 sticks) unsalted butter, melted

3 tablespoons honey

1 1/2 cups raspberries

1. Preheat the oven to 400°F. Grease the cups of a muffin pan with nonstick cooking spray or butter or fill with paper liners.

2. In a medium bowl, stir the cornmeal with the flour, sugar, baking powder, baking soda, and salt.

3. In another medium bowl, whisk the eggs and buttermilk, then whisk in the butter and honey. Using a rubber spatula or large spoon, stir in the flour mixture until the batter is evenly combined and no dry streaks are visible. Add the raspberries and gently mix until everything is barely blended—to keep the muffins light it's important to not overmix the batter.

4. Spoon the batter into the prepared muffin cups, filling them equally. Bake until a bamboo skewer or toothpick inserted into the middles of the muffins comes out clean and the tops are golden brown, about 20 minutes. Let cool in the pan for 5 minutes and then use a small paring knife to pop them out of the cups.

Dried Apricot-Cherry Puffs

Makes 6 puffs

These "puffs" are similar to turnovers but shaped like miniature Frisbees. Instead of using fresh fruit, cooked dried fruit is encased in flaky dough.

They can be formed the night before and baked in the morning while the coffee brews; I like them best on the day they're baked.

Cooking the dried fruit in the butter and brown sugar intensifies its flavor, making it so much better than if you were to use the fruit plain. Remember that it's the little things that count, particularly when you're working with only a few ingredients.

WHAT YOU'LL NEED
Rolling pin

4-inch round cookie cutter (if you have one)

Baking or cookie sheet

2/3 cup dried apricots

2/3 cup dried cherries

4 tablespoons (1/2 stick) unsalted butter

1/3 cup firmly packed light brown sugar

2 sheets store-bought puff pastry (see page 117), defrosted according to the package directions

1 large egg, lightly beaten

1 tablespoon granulated sugar

1. Preheat the oven to 400°F.

2. Cut the dried apricots the same size as the dried cherries (I like to use scissors to cut dried fruit—it's easier). In a medium saucepan, melt the butter with the brown sugar over medium-low heat. Add the apricots and cherries, stirring until everything is blended. Set the filling aside to cool to room temperature.

3. Unfold one of the thawed sheets of puff pastry (leave the second sheet in the fridge) by carefully opening it to see if it's cold but pliable. If it starts to crack, let it defrost on the counter for 5 minutes and test it again. Once it's fully flexible, unfold it and check for any cracks along the seam. If there are any, simply push the edges back together and smooth them out.

4. Roll out the puff pastry on a lightly floured surface into an 11- by 12-inch rectangle that's evenly about 1/8 inch thick. Using the cookie cutter or a 4-inch plate as a template, cut it into 6 rounds and place on the baking sheet. Repeat with the second sheet of puff pastry. Put all the pastry rounds back in the refrigerator to keep them cold.

5. When you're ready to fill the puffs, remove the pastry from the fridge and place 2 tablespoons of the filling in the middle of 6 of the rounds. Brush the outer 1/4 inch of the circle with the egg. Top with the other 6 pastry rounds. Using your fingers, press the edge of each pastry firmly together. With a paring knife, make three small slits in the top of each pastry. Brush with the remaining egg wash and sprinkle with the granulated sugar.

6. Bake until the pastry is a deep golden brown, about 20 minutes.

Blueberry–Cinnamon Sugar Buns

Makes 12 buns

Puff pastry is a miraculous thing indeed, but thank goodness, with so many good brands available, we don't have to make it from scratch. Store-bought puff pastry allows you to make these buns anytime, because they can be assembled in the pan and baked in the morning. I'm not big on sweets early in the day, but these buns are fabulous, bursting—literally, because they pop open—with blueberries.

Make sure you use fresh blueberries. Frozen berries don't work because they become too wet. Let the buns cool in the pan for not more than 10 minutes (or they will be impossible to remove). Use a spoon to scoop them out.

WHAT YOU'LL NEED
Standard 12-cup muffin pan

Pastry brush

1/2 teaspoon ground cinnamon

1/3 cup firmly packed brown sugar

1/3 cup granulated sugar

4 tablespoons (1/2 stick) unsalted butter

2 sheets store-bought puff pastry (page 117), defrosted according to the package directions

1 cup fresh blueberries

1. Preheat the oven to 350°F.

2. In a small bowl, stir the cinnamon with the brown sugar and granulated sugar. Melt the butter in a saucepan or the microwave.

3. Unfold one of the thawed sheets of puff pastry (leave the second sheet in the fridge) by carefully opening it to see if it's cold but pliable. If it starts to crack, let it defrost on the counter for 5 minutes and test it again. Once it's fully flexible, unfold it and check for any cracks along the seam. If there are any, simply push the edges back together and smooth them out.

4. Brush the sheet of puff pastry with a little melted butter and sprinkle with 2 tablespoons of the cinnamon sugar. Put half of the blueberries on the pastry and, with your hands, spread them out so they're spaced somewhat evenly.

5. Roll the puff pastry up in a log. Pinch the long seam together and brush on all sides with melted butter. Sprinkle all sides with some of the cinnamon sugar and pat it on so it adheres. Cut the log into 6 equal slices. (The easiest way to do that is first to cut the log in half crosswise and then cut each half into 3 equal pieces.)

6. Brush the cut sides of the rolls with melted butter and then sprinkle with cinnamon sugar. Put the rolls spiral-side up in the muffin cups. Make 6 more rolls with the second sheet of puff pastry. Sprinkle the tops of the rolls in the pan with any remaining cinnamon sugar.

7. Bake the rolls until golden brown, about 25 minutes. Let cool for 5 minutes and then, with a soup spoon, scoop or nudge the buns out of the pan. If you find that they're sticking, put the pan back in the oven to warm for a few minutes.

8. Serve the cinnamon buns warm or at room temperature.

Breakfast Fall Fruit Crumble

Serves 8

This crumble is perfect for breakfast, especially if you serve it with yogurt. Bake it fresh on Sunday morning and reheat leftovers during the week. Here you don't need to peel the apples and pears.

WHAT YOU'LL NEED

9- by 13-inch baking dish

2 red apples, any kind except Red Delicious

2 ripe pears

1/2 cup dried sweetened cranberries

1/2 cup granulated sugar

Grated zest of 1 lemon

Crumble Topping

6 tablespoons (3/4 stick) cold unsalted butter

3/4 cup unbleached all-purpose flour

1/4 cup granulated sugar

1/4 teaspoon ground cinnamon

1/8 teaspoon kosher salt

1/3 cup quick-cooking oats

1/3 cup sliced almonds

1. Preheat the oven to 375°F. Grease the bottom and sides of the baking dish with nonstick cooking spray or butter.

2. From the top, core the apples by cutting off the sides and removing the rectangular piece of core. Slice the apples 1/4 inch thick. Cut the pears and discard the cores, then slice 1/2 inch thick. Put the fruit into a medium bowl and toss with the cranberries, sugar, and lemon zest. Spread evenly in the bottom of the prepared baking dish.

Crumble Topping

3. Cut the butter into 3/4-inch pieces. Put in a bowl with the flour, sugar, cinnamon, and salt. Using your fingers or a fork, break up the butter until it's the size of small peas and is mixed with the dry ingredients. Stir in the oats and almonds. Distribute the crumble topping evenly over the fruit.

4. Bake the crumble until the topping is golden, 35 to 40 minutes.

5. Let the crumble cool slightly before serving. It can be reheated.

Breakfast Breads

I love breakfast breads, whether they're made out of bananas, carrots, pumpkin, or zucchini. There's just something so seductive about waking up in the morning, coming into the kitchen, and seeing a loaf on the counter just waiting to be sliced and put in the toaster oven. What could be simpler or more satisfying? Add a little pat of butter or a schmear of cream cheese perhaps, but plain is fine too.

These breads are all made by hand, but you can use your mixer on low speed too.

FB: What does a recipe mean really when it says softened or room-temperature butter?

EL: When I say "softened" butter, I mean butter that's been allowed to soften at room temperature, as opposed to butter taken straight out of the refrigerator. That's "cold" butter. How long butter needs to sit out to become soft depends on the temperature of the room. It could be anywhere from fifteen minutes up to an hour. What you want is butter that you can make a finger dent in. Or a stick of butter that can bend.

FB: This stick seems too soft, because I can't even pick it up, it's so oily.

EL: That butter is too soft. You don't want it greasy. If it's really warm, as it is today, it will take only fifteen minutes or so to soften the butter at room temperature.

FB: Can you soften it in the microwave?

EL: Yes but it's not ideal. You have to be careful not to melt it. Try it on the lowest power at ten-second intervals, and turn it over to make sure it's not melting.

Banana Bread

Makes 1 loaf, about 12 slices

WHAT YOU'LL NEED
9- by 5-inch loaf pan

1 cup firmly packed light brown sugar

12 tablespoons (1 1/2 sticks) unsalted butter, softened

3 large eggs

1 cup (about 2 large) super-ripe bananas

1 3/4 cups unbleached all-purpose flour

1 1/4 teaspoons baking powder

1/4 teaspoon kosher salt

1. Preheat the oven to 350°F. Grease the bottom and sides of the loaf pan with nonstick cooking spray or butter.

2. In a medium bowl, use a wooden spoon (or any other stiff spoon) to mix the brown sugar with the butter until smooth. Stir in the eggs one at a time, mixing until well combined before adding the next egg.

3. Stir in the bananas, then add the flour, baking powder, and salt, stirring until the mixture is smooth.

4. Spread the batter into the prepared pan. Bake until a bamboo skewer or toothpick inserted in the middle comes out clean, about 45 minutes. Let the banana bread cool for 15 minutes and then unmold.

5. To remove, run a small knife around the bread to loosen it from the pan and then turn it out onto a cutting board or plate. Cool completely. Cut into slices. The bread will keep at room temperature, wrapped in plastic, for 4 days or frozen for 2 months.

Carrot Bread

Makes 1 loaf, about 12 slices

WHAT YOU'LL NEED

9- by 5-inch loaf pan

Food processor or blender

8 medium carrots

1 1/3 cups unbleached all-purpose flour

1 teaspoon baking soda

1/4 teaspoon baking powder

3/4 teaspoon kosher salt

6 tablespoons (3/4 stick) unsalted butter, softened

1 cup granulated sugar

2 large eggs

1/3 cup buttermilk or 1/3 cup whole milk mixed with 1/2 teaspoon lemon juice

1. Preheat the oven to 350°F. Grease the bottom and sides of the loaf pan with nonstick cooking spray or butter.

2. Peel and slice 3 of the carrots into 1/4-inch rounds. Bring a medium saucepan of salted water to a boil, add the carrots, and cook until soft, about 10 minutes. Drain. Let cool and then puree in the food processor or blender. Coarsely grate the remaining 5 carrots (you should have 2 cups). Set both the pureed carrots and grated carrots aside.

3. Measure the flour, baking soda, baking powder, and salt onto a piece of parchment paper or into a bowl. Set aside.

4. In a medium bowl, use a wooden spoon (or any other stiff spoon) to mix the butter and sugar until smooth. Stir in the eggs one at a time until combined. Stir in the buttermilk, carrot puree, and grated carrots. Add the flour mixture and mix until well blended.

5. Spread the batter in the prepared pan. Bake until a bamboo skewer or toothpick inserted in the middle comes out clean, about 50 minutes. Let the bread cool for fifteen minutes.

6. To remove, run a small knife around the bread to loosen it from the pan and then turn it out onto a cutting board or plate. Cool completely. Cut into slices. The bread will keep at room temperature, wrapped in plastic, for 4 days or frozen for 2 months.

Pumpkin Bread

Makes 1 loaf, about 12 slices

9- by 5-inch loaf pan

1 1/3 cups unbleached all-purpose flour

1 teaspoon baking soda

1/4 teaspoon baking powder

1/2 teaspoon ground cinnamon

1/4 teaspoon ground nutmeg

1/4 teaspoon ground cloves

3/4 teaspoon kosher salt

6 tablespoons (3/4 stick) unsalted butter, softened

1 cup plus 2 tablespoons granulated sugar

2 large eggs

1/3 cup buttermilk or 1/3 cup whole milk mixed with 1/2 teaspoon lemon juice

1 cup pumpkin puree

1 cup pecan pieces

1. Preheat the oven to 350°F. Grease the bottom and sides of the loaf pan with nonstick cooking spray or butter.

2. Measure the flour, baking soda, baking powder, cinnamon, nutmeg, cloves, and salt onto a piece of parchment paper or into a bowl. Set aside.

3. In a medium bowl, use a wooden spoon (or any other stiff spoon) to mix the butter and the 1 cup sugar until smooth. Stir in the eggs one at a time until combined. Mix in the buttermilk and pumpkin puree. Stir in the flour mixture and mix until well blended.

4. Spread the batter into the prepared pan and sprinkle the pecans and remaining 2 tablespoons sugar on top. Bake until a bamboo skewer or toothpick inserted in the middle comes out clean, about 1 hour. Let the pumpkin bread cool for 15 minutes.

5. To remove, run a small knife around the bread to loosen it from the pan and then turn it out onto a cutting board or plate. Cool completely. Cut into slices. The bread will keep at room temperature, wrapped in plastic, for 4 days or frozen for 2 months.

Zucchini Bread

Makes 1 loaf, about 12 slices

WHAT YOU'LL NEED

9- by 5-inch loaf pan

2 medium firm zucchini

2 1/3 cups unbleached all-purpose flour

1 1/2 teaspoons baking powder

1 1/4 teaspoons baking soda

1 teaspoon kosher salt

3/4 cup vegetable oil

3/4 cup granulated sugar

3/4 cup firmly packed brown sugar

3 large eggs

1. Preheat the oven to 350°F. Grease the bottom and sides of the loaf pan with nonstick cooking spray or butter.

2. Coarsely grate the zucchini; you should have about 2 1/2 cups loosely packed. Set aside.

3. Measure the flour, baking powder, baking soda, and salt onto a piece of parchment paper or into a bowl. Set aside.

4. In a medium bowl, stir the oil, granulated sugar, and brown sugar together until smooth. Stir in the eggs one at a time until combined. Stir in the flour mixture. Add the grated zucchini and mix until combined.

5. Spread the batter into the prepared pan. Bake until a bamboo skewer or toothpick inserted in the middle comes out clean, about 50 minutes. Let the zucchini bread cool for 15 minutes.

6. To remove, run a small knife around the bread to loosen it from the pan and then turn it out onto a cutting board or plate. Cool completely. Cut into slices. The bread will keep at room temperature, wrapped in plastic, for 4 days or frozen up to 2 months.

Golden Raisin Toasting Bread

Makes 1 loaf, about 12 slices

This loaf is meant to be sliced and toasted. I love it spread with sweet butter. To toast it, put it under the broiler or in a toaster oven. It's so tender and crumbly that it will fall apart if you try to put it in a regular toaster. A little good-quality jam couldn't hurt.

WHAT YOU'LL NEED
9- by 5-inch loaf pan

2 1/2 cups unbleached all-purpose flour

1 1/2 cups firmly packed light brown sugar

1/2 teaspoon kosher salt

8 tablespoons (1 stick) unsalted butter, softened

1 teaspoon baking powder

1 teaspoon ground cinnamon

1 large egg

3/4 cup buttermilk or 3/4 cup whole milk mixed with 1 teaspoon lemon juice

1 cup golden raisins

1 tablespoon unsalted butter, melted and cooled

1. Preheat the oven to 350°F. Grease the bottom and sides of the loaf pan with nonstick cooking spray or butter.

2. In a medium bowl, use a wooden spoon (or any other stiff spoon) to mix the flour with the brown sugar and salt. Add the softened butter and mix until smooth. Remove 1/2 cup of the mixture and set aside in a small bowl. Stir the baking powder and cinnamon into the larger mixture. Stir in the egg, buttermilk, and raisins until combined.

3. Spread the batter into the prepared pan. Stir the 1 tablespoon melted butter into the reserved brown sugar/flour mixture. Sprinkle over the top of the batter in the pan.

4. Bake until a bamboo skewer or toothpick inserted in the middle comes out clean, about 1 hour and 10 minutes. Let the bread cool for 15 minutes.

5. To remove, run a small knife around the bread to loosen it from the pan and then turn it out onto a cutting board or plate. Cool completely. Cut into slices just before toasting. The bread will keep at room temperature, wrapped in plastic, for 3 days or frozen for 2 months.

Cinnamon Coffee Swirls

Makes 16 rolls

These may not be as humongous as those airport cinnamon buns that are as big as your head, but don't be put off by their dainty appearance. The cinnamon rolls are slyly rich, but worth every caloric bite.

WHAT YOU'LL NEED
9-inch baking pan

8 tablespoons (1 stick) unsalted butter, softened

1/2 cup granulated sugar

1 tablespoon ground cinnamon

1 tablespoon plus 1 teaspoon instant coffee granules

1/4 teaspoon kosher salt

2 sheets store-bought puff pastry (see page 117), defrosted according to the package directions

3/4 cup confectioners' sugar, sifted

About 1 tablespoon water

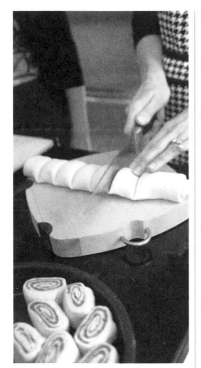

1. Preheat the oven to 400°F. Grease the bottom and sides of the baking pan with nonstick cooking spray or butter.

2. In a small bowl, mix the softened butter with the granulated sugar, cinnamon, 1 tablespoon of the coffee, and the salt.

3. Unfold one of the thawed sheets of puff pastry (leave the second sheet in the fridge) by carefully opening it to see if it's cold but pliable. If it starts to crack, let it defrost on the counter for 10 minutes and test it again. Once it's fully flexible, unfold it and check for any cracks along the seam. If there are any, simply push the edges back together and smooth them out.

4. Spread half of the butter mixture onto one of the puff pastry sheets. Roll it up like a carpet and cut into 8 rounds. Repeat with the second pastry sheet. Arrange the 16 rolls in the prepared pan, cut side up.

5. Bake the rolls until golden brown, about 30 minutes. Let cool in the pan for 5 minutes so that the butter can be re-absorbed by the pastry. Put a serving plate or platter on top of the pan and flip over to turn the rolls out onto the plate. Let sit 5 more minutes. While the rolls are cooling, whisk the confectioners' sugar with the remaining 1 teaspoon coffee and 1 tablespoon water in a small bowl until smooth. If it's too thick to drizzle off the end of a spoon, stir in another teaspoon of water. Drizzle the glaze over the rolls using a slotted spoon or table fork.

Currant-Walnut Galette

Makes 8 servings

"Galette" can mean many things. Most people identify a galette by its free-form pastry shell, a rustic tart that can contain either sweet or savory ingredients. In France, a galette can be anything from a thin, flaky cake, sometimes made with yeast, or a king's cake, made for the feast of the Epiphany. In Breton, it's a buckwheat crepe filled with savory ingredients. What I've made here is a simple, thin, yeasted cake, rich with butter and packed with nuts and currants. It's kind of the non-coffee-cake coffee cake. Not too sweet, but crisp and light. If you've never used yeast before, this cake is a good way to start. There's no kneading or rising of dough required.

WHAT YOU'LL NEED

Baking or cookie sheet

Parchment paper

Rubber spatula

1/4 cup warm water

1 envelope or 2 1/4 teaspoons instant dry yeast

12 tablespoons (1 1/2 sticks) unsalted butter, softened

1/3 cup granulated sugar, plus more for the pan

1 large egg

1 3/4 cups unbleached all-purpose flour

Grated zest of 1 lemon

1/2 cup currants

1/2 teaspoon kosher salt

2 tablespoons walnuts

2 tablespoons firmly packed light brown sugar

FB: It says here, quarter cup of warm water. Do I just go to the tap?

EL: Yes, that's fine. But warm, like bath water.

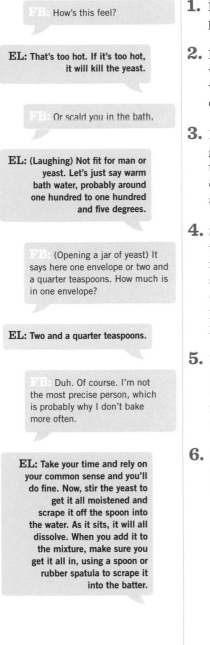

FB: How's this feel?

EL: That's too hot. If it's too hot, it will kill the yeast.

FB: Or scald you in the bath.

EL: (Laughing) Not fit for man or yeast. Let's just say warm bath water, probably around one hundred to one hundred and five degrees.

FB: (Opening a jar of yeast) It says here one envelope or two and a quarter teaspoons. How much is in one envelope?

EL: Two and a quarter teaspoons.

FB: Duh. Of course. I'm not the most precise person, which is probably why I don't bake more often.

EL: Take your time and rely on your common sense and you'll do fine. Now, stir the yeast to get it all moistened and scrape it off the spoon into the water. As it sits, it will all dissolve. When you add it to the mixture, make sure you get it all in, using a spoon or rubber spatula to scrape it into the batter.

1. Preheat the oven to 350°F. Line the baking sheet with parchment paper.

2. Put the warm (bath temperature) water in a small bowl and, with a small spoon, stir in the yeast until it dissolves. Don't worry if it doesn't all dissolve. Just push any goopy yeast left on the spoon into the bowl and let it sit for 10 minutes.

3. In a medium bowl, use a wooden spoon to mix the butter and granulated sugar until smooth. Add the yeast mixture and then the egg and mix until well combined. If it looks curdled, don't worry, it's fine. Stir in the flour, lemon zest, currants, and salt until the dough just comes together.

4. Sprinkle a tablespoon or so of granulated sugar in the middle of the parchment-lined baking sheet and use your fingers to spread it out into an approximate 10-inch circle. With the rubber spatula, scrape the dough in a mound onto the center of the sugar on the sheet. Cover the dough with a piece of plastic wrap and press it into an evenly thick, 10-inch circle (the plastic helps keep your fingers from sticking to the dough.)

5. By hand, using a sharp knife, finely chop the walnuts into 1/8- to 1/4-inch pieces. In a small bowl, stir the nuts with the brown sugar. Sprinkle the mixture evenly over the dough. You can refrigerate the galette dough the night before, but let it sit at room temperature for 15 minutes before baking in the morning.

6. Bake until the galette is evenly golden brown and is as firm in the center as it is on the edge, about 15 minutes. Cut into wedges and serve warm.

Toasty Granola

Makes 2 cups

Many people don't realize you can make your own granola. The advantage to putting forth a little bit of effort in the kitchen is that you can include ingredients to suit your taste. A different nut here, less sugar there. Dried fruit? Go ahead and add it. This recipe makes a kind of dry, loose granola, rather than clumpy, and you get a little kick of candied ginger every few bites.

WHAT YOU'LL NEED
Rimmed baking sheet

1 cup old-fashioned oats

1/2 cup sliced almonds

1/4 cup walnut pieces

1/4 cup currants

1 tablespoon chopped candied ginger

1/8 teaspoon kosher salt

2 tablespoons honey

2 tablespoons real maple syrup

1. Preheat the oven to 300°F.

2. In a medium bowl, stir the oats with the almonds, walnuts, currants, candied ginger, and salt. In a small bowl, stir together the honey and maple syrup. Add to the oat mixture and stir until everything is well combined.

3. Spread the mixture out in a single layer on the baking sheet. Bake, stirring every 10 minutes or so, until the mixture turns a deep golden brown, about 25 minutes.

4. Let cool on the pan. Transfer to an airtight container and store at room temperature for up to 2 weeks.

Oat-Streusel Coffee Cake

Makes 1 cake, serving 12

Because I work around sugary temptations all day, I like to start off in the morning with something simple, delicious, and not too sweet. This coffee cake fits the bill. It's a moist cake, topped with a crunchy streusel. In every slice you get a sliver of topping—just enough to satisfy that morning sweet tooth, yet not so much to send you crashing by your morning coffee break.

WHAT YOU'LL NEED
9- by 13-inch cake pan

Streusel
8 tablespoons (1 stick) cold unsalted butter

1/2 cup quick-cooking oats

1/2 cup walnut pieces

1/2 cup firmly packed brown sugar

1/2 cup unbleached all-purpose flour

1 teaspoon ground cinnamon

1/4 teaspoon kosher salt

Coffee Cake
8 tablespoons (1 stick) unsalted butter, softened

1 1/4 cups granulated sugar

2 large eggs

1 cup buttermilk or 1 cup whole milk mixed with 1 teaspoon lemon juice

1/2 teaspoon pure vanilla extract

3 cups unbleached all-purpose flour

4 teaspoons baking powder

1 teaspoon kosher salt

Streusel

1. Cut the cold butter into small (1/4-inch) cubes. Put the cubes in a medium bowl and stir in the oats, walnut pieces, brown sugar, flour, cinnamon, and salt until everything is well combined. The streusel can be made ahead and kept in a covered container in the refrigerator for up to 2 weeks.

Coffee Cake

2. Preheat the oven to 350°F. Grease the bottom and sides of the baking pan with nonstick cooking spray or butter.

3. In a medium bowl, use a wooden spoon (or any other stiff spoon) to mix the softened butter and sugar together until smooth. Stir in the eggs one at a time until combined. Stir in the buttermilk and vanilla and mix thoroughly. Add the flour, baking powder, and salt and mix until combined.

4. Spread about half of the batter in the prepared pan (the batter will be thick and a bit difficult to spread). Evenly sprinkle with half of the streusel, then spread the remaining batter on top of the streusel. Sprinkle the remaining streusel over the batter.

5. Bake until a bamboo skewer or toothpick inserted in the middle comes out clean, about 35 minutes.

6. Cool the cake in the pan for 10 to 15 minutes. Cut it into approximate 3-inch squares for serving.

Pain au Chocolat Sticky Buns

Makes 12 buns

If you're a fan of *pain au chocolat,* you may find it hard to believe that it could be improved upon, but this recipe is proof that miracles do exist. The gooey brown-sugar topping normally used for sticky buns is combined with chocolate and puff pastry to create the ultimate breakfast indulgence.

Don't skimp on cheap chocolate. Use the best quality you can get your hands on—it will pay off in dividends of flavor.

WHAT YOU'LL NEED
9- by 13-inch baking pan

1/2 cup pecan pieces

1 cup firmly packed brown sugar

8 tablespoons (1 stick) unsalted butter, softened

2 tablespoons dark corn syrup

2 sheets store-bought puff pastry (see page 117), defrosted according to the package directions

1/2 cup chopped (1/4- to 1/2-inch pieces) dark chocolate (58 to 62 percent cacao)

1. Preheat the oven to 350°F.

2. Spread the pecan pieces in one layer in a small baking pan and put in the preheated oven. Set a timer for 10 minutes and check the nuts to see if they're a light golden brown. If not, toast 2 minutes longer. Set aside to cool.

3. In a small bowl, stir 1/2 cup of the brown sugar, 4 tablespoons of the butter, and the corn syrup and spread in the baking pan.

4. Unfold one of the thawed sheets of puff pastry (leave the second sheet in the fridge) by carefully opening it to see if it's cold but pliable. If it starts to crack, let it defrost on the counter for 10 minutes and test it again. Once it's fully flexible, unfold it and check for any cracks along the seam. If there are any, simply push the edges back together and smooth them out.

5. Spread the puff pastry sheet with 2 tablespoons of the remaining butter. Sprinkle 1/4 cup of the remaining brown sugar, 1/4 cup of the pecan pieces, and 1/4 cup of the chocolate over the butter. Roll the pastry up like a carpet, pinch the ends closed, and cut into 6 rounds. (The easiest way to do that is first to cut the log in half crosswise and then cut each half into 3 equal pieces.) Make 6 more rounds with the second pastry sheet. Arrange the 12 rolls in the pan, cut-side up on top of the sugar-butter-syrup mixture.

6. Bake the rolls until golden brown, about 30 minutes. Let cool in the pan for 5 minutes so that the butter can be re-absorbed into the pastry. Put a serving plate or platter on top of the pan and flip over to turn the buns out onto the plate.

Pain Perdu with Plums

Makes 6 servings

We Americans call it French toast. The French call it *pain perdu*. No matter what you call it, this version is baked in the oven so it doesn't get soggy and develops a crispy, golden-brown exterior. The fresh plums, sautéed for a topping, take this familiar breakfast dish to another level. Alternatives to the plums are peaches or apricots.

WHAT YOU'LL NEED
Baking dish or shallow bowl

Baking or cookie sheet

1/2 cup plus 2 tablespoons granulated sugar

1/2 cup firmly packed brown sugar

3/4 teaspoon ground cinnamon

Pinch ground ginger

1 cup whole milk

4 large eggs

1 1/2 teaspoons pure vanilla extract

Pinch kosher salt

6 (3/4-inch-thick) slices challah or rich sandwich bread

Plum Topping
4 ripe red plums

1/3 cup granulated sugar

1/4 teaspoon lemon juice

1. Preheat the oven to 375°F.

2. In a small bowl, stir the 1/2 cup granulated sugar with the brown sugar, cinnamon, and ginger. Spread the mixture out on a plate and set aside.

3. In the baking dish or shallow bowl, whisk the milk with the eggs, remaining 2 tablespoons granulated sugar, the vanilla extract, and salt until the eggs are broken up and well blended with the milk.

4. Dip a bread slice in the egg mixture and turn it to coat both sides. Leave it in for a few seconds and press on it a little bit so it soaks up the liquid. Transfer the soaked bread to the plate with the sugar-spice mixture, turn it over to coat both sides, and put on the baking sheet. Repeat the process of soaking the bread slices and coating them with the sugar mixture.

5. Bake the bread slices for 15 minutes. Turn them over and bake for 10 minutes longer, or until golden brown. While the bread is cooking, make the plum topping.

Plum Topping
6. Halve the plums and twist to separate the halves. With a paring knife, pop out the pits and cut the plums into 1-inch pieces. Put them in a medium sauté pan or skillet with the sugar and lemon juice. Cook over medium heat until they are warmed through and begin to give off some liquid, about 3 minutes.

7. Transfer the bread slices to each of 6 plates. Top with a spoonful of plums and serve hot.

Peach-Blueberry Breakfast Upside-Down Cakes

Makes 8 muffins

Unlike traditional upside-down cakes that are served for dessert, these don't have a caramel brown-sugar topping, making them more like an upside-down muffin. Perfect way to get in your morning fruit serving.

WHAT YOU'LL NEED

Standard 12-cup muffin pan

3 ripe but firm peaches

1 1/4 cups blueberries

3/4 cup unbleached all-purpose flour

1 teaspoon baking powder

1/4 teaspoon ground cinnamon

1/2 teaspoon kosher salt

1/2 cup sour cream

3/4 teaspoon pure vanilla extract

5 tablespoons unsalted butter, softened

1/2 cup granulated sugar

2 large eggs

1. Preheat the oven to 350°F and put the oven rack in the middle. Grease the bottoms and sides of 8 of the muffin cups with nonstick cooking spray or butter and evenly coat with flour, tapping out the excess.

2. Peel and pit the peaches (I use a serrated or paring knife to peel peaches). Cut them into 1/2-inch slices. You'll need 16 slices. Place 2 peach slices in the bottom of each of the prepared muffin cups. Top with 1 tablespoon of blueberries.

3. Over a bowl or piece of parchment, sift the flour, baking powder, and cinnamon together in a sifter or in a fine strainer by gently tapping your hand against the edge. Add the salt (you can just leave it on top of the flour pile because it gets mixed in later). Set aside.

4. In a small bowl, stir the sour cream with the vanilla.

5. In a medium bowl, use a wooden spoon to mix the butter and sugar together until smooth. Stir in the eggs, then the sour cream mixture. Stir in the flour mixture until just blended. Spoon the batter into the cups and spread to cover the fruit evenly.

6. Bake until a bamboo skewer inserted in the middles of the cakes comes out clean, about 20 minutes. Let cool for 5 minutes.

7. Unmold the cakes by running a small knife around the inside edge of each muffin cup and, with the tip of the knife, at the bottom of the pan. Put a baking sheet or cutting board on top of the muffin pan and then flip both over in one move. You may have to tap the sheet pan gently on the counter to release the cakes. Serve warm or at room temperature. They can also be reheated.

Raspberry-Lemon Yogurt Coffee Cake

Makes 1 cake, serving 9

Crunchy with nuts and tangy from yogurt, this cake is great for breakfast as well as for an afternoon pick-me-up. You can substitute blueberries or blackberries, but not strawberries because they give off too much liquid. Sour cream can also be swapped for the yogurt.

WHAT YOU'LL NEED

9-inch square cake pan

1/2 cup walnuts

3/4 cup granulated sugar

1 teaspoon ground cinnamon

8 tablespoons (1 stick) unsalted butter, softened

2 large eggs

1/2 cup yogurt (whole milk or low-fat)

1 1/4 cups unbleached all-purpose flour

Grated zest of 1 lemon

1 1/2 teaspoons baking powder

1/2 teaspoon baking soda

1/4 teaspoon kosher salt

1/2 pint raspberries

1. Preheat the oven to 350°F. Grease the bottom and sides of the cake pan with nonstick cooking spray or butter and evenly coat with flour, tapping out the excess.

2. Spread the walnuts in one layer in a small baking pan and put in the (preheated) oven. Set a timer for 10 minutes and check the nuts to see if they're a light golden brown. If not, toast 2 minutes longer. Cool and then, by hand, chop the toasted walnuts into 1/4-inch or so pieces. Transfer to a small bowl and stir in 1/4 cup of the sugar and the cinnamon. Set aside.

3. In a medium bowl, use a wooden spoon (or any other stiff spoon) to mix the butter and remaining 1/2 cup sugar together until smooth. Stir in the eggs, then add the yogurt and mix thoroughly. Stir in the flour, zest, baking powder, baking soda, and salt.

4. Spread half the batter in the prepared pan and evenly sprinkle the raspberries over the batter. Gently spread the rest of the batter over the raspberries. Sprinkle the walnut mixture over the top.

5. Bake until a bamboo skewer or toothpick inserted in the middle comes out clean, about 35 minutes.

6. Cool the cake in its pan for 10 to 15 minutes. Cut into approximate 3-inch squares for serving.

Pistachio Ginger Cake

Makes 1 cake, serving about 10

The combination of pistachios and ginger make this Bundt cake a little more sophisticated and unexpected than your typical coffee cake. I love it for breakfast, but I have to say that it makes a delicious dinner-party dessert as well—served with whipped cream, of course.

If all you can find are salted pistachios, rinse them off and dry them in a clean kitchen towel.

WHAT YOU'LL NEED

10-inch nonstick Bundt pan

Food processor

1/3 cup fine dry bread crumbs

1 1/4 cups shelled unsalted pistachios

2 cups unbleached all-purpose flour

2 cups granulated sugar

16 tablespoons (2 sticks) unsalted butter, melted

1 cup plain yogurt (whole milk or low-fat)

2 large eggs

2 teaspoons baking powder

1 teaspoon ground ginger

1/2 teaspoon kosher salt

1. Preheat the oven to 350°F.

2. Grease the Bundt pan with nonstick cooking spray, making sure you coat the center tube and crevices of the pan well. Sprinkle all sides and the tube with the bread crumbs, rotating and tilting the pan to coat well. Tap out any excess crumbs.

3. Rinse the pistachios if necessary (see headnote). Spread them in one layer in a small baking pan and put it in the (preheated) oven. Set a timer for 10 minutes and check the nuts to see if they're a light golden brown. If not, toast 2 minutes longer. Put the warm nuts in a colander and rub them with a clean kitchen towel to remove some of the skins. (If you don't have a colander, just rub them in the towel.) Don't worry about getting all the skins—you just want to remove the loose pieces.

4. In the food processor, process the pistachios with 1 cup of the flour until finely ground.

5. In a medium bowl, whisk the sugar with the melted butter until combined. In a small bowl, whisk the yogurt with the eggs and then whisk them into the bowl with the sugar and butter. Stir in the ground pistachios, remaining 1 cup flour, baking powder, ginger, and salt until everything is well blended.

6. Evenly spread the batter into the prepared pan. Bake until a bamboo skewer inserted in the middle comes out clean, about 50 minutes.

7. Let the cake cool for 20 minutes. Unmold by inverting the pan onto a cake plate or platter. If necessary, lift the plate and give it a tap on the counter to release the cake.

Oat Trail Bars

Makes 9 bars

Eaten on the run or in a bowl topped with yogurt, these homemade, no-bake bars are not only wholesome and good for you (without any preservatives), they are also much tastier than the ones you buy.

Since they aren't cooked, old-fashioned oats cannot be substituted here; instant (1-minute) oats have a finer texture that works better in the recipe.

WHAT YOU'LL NEED
9-inch square baking pan

1/2 cup pecans

1/2 cup cashews

16 tablespoons (2 sticks) unsalted butter

2/3 cup firmly packed light brown sugar

1/4 cup corn syrup

5 cups instant (1-minute) oats

3/4 teaspoon kosher salt

2/3 cup chopped fresh dates

1/2 cup dried cranberries

1. Preheat the oven to 350°F. Spread the pecans and cashews in one layer in a small baking pan and put in the oven. Set the timer for 10 minutes and check the nuts to see if they're a light golden brown. If not, toast 2 minutes longer.

2. Grease the baking pan with nonstick cooking spray or butter. This is just so that the plastic wrap will adhere to the pan, so don't obsess about coating it well. Line the pan with a piece of plastic wrap, making sure it evenly runs up the sides of the pan and pressing it neatly into the corners.

3. Stir the butter with the brown sugar and corn syrup in a medium saucepan. Cook over medium heat until the butter is melted and stir until smooth. Reduce the heat and add the oats and salt, stirring until everything is well coated. Remove the pan from the heat and stir in the dates, cranberries, and nuts.

4. Using your fingers or the bottom of a drinking glass, press the mixture into the prepared pan. Refrigerate until the mixture is set, about 3 hours.

5. Lift the big bar out of the pan using the plastic wrap "handles" and peel the plastic away from the sides. Cut into 3-inch squares.

Sources

These days the national supermarket chains and big box stores are carrying more and more quality products. That being said, I also shop at my local specialty grocery store, Whole Foods, or Trader Joe's. While the chains will have the basics, I can count on these stores to carry some of the higher-quality ingredients I depend on for baking.

If you like to shop online, you probably are aware that an Internet search of any baking ingredient or piece of equipment will bring up a list that's in the thousands. To save you some time, here are a few of my favorite sites:

www.surlatable.com
Kitchen equipment

www.chefscatalog.com
Baking equipment

www.chefshop.com
Chocolate and spices

www.williams-sonoma.com
Kitchen equipment

www.chocosphere.com
Good-quality chocolate at good prices

www.thespicehouse.com
Vanilla, cocoa, and baking spices

www.kingarthurflour.com
Baking ingredients and equipment

www.worldwidechocolate.com
Good-quality chocolate at good prices

www.zingermans.com
Chocolate and vanilla

Metric Equivalents

The recipes in this book use standard U.S. measurements. The information below is intended to help cooks outside the United States successfully work with these recipes.

Weight

FORMULAS	
Ounces to grams	ounces × 28.35
Pounds to grams	pounds × 453.5
Pounds to kilos	pounds × .45

EXACT EQUIVALENTS	
1 ounce	28.35 grams
1 pound	453.59 grams, .45 kilograms

APPROXIMATE EQUIVALENTS	
1/4 ounce	7 grams
1/2 ounce	14 grams
1 ounce	28 grams
1 1/4 ounces	35 grams
1 1/2 ounces	40 grams
1 2/3 ounces	45 grams
2 ounces	55 grams
2 1/2 ounces	70 grams
4 ounces	112 grams
5 ounces	140 grams
8 ounces	228 grams
10 ounces	280 grams
15 ounces	425 grams
16 ounces (1 pound)	454 grams

Volume

FORMULAS	
Cups to milliliters	milliliters × 2.4
Cups to liters	cups × .24

EXACT EQUIVALENTS	
1 teaspoon	4.9 milliliters
1 tablespoon	14.8 milliliters
1 ounce	29.57 milliliters
1 cup	236.6 milliliters
1 pint	473.2 milliliters

APPROXIMATE EQUIVALENTS	
1/4 cup	60 milliliters
1/3 cup	80 milliliters
1/2 cup	120 milliliters
2/3 cup	160 milliliters
3/4 cup	177 milliliters
1 cup	230 milliliters
1 1/4 cups	300 milliliters
1 1/2 cups	360 milliliters
1 2/3 cups	400 milliliters
2 cups	460 milliliters
2 1/2 cups	600 milliliters
3 cups	700 milliliters
4 cups (1 quart)	.95 liter
4 quarts (1 gallon)	3.8 liters

Length

FORMULA	
Inches to centimeters	inches × 2.54

Temperature

FORMULA
Fahrenheit to centigrade
subtract 32 from Fahrenheit,
multiply by 5, then divide by 9
(F−32) × 5 ÷ 9

APPROXIMATE EQUIVALENTS			
250°F	120°C	**350°F**	180°C
275°F	135°C	**375°F**	190°C
300°F	150°C	**400°F**	200°C
325°F	160°C	**450°F**	230°C

Acknowledgments

Writing a book involves a support team of many people. We would like to thank Jane Dystel, our agent; Michael Sand, our editor; Deri Reed and Peggy Freudenthal, our copy editors; Noreen Morioka and the design team at AdamsMorioka, Inc.; Kim Yost Goddard, our photographer; and Sebia Petrovich, our Fearful Baker coordinator.

Fearful Bakers

Jeanette Boudreau entertainment lawyer

Hadley Brooke student, athlete, and aspiring cook

Adrian Buechner glassblowing business owner, mom, and nature-lover

Andrea Burnett PR professional, mom, and aspiring baker

Monica Dashwood president of a professional and personal growth company for women

Michelle DeGuara stylist and now baker with her grandkids

Sharon Eidler wanna-be baker

Kevin George innovator of ice cream by day, motivator of twins by night

Jeffrey C. Gleason photographer and undying fan of the culinary arts

Ed Goldberg aspiring cellist and alpaca farmer

Brooke Gray photographer/freelance writer and PR consultant

Paula Harris owner of a pet provisions shop

Jayne Hillman just another (former) Fearful Baker

Lori Howard educational consultant and Latin dance devotee

Bob Kenney marketing consultant

Betsy Lawrence mother of one human, two canines, part-time teacher

Sofia Levy college student

Phyllis Lucas Haddow artist

Judy Lund retired medical assistant and ex–Fearful Baker

Will McCoy cookware shop district manager and food fanatic

Vicki Baldwin McNally fearless tennis player, mother of three athletes, and wife of a baker

Helen Burke Montague school counselor and passionate gardener

Sian Perry publicist

Beth Rasmussen food and travel enthusiast and energy industry professional

Joanna Rees venture capitalist and mother

Joel Riddell radio show executive producer and co-host of *TV Dinner*

Mike Roy businessman

Celia Sack owner of Omnivore Books on Food

Andrea Underhill up-and-coming actress

Ethan Underhill college student

Stephanie Underhill administrator and bibliophile

John Washko hotelier and art gallery co-owner

Recipe Testers

Angela Brassigna

Kia Brown

Megan Chromik

Dave Cleveland

Janet Rikala Dalton

Theresa Ebilane

Nicole Lago

Robyn Lenzi

Kathleen Mariano

Mary Sue Murray

Diana Ortega

Lisa Pannone

Joanne Paradis

Kate Petcavich

Beth Rasmussen

Hadley Reynolds

Erin Loftus Sweetland

Allen Underhill

Baker Models

Marcia Anselmo retired elementary school principal

Sarah Cole mother

Kevin George innovator of ice cream by day, motivator of twins by night

Aaron Naisbitt financial investments pricing coordinator

Kelli Nolan stay-at-home mom

Beth Rasmussen food and travel enthusiast and energy industry professional

Joanna Rees venture capitalist and mother

Christina Lohrisch Ruggles stay-at-home mom

Maddy Stewart student

Hannah Wilcox student

Index

About the Authors

Emily Luchetti, executive pastry chef at two busy and high-profile restaurants in the San Francisco Bay Area—Farallon and Waterbar—has developed a nationwide following for her innovative but approachable dessert creations. With six successful cookbooks under her belt, plus awards, public appearances, television shows, and cooking demonstrations too numerous to count, she's expanded her already formidable reputation globally.

Luchetti began her cooking career more than twenty years ago with Chef Mark Franz as part of the opening team of Stars Restaurant in San Francisco. Her passion for making desserts eventually took sway, and in 1987 she became their pastry chef, a position she held until 1995. Also, from 1994 to 1995, she was the co-owner with Jeremiah Tower of StarBake, a retail bakery. Two years later she again joined Mark Franz when he teamed up with entrepreneur Pat Kuleto to open Farallon. Emily's James Beard Foundation Award in 2004 for Outstanding Pastry Chef helped put Farallon on the map as a destination for dessert fanatics worldwide.

Luchetti has written several award-winning cookbooks: *Stars Desserts* (HarperCollins, 1991), which won the Martini & Rossi Dessert Cookbook of the Year award, *Four-Star Desserts* (HarperCollins, 1996), which was nominated for a James Beard Foundation Cookbook Award, *A Passion for Desserts* (Chronicle Books, 2003), and *A Passion for Ice Cream* (Chronicle Books, 2006), which won the 2007 IACP Cookbook Award. She also created the dessert recipes for *The Farallon Cookbook* (Chronicle Books, 2001) and in 2007 her first two books were combined to create the well-known *Classic Stars Desserts* (Chronicle Books).

Luchetti and her husband Peter divide their time (when they're not traveling) between their home in Marin County and their working ranch in Lake County, California.

Lisa Weiss is a cookbook author who trained at the California Culinary Academy and has collaborated with some of the best chefs in the country. Originally, she was a graphic artist who became a partner in a small San Francisco Bay Area advertising agency. When she realized that her weekend forays into the kitchen were becoming more creatively rewarding than her job at the drawing board, she decided to switch careers and in 1984 enrolled in the CCA. With her background in graphic design, food styling was a natural progression. Food styling eventually led to recipe development, testing, and freelance food writing for publications such as *Cook's Illustrated* and *Cooking Light*. Weiss tested all the recipes for Bruce Aidells's and Denis Kelly's contribution to *The Joy of Cooking* (Scribner, 1997), and then again for their best-selling *The Complete Meat Cookbook* (Houghton Mifflin Harcourt, 1998).

The Fearless Baker is Weiss's seventh cookbook collaboration. Earlier highlights include the critically acclaimed *The Farallon Cookbook* (Chronicle Books, 2001) co-written with Mark Franz; *Bruce Aidells's Complete Book of Pork* (William Morrow Cookbooks, 2004), which was an IACP Cookbook Award finalist; *Boulevard: The Cookbook* (Ten Speed Press, 2005) by Nancy Oakes and Pamela Mazzola (Ten Speed Press, 2005); *Chocolate & Vanilla* (Clarkson Potter, 2006) by Gale Gand; and *Pintxos: Small Plates in the Basque Tradition* (Ten Speed Press, 2009), co-written with Bay Area chef Gerald Hirigoyen. Cecilia Chiang's *The Seventh Daughter: My Culinary Journey from Beijing to San Francisco* (Ten Speed Press, 2007), a memoir and cookbook co-written with Weiss, was nominated for a James Beard Foundation Cookbook Award (Asian category) in 2008.

Weiss and her husband Dan live in Marin County, California, and visit Los Angeles frequently to spend time with their two grown children.